Monitoring Performance in the Public Sector

Monitoring Performance in the Public Sector

FUTURE
DIRECTIONS
FROM
INTERNATIONAL
EXPERIENCE

John Mayne & Eduardo Zapico-Goñi editors

WITH A
FOREWORD BY
JOSEPH S. WHOLEY

TRANSACTION PUBLISHERS
NEW BRUNSWICK (U.S.A.) AND LONDON (U.K.)

BHR 7907 - 0/2

Library of Congress Catalog Number: 96–43358
ISBN: 1–56000–292–1
Printed in the United States of America

Library of Congress Cataloging-in-Publication Data

Monitoring performance in the public sector : future directions from
    international experience / John Mayne and Eduardo Zapico-Goñi ; with
    a foreword by Joseph S. Wholey.
        p.   cm. — (Comparative policy analysis series)
    Includes bibliographical references and index.
    ISBN 1–56000–292–1 (alk. paper)
    1. Administrative agencies—Evaluation. 2. Executive departments—
Evaluation. I. Mayne, J. (John) II. Zapico-Goñi, Eduardo.
III. Series.
JF1351.M575   1996
351.009'1—dc20   96–43358
                                                            CIP

Contents

Part III: Comparing Performance Monitoring in Policy Areas

Foreword

Joseph S. Wholey

A host of promising public sector reform efforts are under way throughout the world. In governments challenged by budget deficits and declining public trust, these reform efforts seek to improve resource allocation and other policy decision making, to improve public management, to improve program efficiency and effectiveness, and to help rebuild public confidence in government.

Whether through regular measurement of program inputs, activities, and outcomes, or through episodic "one-shot" program evaluation studies, performance monitoring plays a central role, as this book argues, in the most interesting of the current reform efforts. Performance monitoring helps clarify the purposes and goals of public sector activities and helps communicate the costs, results, and value of public programs. A large number of countries are identified in the book where performance monitoring is seen as a critical element in public sector reform efforts.

As performance monitoring and public sector reform efforts evolve, it is important that we discover how performance monitoring can help improve policy decision making, public management, program efficiency and effectiveness, and public trust. In the pages that follow, case studies and cross-case analyses describe and evaluate a number of performance monitoring efforts as they have evolved over the past twenty years.

Critical initial steps in effective performance monitoring are the identification and clarification of the goals and objectives in terms of which performance will be assessed (as well as the identification of key external factors that could influence the extent to which goals and objectives are achieved). "Performance" is not an objective reality out there waiting to be measured and evaluated. Instead, "performance" is socially constructed reality that exists in people's minds.

The "performance" of a program will be found in the network of inputs, activities, outputs, and outcomes (intended and unintended outcomes, intermediate and end outcomes) that are most important from the perspectives of the program's key stakeholders. Often "performance" will be found in comparisons between actual levels and projected target levels of inputs, activities, outputs, or outcomes. We have to work with customers and other important stakeholders to define the "performance" of important programs in terms that capture important competing and often conflicting goals of parliament, interest groups, grantees and other partners, and "customers" served by the program, as well as agency and program executives, managers, budget officials, and other staff. In any specific case, the key dimensions of "performance" may be a program's direct or indirect costs, the services that the program delivers, intermediate outcomes such as customer satisfaction or actions taken by partners including other levels of government, or end outcomes such as environmental quality or health status.

Performance should be defined broadly enough to capture the key dimensions of performance that are of interest to important stakeholders. Only after this step is it possible to assess the relevance and utility of potential performance measures. One of the new challenges offered in this book is the need to consider dimensions of performance beyond the traditional ones of economy, efficiency, and effectiveness. With an increasingly complex, interdependent, and uncertain public sector environment, for some stakeholders, meeting objectives fixed some time ago may not be as an important dimension of performance as is the capacity of the program or organization to adapt to current and future change.

After performance has been defined and specific performance measures have been selected, performance can be monitored through agency and program data systems, through customer surveys, or ratings by trained observers, through evaluation studies or performance audits, or through other special studies. To get organizations to actually carry out such measurement requires considerable thought on what incentives exist, both tangible and nontangible, to encourage and support this kind of activity. Getting the incentives right is one of the interesting themes of this book.

Once we have a clear concept of the important dimensions of program performance, the key questions are whether and to what extent the political, bureaucratic, and financial costs of performance monitoring will be justified by the use of performance monitoring in policy decision making and public management. As we gain experience with performance monitoring and its uses, performance monitoring systems can and should evolve. Performance monitoring should itself become more cost-effective over time.

What we need at this point is a network of researchers and evaluators working to produce "lessons learned" case studies of the use of performance monitoring as well as cross-case analyses that will identify circumstances under which performance monitoring can contribute to improvements in budget decision making, program efficiency and effectiveness, and public confidence in government. The chapters below provide a good start on the needed work.

Part I

Performance Monitoring: An Overview

1

Effective Performance Monitoring: A Necessary Condition for Public Sector Reform

John Mayne and Eduardo Zapico-Goñi

Overview

The public sectors in most countries are going through profound restructuring, trying to provide improved services while at the same time having to drastically downsize in the face of major fiscal problems. And to compound matters, the citizenry feel that they are not getting value for their taxes: that they are overtaxed and that they should be getting better services. In many countries, the role of government in society is being reexamined.

A significant element of this restructuring of the public sector is the initiatives underway to reform public administration, to "reinvent government" to use a popular expression. Reforming public administration is seen as necessary to meet the dual challenges of improved services with fewer resources. A reformed public administration would be streamlined and lean, able to innovatively respond to constant changes and challenges, and deliver quality services to its citizens at lower cost.

It is a thesis of this book that effective monitoring of the performance of government services and programs is essential to successful public sector reform. Reform efforts in a large number of countries

3

argue this. A second thesis is that effective performance monitoring in the mid–1990s has a different focus, plays a different role and operates in a different environment than the performance monitoring of the 1960s, 1970s, and 1980s. Again, a comparative analysis of the efforts to "reinvent" performance monitoring in a number of countries confirms this. Thirdly, we have indeed learned a number of important lessons from earlier attempts at developing effective performance monitoring practices in the public sector of many countries and these lessons are transferable. Finally, we suggest there is a need to revise the traditional perception and measurement of "performance" in the public sector to reflect the realities of public management in the late–1990s.

This book is one in a series of books looking at evaluation and public administration from an international perspective. Previous books have reviewed the development of evaluation in national governments (Rist 1990), examined the role of evaluation and auditing in budgeting (Gray, Jenkins, and Segsworth 1993), and have looked at the ability of governments to learn from evaluation (Leeuw and Sonnichsen 1994). In a more recent book Toulemonde and Rieper (1996) address the challenging task of evaluating areas where multiple levels of government are jointly delivering programs and services.

This present book continues this comparative tradition but broadens the focus to include performance measurement in addition to evaluation, that is, it looks at both ongoing and periodic approaches to examining the performance of government programs. It perhaps is less descriptive than previous books, in part reflecting the fact that much has been written about performance measurement. Each chapter tries to develop lessons learned, usually from an international comparative perspective, and provide a guide to future developments in its area of focus.

Several themes of earlier books are further developed: the challenge of bringing information on the performance of programs to bear on budgeting decisions and the importance of such information to the success of governments learning from their experiences. In the book, evaluation is rediscovered as a potential tool for incorporating new criteria of organizational performance, more appropriate to the current public sector environment of complexity, interdependence, uncertainty and instability. It stresses the importance of organizational and interorganizational learning, the focus of two other books in this series.

What do We Mean by Performance Monitoring?

Unlike the private sector, public sectors do not have a single "bottom line." What, then, does performance monitoring mean for the public sector? We use the term quite broadly to include any management system that measures some aspect of performance, whether on a relatively ongoing basis as is the case for most performance measurement systems or on a more periodic basis as occurs with policy and program evaluations, and with audits. Most approaches to monitoring today involve some form of automated data retrieval.

Perhaps more interesting is what is meant by *performance* in the public sector? A large number of terms and definitions have been used in the literature to describe aspects of program performance. While some lament this proliferation, in our view it merely confirms that there are a variety of aspects of performance that are of interest to different people. It is, therefore, necessary to ensure that the term is appropriately defined.

We are using the term broadly. A *well-performing public program or service* is one that is providing, in the most cost-effective manner, intended results and benefits that continue to be relevant, without causing undue unintended effects. This definition covers the types of performance measures that have been discussed in the literature.

The best known performance measures are the traditional 3Es of *economy* (minimizing the consumption of inputs), *efficiency* (the relationships between inputs and outputs), and *effectiveness* (outcomes achieved as compared to expectations).[1] Within these, any number of more specialized terms can be defined, such as technical vs. economic efficiency, and administrative vs. policy effectiveness (Carter 1988). To further complicate the picture, authors have added several more "Es" to the menu: equity, entrepreneurship, excellence (Gunn 1988), as well as efficacy and electability (Bovaird, Gregory, and Martin 1988; Flynn, Gray et al. 1988) and ethics (Jackson 1991). And as argued elsewhere in this book, the 3Es themselves may not always be the most appropriate measure of performance, especially under conditions such as uncertainty (see chapters 3 and 11).

It is, however, doubtful that any one set of terms will emerge as the "best" definition. Rather, in any discussion of performance monitoring, we need to be quite clear on what aspects of performance we are talking about and not assume that others are using the same term to refer to the same concept. Our definition is given above.

Trends in Public Sector Reform

Public administration is changing and evolving. Most countries, faced with continuing and increasing resource pressures and with the need to respond to the global competitive challenge, are struggling to restructure the management of their public sectors.

The United Kingdom has its Financial Management Initiative (Cmnd. 8616 1982), the Next Steps (Improving Management in Government: The Next Steps 1988) and Citizen's Charter (Cmnd. 1599 1991). France has a policy of Renewal of the Public Service (OECD 1992: 41) and La Charte des Services Publics (1993). Canada has Public Service 2000 (Government of Canada 1990) and its service standard initiative (Treasury Board Secretariat 1994). New Zealand has perhaps gone through the most drastic restructuring (Boston, Martin et al. 1991). Australia has pushed through a wide range of reforms (Keating and Holmes 1990). Finland (Finish Ministry of Finances 1992) and Norway (Royal Norwegian Ministry of Labour and Government Administration 1992) have similarly undertaken major reform steps, challenging many of their previous strongly held beliefs about the role of government in society. In Spain, both the ministry of public administrations (Ministry of Public Administrations 1990) and the ministry of finance (Spanish Ministry of Finance 1993) have initiated several client-oriented projects and are discussing major reforms. The United States has its National Performance Review (National Performance Review 1993).

These reforms arose from the realization that the public sector (a) had become involved in activities it could not efficiently carry out; (b) was being managed in a very inefficient and hence expensive way, consuming too large a share of the domestic product; and (c) needed to provide better services to its citizens and do so in a more open way. The necessity to reduce and streamline became evident, often painfully so. The demand for more transparency became clear.

In the reform movements that responded to these pressures, at least three broad interrelated trends in public administration can be seen: a search for quality and excellence at affordable prices, managerialism, and partnerships with the public.[2] In each of these aspects, we will argue that the capability to effectively monitor the performance of the public sector is essential for success.

Affordable Excellence

Governments are trying to create well-managed public sectors, public sectors that are responsive to the publics they serve, deliver the results promised for their citizens, and can do so with reduced resources in the most efficient way possible. With the search for excellence well under way in the private sector (Peters and Waterman 1992), we now expect the same for the public sector.[3]

And considerable effort has been made to adopt in the public sector the more successful initiatives in the private sector, with some success. The phrases "total quality management (TQM)," "quality management," "a learning organization," "service quality," and "continuous improvement" are now common in many public services. There are several requirements common to these initiatives to reinvent government:

- the prime importance of focusing on the clients of public services, of seeing citizens as the customers for government goods and services and the need to treat them as the "buyers" of public sector products;
- the need for adequate training and empowerment of staff to achieve this client orientation;
- the necessity of challenging and streamlining existing bureaucratic practices and procedures to provide the needed flexibility; and
- the necessity to take into account the diminishing resources available to the public sector and to be more productive and innovative.

In addition, a key common element is the need to know how well you are actually performing in relation to expectations. Excellence implies knowing how well you are doing and improving based on this information. It implies a learning organization.

Specific efforts at improving service to the public at affordable prices are quite evident in many countries. The Finnish government's goal for the 1990s is "to improve performance and productivity" (Finish Ministry of Finances 1992: 2). The Norwegian government's Renewal Program has two aims: "1) enhanced public services and 2) optimum utilization of the Government's resources" (Royal Norwegian Ministry of Consumer Affairs and Government Administration 1988: 1). In Canada, in the first report to the prime minister on the Public Service 2000 initiative, the clerk of the privy council and secretary to the cabinet gives as a priority for 1992 "to deliver meaningful progress to Canadians in the area of service. . . . [by] achieving perceptible improvements in the efficiency and quality of service delivery, at lower cost . . . " (Tellier 1992: 16). The Spanish government has identified as a main challenge for public administration to guarantee the provision of public services to all citizens under the criteria of effectiveness and efficiency (Ministry of Public Administrations 1990: 19).

Managerialism

Governments are trying to create good managers in the public service. Most countries are trying to turn their public servants into managers rather than administrators, adopting many characteristics and values from the private sector. The term "manager" is used here to identify a management style that expects and encourages individuals to use the resources and authorities entrusted to them to innovatively achieve agreed upon results. The term "administrators" is used to describe a management style that is more concerned about following proper procedures, that does not encourage innovation, and that rewards caution. Managers focus on achieving ends, administrators on the means being used (Aucoin 1990: 118) .

While this dichotomy is perhaps a little simplistic, it does capture many of the changes being attempted in public administration. Reform in all of the countries mentioned includes the following features:

- empowerment of individuals and organizations by increasing their flexibility for action, reducing rules and regulations they must follow, and encouraging innovation and risk taking;
- reforming personnel policies to allow practices which encourage innovation, flexibility, and risk taking, foster motivation, and provide opportunity and appropriate rewards;
- decentralization of decision making to smaller units situated closer to the front-line delivery of services; and
- decentralization of organizations out of the traditional public sector into the quasi public sector through the use of agencies or into the private sector through privatization.

Finally, the counterbalance to greater flexibility is the importance of a strong focus on achieving results and on managerial accountability. Managerialism means managing to some end result and doing so based on facts and information and not solely on experience.[4] Again the need to know current performance is key, both to manage by and to be able to account for what has been achieved with taxpayers' money. At a system-wide level, a key issue in public sector reform is how to balance managerialism with the need for public accountability: the desire to decentralize authorities and responsibilities away from the centers of government without loosing complete control, and the ability for central government to be able to know and account for what is happening in the decentralized units and also government-wide.

These reforms to develop good managers are proceeding with different degrees of vigor and with different degrees of success. Research is only now beginning to examine the extent to which these reforms are meeting their objectives.[5] We leave it to others to comment on their success. Our interest in this introductory chapter is in the stated objectives of management reform. In the concluding chapter, we will take into account the arguments and evidence other contributors have provided that recognize the limitations and strengths of managerialism in the public sector.

Public Partnership

Accountability for results is an essential feature of managerialism. Managers focus on achievements not process and are to be held accountable in their organization for their success or lack thereof. But we suggest that there is a broader form of accountability that is occurring as part of the efforts to reform the public sector. This third theme of reform—that new partnerships with the public are required—is perhaps not as readily recognized as managerialism and excellence, but we argue that it is an inescapable aspect of public sector reform. Pollit (1990: 149) for one, discusses a "public-service orientation" as an alternative to managerialism.

Part of this is evident from the need to involve the public in a more substantial way in governance. President Clinton pledged to "listen to the people." Excellence in the public sector requires treating the public as the clients, consumers and indeed partners of government services. A deputy minister and minister for public sector renewal in the Canadian federal government put it this way:

> . . . the consumers of government services will have to act less as recipients and more as partners. They will have to be partners in the substantial decision-making about the kind and quality of services being offered. They will have to be partners in devising the necessary changes in delivery mechanisms, and they will have to be

partners in the graduation process from a number of government services. (Massé 1993)

By focusing on the citizen as consumer of services and as partner in governance, *the modern public sector of the year 2000 must involve a new partnership between the citizen and the public servant.* Several factors ensure this more direct public partnership:

- the focus on the citizen as consumer means that the public servant's goals will frequently be set in terms of understanding and meeting the citizen's expectations;
- consultation with the public is often an important element of reform movements;
- a call for more openness and transparency in government; and
- explicit requirements to set service goals and publicly report against them are elements of many reform efforts.

This focus on the need to involve citizens more in governance is not a new theme and is reflected in the reform movements of many countries. In a 1985 report to the Norwegian Parliament it is stated that, "The public administration must respond to the public rights, wishes, and needs . . . " (Government of Norway 1985: 342).

Several countries have pursued initiatives to develop and display client service standards for the services provided to their citizens. In the United Kingdom, the Citizen's Charter initiative (Cmnd. 1599 1991) is based on consulting with citizens, publishing standards for service and performance against the standards. The Canadian service standards initiative (Treasury Board Secretariat 1995) is based on the same consultation and publishing elements, as well the need to inform service clients of the costs involved in providing services. As such, both these initiatives involve engaging the citizenry and reporting to the public, beyond the normal reporting through Parliament.

President Clinton issued an executive order in September 1993 to require federal agencies to establish customer-service standards, benchmarked against the best in business, by September 1994. Several states in Australia have made the publication of citizen charters an essential element of their reform efforts.

The public sector can "account to" the citizens in two ways: by providing good service, and by demonstrating to their public that they are giving value for money. Our interest here is in the second approach which requires that current levels of performance are in fact known.

Affordable excellence, managerialism, and public partnerships are not the only trends in public sector reform, but they capture key aspects of the reform of interest to us. Each, as argued below, requires effective performance monitoring to succeed.

Effective Public Sector Reform Requires Performance Monitoring

There are a number of prerequisites for effective reform of the public sector including: political will, enlightened and credible public service leadership, and a realistic reform strategy. Meaningful and effective monitoring of the performance being achieved by public sector policies, programs, and services is also critical. Let us consider each of the three elements of public sector reform discussed earlier.

Affordable excellence in the public sector is not possible without good performance information. Measurement is a key element of the TQM and quality improvement initiatives. All discussions of quality management and continuous learning point to the importance of measurement and monitoring. For example, in the PDCA cycle—Plan, Do, Check, Act—"the 'check' step, the one many organizations admit they are weakest at, is continuous monitoring" (Johnston and Daniel 1993).

If public servants are to become good managers, focused on the results they are trying to achieve rather than the procedures they follow, they must have reliable information on the performance being achieved. This is perhaps more so now than in the past when, once a program or service was in place, circumstances changed only rarely and one could manage by procedures, procedures which had worked well in the past. Today the government is operating in increasingly complex social and economic situations where "gut-feel" management is insufficient and in an era of constant change where to be effective, managers must respond with informed decisions. The more managers and their staff are empowered and required to make decisions, the more they need reliable and current performance information. Empowerment provides the opportunity to manage and be in control. Performance information provides the practical means to manage and be in control (OECD 1993). Without it, empowered managers and staff have to fall back on following procedures. Without performance information, central governments have no informed control of decentralized units.

Finally, enhanced public accountability is impossible without credible performance information. Citizens do not, will not, and should not be expected to simply trust politicians and public servants to "deliver the goods." As the source of funds for government programs and services, they are entitled to meaningful and transparent reporting on what their government has achieved for them with their tax dollars. In the past, they have been perhaps satisfied with being told how much money was being spent in an area. The resulting lack of attention on results probably distorted government priorities. But, now facing a high level of taxes, citizens want more and better information on what they are getting.

Good performance information on its own is not going to reform the public sector. But for successful reform it is an essential management tool for managers, allowing them to achieve affordable excellence and to create meaningful partnerships with the public. A review of public sector reform initiatives in several counties supports this conclusion.

A recent publication from the Organization for Economic Cooperation and Development (OECD) on performance measurement in member countries discusses "Performance measurement: a crucial element in the modernization of the public sector" (OECD 1994: 17).

Public sector reform in Australia is built upon the requirements for clear objectives, effective management systems, and a framework for accountability. A recent report states "Appropriate performance information on program outputs and outcomes is essential to meet those requirements" (Task Force on Management Improvement 1992: 8). It goes on to say that

> Performance information is a key factor in overcoming organizational obstacles to using resource flexibilities, achieving more rational priorities and gaining clearer focus on outcomes. . . . It needs to be recognized that it is performance information which links the various elements of the management cycle. (Task Force on Management Improvement 1992: 8)

A companion document on accountability and its central role in public sector reform, states that "effective management information systems give senior managers the means for monitoring performance without the continual need for elaborate and arduous reporting by people down the line" (Management Advisory Board and Management Improvement Advisory Committee 1993: 19).

In Finland, "the core of Finnish public management reform comprises a change-over to management by results" (Finish Ministry of Finances 1992: 9). "All Ministries and government agencies will introduce result budgeting as quickly as possible" (Finish Ministry of Finances 1992: 2). Of course, management by results is impossible without performance information.

In a 1993 report to the OECD on recent developments in public sector reform, the Norwegian government stressed that "the emphasis on introducing performance-oriented management is to be continued and further developed. Priority areas are to develop performance monitoring systems" (Royal Norwegian Ministry of Government Administration 1993: 3). The report goes on to say that "the aim of the programme is to develop performance indicators and performance monitoring systems within all areas of the public sector" (Royal Norwegian Ministry of Government Administration 1993:7).

A report to the prime minister in 1991 by Angus Fraser, the prime minister's adviser on efficiency, stressed the continuing need for setting clear objectives and targets, and measuring progress against them (Efficiency Unit 1991: 3). This theme is repeated in a detailed 1992 report on how the Next Steps agencies are doing against previously established targets (Cmnd. 2111 1992).

In the United States, the *Government Performance and Results Act of 1993*, commits the government to an extensive regime of setting performance expectations and annual reporting against those expectations to Congress. The purpose of the act is "to improve the efficiency and effectiveness of Federal programs by establishing a system to set goals for program performance and to measure results." The act requires all government agencies to measure their program and project performance and report annually to the president and Congress.

Since 1990, an initiative of the Spanish ministry of finance to implement program budgeting has included efforts to monitor the extent to which managers are meeting their objectives (Revenga 1992: 138; Zapico-Goñi 1992: 52) At the same time, the ministry of public administrations (1990) is implementing a system of performance monitoring of public services aimed at developing an "Observatory of Public Services" to make the performance of public managers more transparent to citizens.

Most countries realize it is an uphill battle to make performance information a useful and essential part of public management. But most also agree that it is necessary to achieve the goals set for reforming public management.

Effective Performance Monitoring in the 1990s: Changes in Focus and Roles

But Haven't We Been Here Before?

Rhetoric is fine and essential, but often not realized. Performance measurement is hardly a new idea. Much of the rhetoric surrounding performance monitoring today is unchanged from that of twenty to thirty years ago: How can we know where we are going without clear objectives and measurement of performance to know if we are achieving what was intended? Haven't we heard this all before? A fine theory some say but it did not work in practice.[6] Many reasons are offered: important aspects of performance are not measurable, measurement quickly distorts behavior, measurement results in information overload and is expensive to maintain, and besides, no one uses performance information for decision making.

Indeed, hasn't even the management concept behind it been discredited: the naive rationalist model of decision making? The idea that public sector decision making is (or should be) based on a rational analysis of alternatives is viewed by most as much too simplistic, with some questioning the need for empirical information at all. French (1992), for example, suggests that governance in the 1990s has little to do with facts and everything to do with appearances and symbolic politics.

These are key issues; if performance monitoring is not likely to be successful in practice and yet is essential to the kind of public sector reform being pursued, then we should be rethinking the kinds of reform being contemplated. In the field of performance measurement, skeptics abound, especially those who have suffered through earlier and often unsuccessful attempts at building performance measurement systems in the public sector. Indeed, given the widespread rhetoric on the need and the historical track record, it is surprising that the practice of performance monitoring receives so little attention.

One response to criticism of performance monitoring efforts could be that we just have to try harder with more diligence. This may be true but is not very comforting. Two key factors mitigate the pessimism and suggest performance monitoring can be successful this time around: the circumstances *are* different and we *have* learned.

Public-Sector Imperatives and Opportunities in the 1990s

The demand for performance information. A key imperative for performance information today is the need to reform the public sector to make it more entrepreneurial. This concept was absent in the 1970s when public sectors were expanding and looking for new ways to spend money. As we have argued above, current public sector reform objectives (affordable excellence, managerialism, public accountability) *require* good performance information—the demand for performance information is there. As a recent OECD report said, "It would be very difficult to talk about results and performance with managers who are rigidly governed by rules and regulations and where results and performance are not a priority" (OECD 1994: 21). Unlike the 1970s and 1980s, performance information is not being touted because it is "obviously" good management, something good managers should obviously undertake. Rather, it is now seen as essential to modern management and is critical if we are to take performance and results, and accounting for them, seriously.

One important caveat. The demand can be there, but in a generic and perhaps abstract sense. The key is making this demand real and practical in organizations and for managers. This remains a real challenge: how to translate the imperative for performance measurement into practical guidance; how to get an organization and its employees to find it in their interest to measure the performance of their programs and services? Several chapters in this book address this issue.

The need to focus externally on clients. As a result of a client-focused and service-oriented public sector, a key focus for performance measurement today is (or should be) *external* to the organization, on the clients of services and the results being achieved. While the earlier rhetoric included performance external to the organization, in practice most performance measurement efforts went into developing internal operational performance measures, measures that—consistent with the needs of administrators as opposed to managers—focused on inputs and procedures, not results. This newer external focus, while posing some challenging measurement problems, ensures that performance measurement deals with matters that are important to governance, namely the benefits being received by the public.

Indeed, the client perspective provides a very useful and practical tool for developing performance measures. Do they make sense to the citizen in the street? If not the measure is probably an internal one, perhaps useful for guiding operations but not sufficient to manage well in the 1990s.

Information technology. A final important condition has changed considerably over the past twenty years. We now have available the technology to make performance information readily available to all managers and their staff. Computer-based information systems on your desk open up a whole new world and allow managers and staff unprecedented ability to have control over performance information and to actually use it from day to day.

Correctional Services of Canada, responsible for federal prisons, has a management information system available to individual managers across the country on their desktop computers. It gives them access to a wide range of budget and operational data, as well as information of relevant current public events. Not only has the system affected decision making—managers, for example, can compare their operations with others across the country—and led to cost savings, it has also changed the culture of the organization.

The importance of information technology is recognized in the reform initiatives of most countries. Norway talks about "Computer technology as Tools of Efficiency" (Royal Norwegian Ministry of Consumer Affairs and Government Administration 1988: 4) and includes the "application of new technology" as one of four elements of its reform program (Government of Norway 1985). Finland has decided to "use data processing techniques in public management in order to ensure access to public services, flexibility, and control of decentralized administrative structures" (Finish Ministry of Finances 1992: 8). In describing its service-improvement initiatives, Canada highlighted information technology as a key element (Treasury Board Secretariat of Canada 1994). It also created a chief informatics officer for Canada. In Spain, the importance of information technology to improve public management and to increase its transparency for citizens is also recognized (Ministry of Public Administrations 1990: 99).

We Have Learned About Performance Measurement

Experience in developing performance-measurement systems is widespread. We argue that the lessons which have been learned can be applied to facilitate new efforts to design and implement effective performance-measurement systems. They should help to shape appropriate indicators and to avoid important obstacles when using them. We are not starting from scratch and those tasked with developing performance information would be foolhardy to ignore the lessons of history.

First of all, however, we need to understand the role performance information can play in the public sector. Performance information can inform or perhaps guide decision making and accountability, but it cannot direct and should not replace decision making and accountability. We need to be realistic about what uses can be made of performance information and not build unreasonable expectations. This point has been learned and relearned, but is often ignored by recent converts to performance information. For example, in 1988 Booth, summarizing fifteen years of experience, suggested a number of lessons which had been learned about the limits of analysis:

- analysis is no substitute for political judgement
- political judgement often involves considerations beyond the scope of analysis
- many imponderables are involved in the making of major decisions and analysis cannot provide all the answers (Booth 1988: 106)

These apply equally well to the use of performance information and have been relearned in the intervening years. But still, in 1994 Stewart and Walsh, concerned about developments in performance measurement in the United Kingdom, felt the need to make essentially the same points: "Performance assessment is . . . not a matter of performance measures, but a matter of judgement which can be informed by performance measures but which can never be determined by them" (Stewart and Walsh 1994: 46).

We agree, and in a similar vein, we are not saying that performance monitoring will solve the problems of public sector reform. Much else is required, among which, we argue, is good performance information.

With these limits in mind, an overview of the main characteristics identified in the design and development of effective performance indicators is a useful starting point for those responsible for new measurement initiatives.

Criteria for "good" performance measures are known. Without pretending to be exhaustive, the following are the essential characteristics of successful performance indicators highlighted by many authors (Bens 1986; Cave, Kogan et al. 1989; Carter 1991; Bledsoe 1983):

• *Validity*—being appropriate to the objective; representing all relevant needs to be met and the related problems to be solved by the organization.

• *Reliability*—making it possible to identify without ambiguity high or low values of the indicator with favorable or unfavorable performance; not susceptible to manipulation and/or challenge; based on data produced by accurate information systems; feasible to obtain accurate observations.

• *Usefulness*—this characteristic can refer to many other additional attributes such as clear, meaningful, and adapted to management needs and capacity; parsimonious (frugal) as opposed to promiscuous (indiscriminate); easily accessible; timely, ready to guide action promptly; purpose-driven as opposed to data-driven; and financially feasible.

Many other characteristics are mentioned in the performance monitoring literature: completeness (Bens 1986: 14), sensitivity (Birch and Maynard 1986), and adequacy among others. They are considered here to be either synonymous or related to the characteristics mentioned above.

It is not our intention to analyze all these characteristics, but to underline one of the main lessons learned: *there is no universally ideal way to design performance-monitoring systems.* Relations among these characteristics involve trade-offs. Normally the more complete the set of performance measures, the less parsimonious and the higher the cost. Indicators of effectiveness are usually more relevant but their measurement is often more difficult or less accurate. A pragmatic balance is necessary and depends on the opportunities and challenges of each organizational situation. The appropriate balance depends on two preliminary questions:

• Why do we want performance monitoring (what is it to be used for)?
• Which type of performance indicators should we have under what circumstances?

Specific lessons from experience help us to reduce resistance to the introduction of performance indicators and facilitate their refinement through a learning process. The conditions considered the most relevant by many are:

- *Involvement* of service providers and recipients of public services in identifying and selecting meaningful performance criteria of success (Office of the Comptroller General 1991);
- *Selectivity* in adopting a *parsimonious* number of indicators (Carter 1991);
- *Sampling* to reduce costs and *balancing* of performance indicators to capture the variety of perspectives of stakeholders and to cover multiple or conflicting objectives (Office of the Comptroller General 1991);
- *Consistency and comparability* of definitions used to produce indicators (Jackson 1988);
- *Controllability* of the measure by the agency being monitored. The measure should represent factors that are not beyond the manager's influence (Hatry 1980; National Audit Office 1991); and
- The need to *continuously update* the performance-indicator system. Performance-indicator development requires a meaningful review and strategy for changing indicators to maintain their significance when appropriate (Office of the Comptroller General 1991).

A major problem in learning these lessons, however, is the "not invented here" syndrome, the tendency for people to discount what has been learned earlier by others. This is perhaps particularly pronounced inside the public service, where consulting and learning from history is not part of most job descriptions. What several governments have done—usually via some central authority—is to produce their own summaries of the performance measurement experiences and lessons learned from earlier times (Office of the Comptroller General 1991; Royal Norwegian Ministry of Labour and Government Administration 1991; U.S. Department of the Treasury 1992; Management Advisory Board and Management Improvement Advisory Committee, 1993). Such summaries are useful and needed.

We know that the form of, and resistance to, effective performance-monitoring systems is contingent on the relevant organizational considerations and the related environment (Flynn, Gray et al. 1988: 35; Jackson 1988: 11–15; Carter 1991: 93), and the reasons why performance measurement has been put in place (OECD 1994: 17–18) . The pattern of performance-monitoring design and use within several organizations in relation to their characteristics has been analyzed by Carter (1991). According to Carter's research, public organizations, such as the National Health Service or the Police Service, with high uncertainty and complexity of tasks, typically have a data-driven, slow, and indiscriminate system of performance indicators. In this case he suggests performance indicators be used descriptively and as "tin-openers" (as signals for further evaluation) rather than "dials" (mechanisms for automatic follow up). Other public organizations such as the Social Security or the prison system with low complexity and uncertainty, with clear lines of responsibility and precise working procedures for personnel, have performance indicators which are purpose-driven, parsimonious, and relatively timely. These performance indicators can be used prescriptively. Carter suggests an evolutionary pattern for performance-monitoring system development: first, pressure for introduction, then resistance and discredit, and finally refinement (Carter 1991: 98). However, Carter's analysis does not call into question the type of performance measures in use (the 3Es). He assumes their relevance for decision making.

Confounding Factors

Our review of literature has identified several factors which make it more or less difficult to define, monitor, and use performance information: uncertainty, diversity, interdependence, and instability. They illustrate the complexity of current public sector management. These factors do overlap and are not mutually exclusive, but it is useful to separate them for clarity. The chapters in this book discuss these factors and seek solutions to overcome or cope with these conditions.

Uncertainty. There is a lack of knowledge and understanding in many cases about what kind of relationship exists between the output and the outcomes being produced. There are frequently many external factors at play in addition to the government intervention being studied. And many are not under the control of a manager or even the organization. Often difficulties are compounded by data collection problems. A rise in crime may reflect an increase in the propensity of the whole society to commit crimes (undesirable TV education, unemployment, legal freedom with regard to drugs consumption, etc.) rather than simply the lowering of police performance in preventing crime. In these situations, it is difficult to develop accurate indicators which can be used as shared criteria of success. This does not preclude the use of performance indicators under conditions of uncertainty, but limits their applications (especially those based on the 3Es) as ideal and unique standards of success for many government programs.

Diversity. Many areas of government activity are characterized by multiple stakeholders and divergent interests. In these instances, there is often no consensus on goals and values. This makes defining success difficult and agreement on performance indicators elusive. This lack of consensus on policy objectives or even conflicting basic values as compared with operational areas might explain the greater progress made in measuring operational performance. In general, there may be no agreement of what good performance entails.

Interdependence. Society and government interventions in society are becoming more complex. Interdependence among problems and solutions is common. This is reflected in the need for cooperative interventions both within and between government organizations. Effective and useful monitoring of performance needs to take all such interdependence into account. For example, internal interdependence makes it difficult to allocate performance ownership—the quality of service provided to a patient depends on a wide range of medical specialists (surgeons, radiologists, anesthetists, etc.), and on chemists, social workers, nurses, janitors and so on (Carter 1989: 133).

Instability. Finally, change in society is becoming the norm. Policies, goals, and objectives are modified over time to reflect current conditions and evolving priorities arising from changing social, economic, and technological conditions. Faced with instability, success in meeting previously agreed objectives and targets may not be the most relevant criteria of good performance.

These confounding factors explain in large part the resistance to and difficulty in designing and implementing performance monitoring. They represent the range of complex management challenges faced today in the public sector. Dealing with them requires individuals and organizations to adopt a continuous and interdependent learning approach to managing and developing appropriate performance monitoring. The design and use of relevant performance indicators must be continuously adjusted to the existing organizational circumstances and priorities. One of the most important lessons from past experiences is to *avoid the mechanical and isolated use of performance indicators in complex public organizations.* This implies the need for a participative, open, adaptive, and learning management style, focused both internally and externally.

Themes and Organization of the Book

This is a book on performance monitoring based on experiences learned from comparative analysis among countries. For the most part, each author has tried to focus on a particular aspect or type of performance monitoring and looked across several countries for lessons learned. This provides a unique perspective on the topic of performance monitoring and allows the experience gained in several countries to be reviewed. The book is trying to explain why there is interest in performance monitoring in a given setting, why performance monitoring has failed or developed in certain settings, and to identify new ways for improving the design and use of performance monitoring.

The book discusses and proposes ways to facilitate the design and implementation of performance monitoring. As we have seen, much has been written in the literature about implementing performance monitoring. This book addresses a number of themes which complement and go beyond the lessons learned summarized above.

- *The critical importance of getting the organizational incentives to support performance monitoring, and getting performance monitoring consistent with the organizational culture.*

How can we make the apparent demand for performance information real to organizations and managers? Past experience strongly suggests that more than an appeal for good management is required. Information is power in and between organizations and can be abused. How can we get the incentives right to foster and support the production of credible and relevant performance information and its constructive use for improving program and service delivery? Why is performance measurement and monitoring working in one setting and not another? Several of the chapters provide insight into this issue.

This book argues that measurement itself is not the limiting factor in having effective performance monitoring. Rather, it is the interest and willingness of the organization to undertake and use performance information which best explains the state of performance monitoring in any setting. Conversely, we also need to best match the performance-information system to the organization or networks of interdependent organizations.

- *The need for a central unit to play an active and effective leadership role in defining criteria for sound performance and implementing practical performance monitoring.*

Effective performance monitoring requires firm leadership. Legitimacy and support from the top are frequently cited as requirements for successful public-sector reform. This is no less true for performance monitoring. Confronting and dealing with resistance to the introduction and use of relevant performance information is one of the critical tasks and responsibilities of central units. We argue that such arrangements as decentralization, contract management, and new accountability regimes require a qualitative change in the role played by the center. There is a need to upgrade the capacity of the center for strategic leadership and interorganizational performance monitoring to avoid fragmentation of the decentralized administrative system as a whole. Several chapters develop this idea and illustrate this type of strategic leadership role.

- *The value of linking ongoing performance measurement with more periodic program and policy evaluations.*

Measuring performance is difficult and expensive. Getting the best use of analytical resources in organizations is essential. Furthermore, it is neither feasible nor practical to monitor all important aspects of performance on an ongoing basis. Many aspects of performance, including cause-and-effect relations and organizational interdependence, are best dealt with through a more in-depth program or policy evaluation. The best monitoring strategy makes use of differing approaches to measurement. Developing such a strategy requires careful planning and management.

- *The emergence of the client/customer/citizen as a key and constructive point of reference for developing performance monitoring.*

We have discussed earlier the advantages of using the customer focus associated with public sector reforms as a key criterion for developing streamlined and useful performance-monitoring regimes. There is a caveat. Many public services are provided by professionals such as doctors in hospitals, and engineers in research and development services. In such cases, it is not always clear who is best situated to define the public benefit and hence what and how to measure. A broad social framework for performance monitoring may be needed to represent adequately the diversity of interests and values.

- *The need to address more than the traditional strictly quantitative aspects of public sector performance.*

Often, performance monitoring in organizations leads to distortions in behavior, as employees or organizations modify their actions to improve the performance indicators chosen (often based on their ease of measurement rather than their importance). A strategic set of performance indicators is usually suggested as the solution. But this will be a solution only if some of the less traditional (sometimes more qualitative) aspects of performance are accounted for. Several chapters suggest that the traditional 3Es approach to performance is increasingly inadequate in the uncertain, diverse, interdependent, and ever-changing environment now characterizing many public services.

Throughout the book, the authors review the experience gained in various settings and in various policy sectors, in relation to these themes we have identified. In part 1, five authors discuss the issue of implementing performance monitoring in government organizations. Terje Nilsen examines the important role played by central units in implementing performance monitoring, comparing the experiences in Norway, the United Kingdom, and Canada. Eduardo Zapico-Goñi discusses the need for budget offices to redefine their role towards a more strategic leadership position in today's public sector and to use more relevant criteria of performance assessment. Sylvie Trosa reviews the experiences in the United Kingdom and France in trying to implement performance monitoring in their central governments, comparing the differing roles played by their respective central units. Rolf Sandahl describes the Swedish experience with attempting to have performance information as an essential element of their central budgeting system, pointing out how the system has evolved over time to reflect the real needs and capabilities of the agencies and the ministries. Finally, Mayne suggests that a key missing element is an effective accountability regime which supports good performance to encourage the need for performance monitoring.

In part 2, experiences with performance monitoring in several specific policy sectors are discussed and reinforce the themes outlined above. Myoung-soo Kim and Javier Casas Guzman describe performance monitoring in the health care systems of Korea and Mexico respectively. The difficulties encountered are surprisingly similar in these two cases, particularly the problems of having a wide variety of organizations which are only loosely related delivering health care. Richard Sonnichsen synthesizes the experience gained in six countries in attempting to measure police performance and suggests some general trends. He discusses the pressure to measure police activities in ways that are meaningful to citizens, and the need to go beyond traditional productivity and workload measures. John Nicholson describes the efforts in Australia and New Zealand to measure policy advice, a key central-government activity which has traditionally been seen as outside the scope of measurement. He suggests the need to go beyond the traditional 3Es perspective on performance.

In the final chapter, we summarize the evidence presented in earlier chapters in relation to the themes presented above and discuss the directions governments need to go to enhance performance monitoring. In particular, we suggest the need to expand the scope of performance beyond the 3Es so that performance monitoring will be able to provide the information needed to manage in an era of uncertainty, diversity, interdependence, and change which characterize the public sector of today.

Conclusions

We have argued that effective performance monitoring is essential to the reform of the public sector. We also note that political leaders in many countries, such as in the United Kingdom, the United States, France, New Zealand, and Australia have pushed for better performance information as part of their reform efforts. However, it is not often pursued with the adequate vigor and common sense, taking into account organizational and situational contingencies. Furthermore, where it is receiving attention, too often the lessons learned from the past twenty years are either not understood and appreciated, or are ignored as irrelevant by recent converts to performance monitoring.

We realize that there are other prerequisites to effective public sector reform, such things as political will, strong leadership, and a realistic reform strategy. These too are necessary. But in addition, we argue, *without effective performance monitoring, public-sector reform as it is envisaged today will not succeed.* Many aspects of reform can seemingly proceed without performance monitoring. The result, however, will be public sectors not in control—managerialism with no accountability, and governments with maverick decentralized units, facing continuing arbitrary resource reductions and an increasingly hostile citizenry. We are suggesting the need to explore new, relevant measures and criteria of performance to shape, adapt, and redefine the limits of public sector reform and its success.

Notes

1. Precise definitions for these terms vary considerably among authors. For a few discussions, see the Canadian Comprehensive Auditing Foundation (1987) and Gray and Jenkins (1992).
2. For a discussion of the nature of public sector reform movements, see Aucoin (1990) and Boston (1991).
3. The literature here is growing at a rapid pace. See, for example, Barzelay (1992) , Osborne and Gaebler (1992) , Cohen and Brand (1993), and Denhart (1993).
4. "Managerialism" has been the subject of numerous books and articles, a few of which are Pollit (1990), Boston (1991), Jenkins and Gray (1993), and Mascarenhas (1993).
5. See, for example, Mascarenhas (1993) who reviews reform in Australia, Britain, and New Zealand; Jenkins and Gray (1993) for a review of the U.K. progress; and Boston, Martin, et al. (1991) for a review of the New Zealand experience. In Australia, the government has published an extensive evaluation of their reform efforts (Task Force on Management Improvement 1992). The journal *Governance* has had a number of special issues on managerial reforms which reviewed progress in a number of countries. See *Governance* 3, no. 2 (April 1990) and 5, no. 4 (October 1992).
6. Laments about performnce measurement have been many. See, for example, Jones (1993).

References

Aucoin, P. 1990. "Administrative Reform in Public Management: Paradigms, Principles, Paradoxes and Pendulums." *Governance* 3, no. 2: 115–37.
Barzelay, M. 1992. *Breaking Through Bureaucracy: A New Vision for Managing Government.* Berkeley: University of California Press.
Bemelmans-Videc, M. L., R.C. Rist, and E. Vedung eds. 1996. *Policy Insturment Choice and Evaluation.* New Brunswick, N.J.: Transaction Publishers.
Bens, C. K. 1986. "Strategies for Implementing Performance Measurement." *Management Information Service Report* XVIII, no. 11.
Birch, S. and A. Maynard. 1986. "Performance Indicators and the Performance Assessment in the UK National Health Service: Implications for Management and

Planning." *International Journal of Health Planning and Management* 1: 143–56.

Booth, T. 1988. *Developing Policy Research.* Gower Publishing Company.

Boston, J. 1991. "The Theoretical Underpinnings of Public Sector Restructuring in New Zealand." In *Reshaping the State: New Zealand's Bureaucratic Revolution*, ed. J. Boston, J. Martin, J. Pallot, and P. Walsh. Oxford University Press.

Boston, J., J. Martin, J. Pallot and P. Walsh eds. 1991. *Reshaping the State: New Zealand's Bureaucratic Revolution.* Oxford University Press.

Bovaird, T., D. Gregory, and S. Martin. 1988. "Performance Measurement in Urban Economic Development." *Public Money and Management* 8, no. 4: 17–22.

Canadian Comprehensive Auditing Foundation. 1987. *Effectiveness Reporting and Auditing in the Public Sector.* Ottawa.

Carter, N. 1988. "Measuring Government Performance." *Political Quarterly* 59, no. 3: 369–75.

Carter, N. 1989. "Performance Indicators: Backseat Driving or Hands off Control ?" *Policy and Politics* XVII, no. 2: 131–38.

Carter, N. 1991. "Learning to Measure Performance: The Use of Indicators in Organizations." *Public Administration* 69: 85–101.

Cave, M., M. Kogan, and S. Hanney. 1989. "Performance Measurement in Higher Education." *Public Money and Management* 9, no. 1: 11–16.

Cmnd. 1599. 1991. *The Citizen's Charter: Raising the Standard.* London: HMSO.

Cmnd. 2111. 1992. *The Next Steps Agencies: Review 1992.* HMSO.

Cmnd. 8616. 1982. *Efficiency and effectiveness in the civil service.* London: HMSO.

Cohen, S. and R. Brand. 1993. *Total Quality Management in Government: A Practical Guide for the Real World.* San Francisco: Jossey-Bass.

Denhart, R. 1993. *The Pursuit of Significance.* Wadsworth Publishing.

Efficiency Unit. 1991. *Making the Most of Next Steps: The Management of Ministers Departments and their Executive Agencies.* London: HMSO.

Finish Ministry of Finances. 1992. *Public Sector Management Reform: Government Decision on Public Sector Management Reform.* Ministry of Finances.

Flynn, A., A. Gray, and W. Jenkins. 1988. "Accountable Management in British Central Government: Some Reflections on the Official Record." *Financial Accountability and Management* I, no. 3: 169–89.

Flynn, A., A. Gray, W. Jenkins, and B. Rutherford. 1988. "Making Indicators Perform." *Public Money and Management* VIII, no. 4: 35–41.

French, R. 1992. "Postmodern Government." *Optimum* 23, no. 1: 42–51.

Government of Canada. 1990. *Public Service 2000 - The Renewal of the Public Service of Canada.* Supply and Services, Canada.

Government of Norway 1985. *Report no. 83 to the Storting: Chapter 19, Modernization of public administration and rules.*

Gray, A. and B. Jenkins. 1992. "Auditing the 3Es: The Challenge of Effectiveness." *Public Policy and Administration* 7, no. 3: 56–70.

Gray, A., B. Jenkins, and B. Segsworth eds. 1993. *Budgeting, Auditing, and Evaluation: Functions and Integration in Seven Governments.* New Brunswick, N. J.: Transaction Publishers.

Gunn, L. 1988. "Public Management: A Third Approach?" *Public Money and Management.* 8, no. 2: 21–25.

Hatry, H. 1980. "Performance Measurement Principles and Techniques - An Overview for Local Government." *Public Productivity Review* I, no. 4: 312–339.

Improving Management in Government: The Next Steps. A Report to the Prime Minister (Ibbs Report). 1988. London: HMSO.

Jackson, P. 1988. "The Management of Performance in the Public Sector." *Public*

Money & Management Winter: 11–15.

Jackson, P. 1991. *Measuring Performance in the Public Sector.* Conference at Rottach-Egern am Tegernsee, Germany: Fédération des Experts Comptables Européens (FEE).

Jenkins, B. and A. Gray. 1993. *Reshaping the Management of Government: The Next Steps Initiative in the United Kingdom.* Roundtable on Rethinking Government Reform: Reform or Reinvention. 11 June, Montreal, Canada.

Johnston, C. G. and M. J. Daniel. 1993. *The Integrated PDCA Approach to Continuous Improvement: Lessons from the Second International Executive Study Tour on Total Quality Management.* The Conference Board of Canada.

Jones, R. 1993. *An Indictment of Performance Measurement in the Public Sector.* Fourth Biennial Conference on Comparative International Government Accounting Research, University of St. Gallen.

Keating, M. and M. Holmes. 1990. "Australia's Budgetary and Financial Management Reforms." *Governance* 3, no. 2: 168–85.

La charte des services publics. 1993. Paris: Direction Générale de la Fonction Publique.

Leeuw, F. L., R. C. Rist, and R. Sonnichsen eds. 1994. *Can Governments Learn? Comparative Perspectives on Evaluation & Organizational Learning.* New Brunswick, N.J.: Transaction Publishers.

Management Advisory Board and Management Improvement Advisory Committee. 1993. *Accountability in the Commonwealth Public Sector.* Australian Government Publishing Service.

Mascarenhas, R. C. 1993. "Building an Enterprise Culture in the Public Sector: Reform of the Public Sector in Australia, Britain, and New Zealand." *Public Administration Review* 53, no. 4: 319–28.

Massé, M. 1993. "Partners in the Management of Canada: The Changing Roles of Government and the Public Service." *Optimum* 24, no. 1: 54–62.

Ministry of Public Administrations. 1990. *Reflexiones para la Modernización de la Administración del Estado.* Madrid, Spain.

National Audit Office. 1991. *Performance Measurement in the Public Service - Experience in the Foreign and Commonwealth Office, HM Customs and Excise, and Department of Education and Science.* Report by the Comptroller and Auditor General. London: HMSO.

National Performance Review. 1993. *Creating a Government that Works Better and Costs Less.* Washington, D.C.

OECD. 1992. *Public Management Developments. Update 1992.* Paris.

OECD. 1993. *Performance Measurement.* PUMA, no. 3: 93. Paris.

OECD. 1994. *Performance Management in Government: Performance Measurement and Results-Oriented Management.* Occasional Paper no. 3. Paris.

Office of the Comptroller General 1991. *Line Managers and Assessing Service to the Public.* Ottawa.

Osborne, D. and T. Gaebler. 1992. *Reinventing Government: How the Entrepreneurial Spirit is Transforming the Public Sector.* New York: Addison-Wesley Publishing.

Peters, J. and R. H. Waterman. 1992. *In Search of Excellence: Lessons from America's Best-Run Companies.* New York: Harper and Row.

Pollit, C. 1990. *Managerialism and the Public Services: The Anglo-American Experience.* London: Basil Blackwell.

Revenga, J. S. 1992. *Presupestos generales del Estado.* Barcelona: Ariel.

Rist, R. C., ed. 1990. *Program Evaluation and the Management of Government:*

Patterns and Prospects across Eight Nations. New Brunswick, N.J.: Transaction Publishers.

Royal Norwegian Ministry of Consumer Affairs and Government Administration. 1988. *The Government's Renewal Program.* Helsinki: Department of Planning and Information Technology.

Royal Norwegian Ministry of Government Administration. 1993. *Public Sector Management Reform in Norway - Recent Developments.* Helsinki.

Royal Norwegian Ministry of Labour and Government Administration. 1991. *Measuring Public Sector Performance in Norway.* Helsinki: Department of Management Policy and Administration.

Royal Norwegian Ministry of Labour and Government Administration. 1992. *Plan for the Readjustment of Central Government Administration in the 1990s: Administrative Policy Guidelines and Measures.* Helsinki.

Spanish Ministry of Finance. 1993. *Informe sobre la Gestión Financiera del Gasto Público en España.* Madrid: Instituto de Estudios Fiscales.

Stewart, J. and K. Walsh. 1994. "Performance Measurement: When Performance Can Never be Finally Defined." *Public Money & Management* 14, no. 2: 45–49.

Task Force on Management Improvement. 1992. *The Australian Public Service Reformed - An Evaluation of a Decade of Public Sector Reform.* Australian Government Publishing Service.

Tellier, P. 1992. *Public Service 2000: First Annual Report to The Prime Minister on the Public Service of Canada.* Ottawa: Privy Council Office.

Toulemonde, J. and O. Rieper, eds. 1996. *The Politics and Practice of Inter-Govermental Evaluation.* New Brunswick, N.J.: Transaction Publishers.

Treasury Board Secretariat. 1995. *Quality and Affordable Service for Canadians: Establishing Service Standards in the Federal Government.* Supply and Services Canada.

Treasury Board Secretariat of Canada. 1994. *Blueprint for Renewing Government Services Using Information Technology.* Ottawa.

U.S. Department of the Treasury 1992. *Criteria for Developing Performance Measurement Systems in the Public Sector.* Washington, D.C.

Zapico-Goñi, E. 1992. "Financial Management Development in Spain." *Public Budgeting and Finance* 12, no. 4: 47–69.

Part II

Designing and Implementing Effective Performance Monitoring

2

Establishing Performance Monitoring: The Role of the Central Unit

Terje Haugli Nilsen

Introduction

In this chapter,[1] we will highlight the role of the central unit in establishing performance monitoring. Our main hypothesis is that if the introduction of performance monitoring on a full-scale basis is to be successful, it must be backed by a competent and active central unit.

The introduction of performance monitoring has met with considerable value-based resistance in public administration. Performance monitoring implies accountability which many try to avoid and, perhaps more importantly, is perceived as being closely linked with market- and management-oriented values and solutions. Within the field of public administration research, the common argument is that market-oriented and management-oriented concepts make only very limited allowance for the diversity and special character of public administration activities (Christensen 1991a).

According to Professor Olsen at the University of Oslo, the management-oriented reforms of recent years have had certain positive effects but he suggests caution:

We have become increasingly aware of the fact that the public administration exists for the sake of the public, and more conscious of results and costs. This is a healthy situation—at least if we regard these tendencies as a trend rather than a desired future state of affairs. When performance management is focused, the argument often applied is that we should think not only of rules and regulations, but also of results. Only when these ideas penetrate our thinking completely in such a way that we abandon our old values, does it become a problem. (Olsen 1993b: 36)

Definitions

We are interpreting performance monitoring in the broad sense outlined by Mayne and Zapico-Goñi in chapter 1 to include both ongoing monitoring of performance and periodic evaluation studies. In this context, central units are defined as, "an organizational unit responsible for development of the government's performance management policies, including performance monitoring."

It is important to note that the central unit's functions, as defined here, include policy *formulation* as well as policy *implementation*. Furthermore, the central unit is assumed to have general responsibility to develop and implement the government-wide performance monitoring policies. As a consequence, the central units are organized at ministerial headquarters and in units which have coordinating functions in the government administration as a whole.

Issues to Consider

The central unit normally has considerable influence on both the policy as well as implementation strategy. It will be of interest to take a closer look at:

- The substance of performance-monitoring policies in various countries: whether the government's performance monitoring policy is based on experience and theory, or whether it is rhetorical in nature; whether the policy is integrated as part of a comprehensive administration policy; whether the policy takes into account the diversity and special character of public administration (Christensen 1991b, Lægreid 1991)
- Which actors are crucial in the development of administration policies; to what extent do politicians take part in policy development in this area; is this an area that politicians entrust to civil servants? (Brofoss 1991, Kleven 1993).

As to implementation strategy, the following will be of interest:

- To distinguish between full-scale implementation on the one hand and experimental implementation on the other;
- To differentiate between various means of implementation used by the central unit. A "soft" approach would use information and guidance, synthesizing and communicating experiences, include the results from experiments, throughout the service. On the other hand, performance monitoring may be enforced by means of rules and regulations which establish a duty for the whole or parts of the public administration to monitor their activities. The use of normative means may vary from general directions to more detailed requirements for systems and procedures; and
- The usefulness of performance monitoring may perhaps increase if it is combined with more in-depth evaluations because performance monitoring in many cases may be insufficient as a method to measure the effects of government programs.

The value of performance monitoring may be greatest at the agency level where it can be utilized in the day-to-day management process. It is of interest to take a closer look at the actual performance and orientation of the central unit and to find out whether or not there is a focus on the agency level. Previous research would suggest that performance monitoring is utilized primarily in agencies where the task structure is homogeneous and where output can be quantified (Christensen 1991b). Trosa in chapter 4 makes the same point. Agencies comprised of a number of homogeneous and comparable units, such as the Department of National Insurance and the Directorate of Labour in Norway, seem to be best suited to performance monitoring.

It may be that central directions concerning development of performance-monitoring systems do not make sufficient allowance for specific management needs at the agency level. This can strengthen resistance towards performance monitoring in cases where it is not in the self-interest of agencies to develop management systems along the lines established by the central unit. In this connection, it is of interest:

- To investigate whether the intention is to produce comprehensive and detailed measurements of results or whether the approach to performance monitoring is of a more strategic character with measurements focused on key data, important and highly prioritized areas, and which are related to the needs of key users of this type of information. Different users will often have different preferences as to the choice of performance indicators;
- To see whether the central unit prefers a confrontational strategy with substantial pressure from central authorities or an experimental approach

where organizational learning is a key element of the improvement process. Is performance-monitoring policy based on a philosophy of organizational learning, the aim of which is to improve the particular agency, or is the policy based on a control philosophy, intended to disclose weaknesses and implement subsequent sanctions; and

- To ascertain whether the performance-monitoring policy takes sufficient account of costs and problems related to measurements.

Method of Analysis

To explore the role of the central unit and questions outlined above, we will use a comparative method. We will study the role of the central unit in three different countries, Canada, the United Kingdom, and Norway, and we will base our comparison on an analysis of documents as well as expert consultation.

The description of each country's experience will be structured as follows:

- Section 1: A description of past performance-monitoring experiments.
- Section 2: A description of the country's performance-monitoring policy. To what extent is the country's approach to performance monitoring based on experience and theory? To what extent is the approach "imported" and how is performance monitoring backed up politically? How and to what extent can performance monitoring be seen as an integral part of a comprehensive administration policy? How is the relationship between performance monitoring and more in-depth evaluations managed?
- Section 3: A description of the central unit and its role. Here we will describe the central unit's role in policy formulation and policy implementation. We will, among other things, discuss the central unit's implementation strategy: its use of normative means, directions and guidelines established at the central level, information, and guidance.
- Section 4: A description of experiences with the use of performance monitoring. Has there been any evaluation undertaken of performance monitoring?

The Implementation of Performance Monitoring in Three Different Countries

Norway

Previous Performance-Monitoring Experiments

The term program budgeting was central to the development of the annual budgets in the 1960s and 1970s in Norway. In 1967, the government set up the Programme Budgeting Commission to investigate the possibilities for program budgeting in the central government. The findings of this body were published in 1972 (Norwegian Official Report). The commission felt that the budgetary system at that time did not provide sufficient information to enable prioritizing. Nor did the budget documents provide a satisfactory basis for assessing the effect of government measures. The commission produced a series of proposals for improving the government budgetary system, among which were:

- The development of a comprehensive program budget and accounts system. Together they would form a complete information and management system which would provide as accurate information as possible about the nature of specific tasks, the objectives of these tasks, and the effects of programs and measures implemented. The commission also proposed that information about the costs of specific measures be improved, in order to facilitate the feedback on effects of these measures.
- All government activities should be grouped according to objectives, starting with the main objectives which were called program areas. The commission proposed the introduction of several new formal management documents—problem notes, programs analysis, program notes, and program reports. Program reports were to contain information about beneficial effects and the utilization of resources. These documents were to be produced at all levels of the public administration.

In the government's *Report to the Storting nr. 57(1973–74)*, the ministry of finance assessed the proposals from the Programme Budgeting Commission and endorsed the suggestion that the budget system be improved. The ministry did not subscribe, however, to the development of a separate information and management system to include a program budget and accounts. The commission's proposal to organize central government agencies according to objectives was not endorsed by the ministry. The ministry proposed, among other things, that the use of program notes on an institutional and ministerial level be extended, and that guidelines concerning the use of program analysis be developed and the long-term budgeting system be improved.

The ministry prepared the way for an experimental approach with trial activities which could form the basis for further development of the government budget system. In all essential areas, the Storting endorsed the guidance outlined in the ministry's report.

A key element of program budgeting was the development of measuring systems which would provide better information about the efficiency of government measures. In this respect, however,— reflecting experience elsewhere—the budget reforms implemented in the 1970s were a failure. The positive effects of the program-budgeting approach of the 1970s can be said to be:

- a better division of the budget according to objectives and agencies;
- the production of guidelines for the use of program analysis;
- a slightly extended use of planning figures and unit costs in budget documents; and
- somewhat greater emphasis on describing budget priorities more clearly.

It is true to say that the proposal to introduce program budgeting as a separate information and management system has now been abandoned completely.

Norway's Current Performance Monitoring Policy

Since the middle of the 1980s, efficiency improvement, improvement in the secretary functions for the political level, and user-orientation have been the public administration goals. Performance management, including performance monitoring, is one of the main tools utilized in this respect.

In 1986, the government budget system was reformed with a main goal to strengthen performance management. Government agencies were given greater freedom to use budget allocations. It became easier for them to reallocate funds between budget posts and to carry unused allocations over to the next year. As a counter-measure, agencies were required to a greater extent to define their objectives and to report to central authorities on the results they achieved. (Norwegian Official Report 1984; Finansdepartementet 1984 and 1985ab)

The development of public budget systems in Norway occurred in a climate characterized by unanimity, as borne out by the fact that the Storting unanimously endorsed all proposals in the government's budget reform (Steine 1988). Similar developmental characteristics can be seen in the budget systems of all Nordic nations.

In 1987, the government presented a program of renewal for the public administration. In this program also, performance management is one of the chief instruments utilized. As part of its program of renewal, the government ordered all agencies to produce corporate plans. The government decided on a full-scale implementation, whereby each government agency was required to produce its first corporate plan by the end of 1990. The implementation strategy also had some experimental features since all ministries were required to carry out one or two pilot projects in order to gain experience. The objective of these corporate plans was to clarify, among other things, the agency's aims and expected results. In addition, the plans would outline which measures and means would be used to reach these goals, and the costs of doing so. Each agency was required to establish measuring systems which would test whether these objectives had been achieved (results measurement). Later in this chapter, we will discuss experiences with this reform.

Performance monitoring has an important basis in the Storting's regulations concerning budgetary allocations. These regulations (§ 2 and § 13) require the government administration to report on both expected results and whether or not this expected output has been met. In the government's long-term program for 1994–97, the public sector and a focus on performance and results are discussed in considerable depth. Performance management is judged to be an important strategy with which to preserve and revitalize the welfare state. Among other things, it mentions: "Greater efficiency in the public administration also requires a stronger focus on the objectives and performance of each agency, and a focus on the needs of users" (Finansdepartementet 1992c: 229). Management and results orientation are also discussed in depth in the *Report to the Storting nr. 35 (1991–92)* regarding the government's public administration and personnel policies, and in the ministry of administration's adjustment plan for government agencies in the 1990s (Arbeids- og administrasjonsdepartementet 1992).

It is also important to note that performance management in the 1990s has received a more prominent place in the government budget. In the annual budgets for 1992, 1993, and 1994, (Finansdepartementet

1992b, 1993, 1994) the government decided that performance management should exert a greater influence on the fiscal budget. The ministry of finance now has a more central role with regard to performance management. Performance management has developed from being an internal administrative management tool to become a more direct instrument for policy decision making and control. At the same time, information about an agency's performance is coupled directly to budget allocations and prioritizing processes.

For example, from the government budget for 1993 (Finansdepartementet 1993: 27):

> In recent years considerable changes have been made to the national budget system. The main goal of this reform has been to transfer budgeting authority to the ministries and the agencies under their jurisdiction. By doing so the way has been prepared for an improvement in performance. A development of this nature requires alternative management mechanisms. In this connection an increased effort is required with regard to prognoses and improved performance management, including quality assurance and learning through performance management. In accordance with this and in keeping with the requirements laid down in § 2 and 13 of the budget allocation regulations regarding the formulation of result requirements and result reporting, increased demands must be placed in respect of the implementation of performance measurement and analysis, as well as reporting which can provide a basis for the introduction of measures which would ensure a more efficient administration of public resources. . . .

And further (Finansdepartementet 1993: 28):

> It is assumed that all ministries will review their measurement and reporting systems to define their development requirements and thereafter establish systems to give these substance. The chief responsibility for providing a basis for results-orientation will lie with the Ministry of Finance and the Ministry of Administration.

> In future stages of the work with result orientation the main focus will be on distinguishing between so-called operations management and strategic management. Operations management and control are often identical with business management, while performance management in relation to effects can often be termed strategic management. The latter stems from the need for overarching political control. One aim of the continuing work will be to focus on strategic management; that is, in relation to effects.

Performance management was also given a prominent place in the government's public administration policy statement to the Storting in early 1994 (Administrasjonsdepartementet 1994).

It should be clear from the above that there is a good legal basis and a solid formal foundation for performance management in Norway. The government budgetary requirement that information concerning performance be reported has been renewed. This means that the ministry of finance has become a central agent and motive force with regard to future developments. There is a focus on the development of budgetary documents and the budgetary process, on ministerial management, and the reporting of performance information between administrative levels, right up to the Storting.

At the same time as the government has given such emphasis to performance management in the Norwegian administration, it has also focused on management development. At the beginning of the 1990s, a total of 450 senior managers in the government administration were taken off the central public pay scale and given individual remuneration, the size of their salaries being tied in with individual agreements and management contracts.

The Central Unit—Functions and Organization

In Norway, the central unit function in the area of performance management is divided between two ministries and one agency—the directorate of public management. One of the ministries, the ministry of administration, is responsible for development and implementation of government administration policies, including performance management. The other ministry, the ministry of finance, is responsible for development and coordination of the budgetary and accounting functions in government administration, including the use of performance monitoring. The directorate of public management, which is under the jurisdiction of the ministry of administration, is the government's professional institution for administrative development. As such, this institution is used by the ministry of administration as well as the ministry of finance, providing professional advice on the development and implementation of public administration policies in this area.

The Ministry of Administration. This ministry has around thirty employees and is responsible for administration policy. From the beginning of the 1980s, performance management has been one of the major instruments in the government's administration policy documents. The ministry of administration's main function has been and continues to be the formulation of a comprehensive government administration policy. The government's renewal program of 1987, which required all government agencies to produce annual corporate plans, was produced and implemented by the ministry of administration. In the 1990s, the ministry of administration devoted a great deal of attention to the implementation and supervision of government administration policy. It now places greater emphasis on producing general guidelines concerning the implementation of administration policy. Examples of such guidelines are

- choosing forms of organization (government institution, public enterprise, state-owned corporation, etc.);
- departmental management; and
- the use of managerial boards in government agencies.

The Ministry of Finance. A major strategy of the government administration policy—both in terms of strengthening the basis for policy management and for improving the government administration—has been to highlight the use of objectives of public resources and to place greater demands on the performance of government agencies. This strategy has resulted in the emergence of the annual budget as an important vehicle for developing performance management in the 1980s and the 1990s. For this reason, the ministry of finance has become a key agent in the development process. The ministry establishes guidelines concerning the content and make-up of the budget, including guidelines as to what the budget should contain about information on performance. In the 1990s, the ministry of finance increased considerably its requirements for information of this kind in the government budget. Note nr. 23 (1994) from the ministry of finance formalizes these requirements. Central elements in the guidelines are a call for a more explicit description of policy objectives, and a demand for greater emphasis on information about objectives and cost-efficiency in the budget. The importance of making performance objectives and requirements as concrete and as verifiable as possible is also emphasized.

These guidelines are directions for the other ministries. In addition to establishing such general demands, the ministry of finance employs less stringent means such as the provision of information, advice and the communication of experience. It also participates in key development projects in connection with other ministries. During the 1990s, the ministry has assumed a more active role as a motive force in this field.

The Directorate of Public Management. The directorate is the government's central body responsible for the development of the government administration. Its main task is to assist the government and its ministries with the formulation and implementation of administration policy. The directorate has no authority over other government agencies. It participates by providing both the ministry of administration and the ministry of finance with professional support in connection with policy formulation and the production of general guidelines and requirements to the government administration. The directorate also produces written guidance which government agencies may use. Examples are:

- advice concerning corporate planning; and
- advice about performance management.

The directorate also offers an educational service and acts as an adviser for government agencies. At present, the directorate is involved in several projects, including the development of performance management in the education sector, the labor market sector and in the police department. Of a total staff comprising approximately 100 person-years, around twenty of these are allocated to work involving the research-based approach to performance management.

Experience of Performance Monitoring in Norway

According to Olsen (1993) and others, the management-oriented reforms of recent years—with their focus on, *inter alia*, performance management—have produced a number of positive effects within the Norwegian public administration. Research results suggest that the increased emphasis on performance management and corporate planning has led to a refocusing of attention within the public administration, towards an outward looking perspective. That is, from an internal—and self-centered—perspective to a focus on the results affecting the population and target groups, and services adapted to users' needs. The effects that researchers have found as the result of a focus on performance management and corporate planning in the Norwegian public administration, are linked to an increased awareness of the agencies' objectives and their utilization of resources. Terms such as "better awareness, improved knowledge, and greater understanding" crop up again and again when different actors describe the effects of these reforms (Nilsen 1991).

However, it is highly uncertain whether the reforms have led to real improvements in productivity and efficiency within the public administration. We lack sufficient data and measurement systems which would confirm whether or not such changes have taken place. According to Christensen (1991b), internal cognitive changes such as increased awareness help to raise the management potential in the public administration in the longer term.

One significant aspect of performance management was a stronger focus on result reporting and evaluation. The introduction of corporate planning, which became mandatory for all government agencies in 1991, was intended to provide support to this concept. Performance-monitoring systems were to be established in individual agencies in order to enhance implementation of management reforms. The reforms carried out in the second half of the 1980s have not, as yet, come up to expectations. Although improved reporting was a key element in the budgetary reform, this has not been followed up. Technical changes in the budgetary routines were introduced so that the budgets would provide information about planned and achieved results. In formal terms this has been implemented, but the practical benefit of this result reporting has been small. The result-oriented aspect of the budgetary reforms has not led to any genuine improvement (Steine 1991).

The social science research environment in Norway is generally unanimous in its judgment that the recent management-oriented reforms have not focused sufficiently on the diversity within the public administration and distinctive features of specific agencies. The introduction of corporate planning in the Norwegian public administration is also interesting in an international context, because it is a full-scale implementation and a reform that embraces all government agencies. Studies carried out by the directorate of public management indicate that 70–80 percent of government agencies had produced their first corporate plan by the end of 1990 (Statskonsult 1991).

In an evaluation produced by Christensen for the directorate of public management in 1991 (Christensen 1991b), it is claimed that in large part the process of introducing corporate planning into central government can be understood from the point of view of a myth perspective. Performance management is not utilized because it solves actual problems, but rather because government agencies wish to give the outside world a semblance of being efficient. According to

Christensen, it is easier to adapt performance management to suit public institutions that have relatively clearly defined and quantifiable tasks, for example, certain types of service and executive agencies. Christensen claims that performance management and corporate planning have been introduced to government agencies without any adjustment to the hierarchical structure, organizational form, tasks, and the personnel. The procedural features of public administration have not been taken into account by the corporate plan concept.

According to Lægreid (1992), corporate planning has weak ties to the population and specific target groups as well as upward to the political leadership. Studies carried out by, among others, Kleven (1993), at the Norwegian Institute for Urban and Regional Research, and by Olsen (1988) conclude that politicians continue to focus on details, despite the fact that on paper the transition has been made to performance management with a broader focus. They conclude that performance management has been imported uncritically from private industry, and that the management form is based on an inadequate understanding of the workings of democracy. Researchers find that in many places the policies remain the same, in spite of new management forms.

Olsen, indeed, claims that corporate planning may have had a disturbing effect on the relationship between politics and administration. Furthermore, a one-sided result-orientation may have conflicted with democratic values:

> The claim that results count most re-introduces a new version of the old division between politics and administration and camouflages the fact that people often attach values to processes and instruments, and not only to objectives. A one-sided result-orientation can cause problems with regard to the ideas that certain individual rights, obligations and moral absolutes cannot be set to one side, regardless of how the total result is affected. Knowledge that a government agency will often have to make allowances for many divergent considerations does not mean that the conditions required to formulate clear objectives are discussed. This is especially problematical when there is disagreement about what good results are, when the culture is compromise-oriented and it is difficult to secure a stable majority. Management presupposes the securement of an efficient operation and rapid adaptation, without this causing problems with regard to constitutional rights, legitimacy and popular control. Change and adjustment is presented as an almost absolute good, without defining how the public sector should be changed, and without a discussion about the value of continuity. The information systems are seen as a management tool. The conditions required so that members of parliament can derive benefit from result reporting is not defined, despite the politicians' traditional scepticism to formal evaluations. (Olsen 1993: 22)

Studies of public administration policy documents and the research that has been carried out on the effects of recent public administration reforms indicate that these reforms, including the use of performance management and performance monitoring, are only to a small extent based on experience and theory, and rather more on rhetoric. The Norwegian reforms have clear parallels with similar reforms in other countries. There is much to suggest that the ideas for these have been imported from other OECD (Organization for Economic Cooperation and Development) nations. In the approach to performance management adopted by the ministry of administration and the directorate of public management, however, there are clear tendencies towards an approach which is based more on experience and research, with, among other things, greater emphasis on the diversity within the public administration and the distinctive features of particular agencies.

The United Kingdom

Previous Performance-Monitoring Experiments

Until the middle of the 1980s in the United Kingdom there appears to have been little systematic development, implementation, and ongoing monitoring of result indicators for management. Before then, developments were dominated by more traditional, research-based evaluation activity, in which detailed analysis was carried out as required for policy development proposals.

Evaluation made its first serious appearance in 1970 when Prime Minister Edward Heath set up the Programme Analysis and Review program (PAR). The objective was to strengthen the capacity for evaluation in Britain's public administration. One significant feature was a plan to link evaluation results to the budgetary process and the size of appropriations. This close link between evaluation and the budgetary process, however, meant that many people compared it with the earlier Programme, Planning, and Budgeting reform (PPB), and in due course PAR was to share the same fate as PPB. The explanation given by many for the lack of success of the PPB reform and the PAR program was that they failed to adapt to the diversity of objectives and tasks within the public sector.

Beginning in 1979, there was a move away from weighty, research-based evaluations to less sophisticated self-evaluations and monitoring. This shift should probably be seen in the light of Prime Minister Thatcher's confirmed distrust of the public sector and her demand for simple measures of productivity and efficiency. Thatcher hand-picked a successful manager from private industry and set him to manage the central efficiency unit, a newly established institution which came directly under the prime minister. With the clear objective of providing a greater focus on productivity and efficiency in the public sector, the central efficiency unit developed a self-evaluation technique (the efficiency scrutiny) for use by public sector institutions. The implementation strategy employed was based on small-scale experiments. The idea was to gain experience before the strategy was implemented fully.

The decision to monitor objectives and performance indicators linked to efficiency and productivity began in earnest with the launch of the Financial Management Initiative (FMI) in 1982. A monitoring unit was established, the Financial Management Unit (FMU), which requested all departments to describe the plans they had for efficiency measures, what they did to achieve objectives and reduce resource utilization, and how they allocated resources. The move away from research-based evaluation towards a more simple expression of performance which could be monitored continuously, is clear from the criteria that the FMU set out as conditions for an efficient agency:

- clearly defined goals and, wherever possible, instruments with which to measure output and performance in relation to established objectives;
- clearly defined responsibility for the resources one has at one's disposal; and
- relevant information, training and the necessary support apparatus in order to efficiently maintain one's performance responsibility.

As a step in the move towards a greater focus on systems for ongoing results, the FMI program placed considerable emphasis on the development of monitoring systems in all departmental areas. In the first phase of the FMI program, there was special management focus on a quite limited range of indicators, chiefly linked to unit costs and internal management, where the objective was to cut costs. This focus must be viewed in the light of a strong political shift to the right, the stated wish for a reduction in costs and a desire for a reduction of the public sector as a whole.

Opposition gradually grew to the limited perspective that had been the basis of the monitoring of results under the FMI program. Both politically and within departments, it was demanded that monitoring be extended and supplemented with evaluations and a comprehensive analysis of results. In a report published by H.M. Treasury (1985), the need for systematic evaluation was acknowledged and given serious discussion. The political debate that arose from the publication of this report led to the adoption of a new requirement: that all new policy proposals or revisions of existing policy should contain a means of evaluation, expected objectives, when the results would be realized, the estimated costs, and how the results would be measured.

On the basis of this requirement, the Financial Management Group (FMG), the FMU's successor, produced a strategy for ensuring that the evaluation of policy measures became a systematic part of policy development. The FMG implemented the following measures to ensure that evaluation would find a place in the work of the departments:

- produced a guide for the evaluation of policy instruments for departmental managers;
- carried out case studies of various types of instruments and activities, with the intention of supplementing the guide with concrete examples; and
- arranged seminars and discussions in which leaders from the departments together with the FMG were able to discuss how the methods had worked and how they could be developed further.

The United Kingdom's Present Performance-Monitoring Policy

Evaluation appears to have suffered a setback when the Next Steps reform was introduced in 1988 (Improving Management in Government: The Next Steps 1988). The Next Steps reform had little of the ambiguity and caution that often characterizes the research approach. In Next Steps, government agencies were primarily portrayed as service-producing units, and the management techniques of private industry were always the ideal. The definition of clear objectives and performance indicators, the ongoing monitoring of these, and performance-related salary bonuses are some of the key elements of Next Steps:

> The identification of the right targets and confidence in the systems which underpin them are at the heart of a healthy arm's length relationship between Department and their Agencies. So too is the ability to use targets sensibly as an effective management tool.

The aim should be for each Agency to have a handful of robust and meaningful top level targets which measure financial performance, efficiency and quality of customer service, over and above whatever subsidiary performance indicators are required for the Agency's internal management purposes. (Making the Most of Next Steps 1991: 3)

One may be tempted to say that performance monitoring never stood more firmly in an administrative context than during Next Steps. The agency director and the cabinet minister enter into contracts (framework documents) in which targets and performance indicators are defined. If the director reaches these targets, a bonus is paid. If the targets are not reached, this bonus will be forfeited. For example, when the labor market picked up, the director of Britain's labor market agency was paid a substantial bonus, which he later lost at the beginning of the 1990s when the labor market declined.

The Next Steps reform established executive agencies, led by a director employed on a fixed-term contract, with an agreement that regulated the agency's performance responsibility through the use of targets and performance indicators. Agencies that receive the status of executive agency were also given considerably extended powers with regard to financial and personnel matters, so that the resources could be utilized as flexibly as possible. By the end of 1993, ninety-two executive agencies had been established, which between them employed around 60 percent of all government officials in the United Kingdom. The aim was to have identified all potential executive agencies and ensure that these had received their status by April 1995. By this time, it was estimated that around 75 percent of government officials would be employed in executive agencies. Those institutions which would not become executive agencies, were chiefly institutions at the uppermost levels of the central administrative apparatus, and first and foremost that part of the administration that had clear secretariat functions in relation to the political leadership.

It appears as though the requirement of ready measurability has weighed heavily in the selection of the targets and performance indicators that are included in framework documents that define the agencies' performance responsibilities in relation to the department, and which also form the basis of bonus payment. For example, the agency for employment's key indicators are the number of people in employment, the number of interviews carried out, the time spent on administrative procedures, the number of complaints, and unit costs. The British map-making agency is managed according to the number of maps developed, the size of internally generated funds, and so forth. The use of such a limited set of indicators to define success may create the wrong incentives. This is perhaps the reason why the Next Steps reform, like the FMI program, has gradually seen a shift in performance management to also include periodical evaluations. In addition to systems for ongoing reporting, at least every third year each agency now carries out a comprehensive review and evaluation of its role, organization and its relationship with the department.

The Central Unit—Function and Organization

As evident from this review, the role and organization of the central unit has differed under the different reforms and has been closely linked to the extent and the substance of the reform itself.

The role of the central unit during the PAR program in the 1970s was chiefly confined to the development of written advice and methodologies, general requests to departments to strengthen their evaluation work, and to providing concrete assistance concerning the implementation of evaluations in a number of departments. Modest in size, the central unit chiefly held the roles of policy formulator and communicator of experiences, but it lacked the administrative apparatus to follow the actual implementation of reforms.

One important feature of the central unit's design in the 1980s would appear to be the division between the formulation of policy and the responsibility for implementation in different organizational units. Policy formulation was the task of the central efficiency unit which, since its establishment in 1979, has been the generator of new reform initiatives, first through the Efficiency Strategy, then the FMI, and finally with the launching of the Next Steps reform.

With regard to the implementation of reforms, especially the FMI and Next Steps, it appears as though this task has been so demanding that the responsibility for implementing reforms has gone to separate organizational units. The responsibility for implementing the Next Steps reform has been divided between the Office of the Minister for the Civil Service (OMCS) in the Cabinet Office with its own Next Steps project team, and H.M. Treasury. In 1992, the responsibility for implementing the reform was transferred to a newly established office under the Office of Public Service and Science (OPSS) in the Cabinet Office, which among other things is responsible for ensuring that the Next Steps reform is coordinated with the Citizen's Charter, an initiative intended to ensure user rights through defined and published quality standards. In the implementation of the Next Steps reform, the Cabinet Office and H.M. Treasury have developed standards and written advice, systematized and communicated experiences, acted as a driving force in the implementation process, assessed new candidates for agency status, and been responsible for implementing the regulatory changes which have been necessary in order to delegate authority for finances and personnel to the new units.

The proximity of the central unit's organization to the prime ministers of recent years is not the least due to the fact that the public administration reforms have received political priority and therefore been given a prominent position of the organizational chart. One noticeable feature of the central unit's development in the United Kingdom is a considerable turnover in organizations, where organizations are established, closed, or moved as new reforms are developed. The consolidation in 1992 of a number of different reform initiatives under the same organizational apparatus (OPSS) reflects the fact that the present prime minister sees a need for a greater coordination of the central unit's work.

Experience of Performance Monitoring in the United Kingdom

It has been difficult to find material about the experiences of performance monitoring during the reforms prior to Next Steps. With regard to this latest and largest reform, however, one of the conditions relating to all executive agencies is that they are obliged to publish annual reports which analyze performance and output, unit costs, and services they provide in relation to target groups. Each year the Cabinet Office publishes a collected review of performance in all agencies taken as a whole. According to the OECD, developments in agencies' performance has been satisfactory:

> Overall—the review showed that agencies have continued to perform well and have met three out of four of their targets, which have become tougher year on year. (OECD 1993: 82)

Experience shows that an agency should be a coherent management unit with clear identifiable aims, and furthermore that an organization should only become an agency if the agency status means significant improvements (see Trosa ch. 4).

Experience indicates that it has been easier to be specific about service requirements and objectives for less politically sensitive tasks. The early agencies in the Next Steps presented relatively little political challenge as to specification of targets. The real test of the reform will appear when experiences begin to come from agencies with highly politically sensitive tasks.

The Next Steps reform has so far been based on imitation of business management rather than an innovation and adaptation to the diverse needs of government. In this way, the reform also contributes to widening the gap between managers and professionals. There is also a risk that the Next Steps approach may push into the background the need for managing interdependencies among organizations. Good results may often depend on cooperation among organizations with interdependent functions.

Canada

Previous Performance-Monitoring Experiments

Performance monitoring in Canada has its roots in program budgeting of the 1960s. Its major focus has been on program evaluation rather than on ongoing performance measurement. Since the 1970s, program evaluation has been characterized by strong central support and a large degree of institutionalization. Program evaluation was mainly seen as an element of the management cycle, but also considered as an element in the budgetary process; two considerations which have proved difficult to combine.

At the end of the 1960s and the beginning of the 1970s, departments established separate planning and evaluation units, responsible for evaluating their programs. The Treasury Board Secretariat was the driving force, promulgated evaluation methods, and maintained a support and advisory function in respect of the departments' evaluation units. This early effort met with little success. According to Dobell and Zussmann (1981), there were three main reasons why the efforts failed: the lack of agreed theory and purpose, departmental resistance, and the failure of the system to consider the information needs of the user.

The auditor general, Parliament's own auditing body, was extremely critical of the quality of the evaluations and received support from the parliament for this view. In 1977, the auditor general was, by means of legislation, given permission to report to Parliament in cases where the government had not established satisfactory procedures for measuring and reporting on the efficiency and effectiveness of the programs. These annual reports to the Parliament were highly critical and left their mark on public debate. The bureaucracy was not overly enthusiastic about having its own evaluation assessed by a parliamentary body.

In 1976, the government issued a performance-monitoring policy which resulted in a lot of performance measurement activity, and a guide on ongoing performance measurement. The Treasury Board Secretariat encouraged departments in this direction and several reports were made to Parliament. But the effort died in the early 1980s, to be replaced by a focus on program evaluation. Still, many departments developed and continue to have operational performance monitoring systems for their own management purposes and for reporting to Parliament.

In 1977, the Office of the Comptroller General (OCG) was established in the Treasury Board and a new evaluation strategy (a Treasury Board policy) was developed in 1981. This new policy stressed the need to address the opposition that characterized the earlier efforts and took its final form in two publications (Office of the Comptroller General 1981a, 1981b)

These documents formed the basis for further developments. They provided a definition of program evaluation, clarified the roles of key agents in the evaluation process, and discussed an appropriate evaluation process. These two documents described in considerable detail the official policy with regard to program evaluation.

The policy focused on evaluation as one of several elements in the management cycle (planning, evaluation, and adjustment). The main objective was to provide clients and users with relevant and timely information and analyses which could help them to allocate resources more efficiently and to reach decisions on improving programs. This produced a form of program evaluation which focused to a lesser extent than found in the literature on true scientific studies attempting to present absolute statements about program outcome and effects (Segsworth 1989: 24).

However, it did open the way for extensive studies of many fundamental conditions: whether the programs are still relevant, whether they are effective in terms of meeting their targets, and whether there are alternative ways of meeting objectives which would be more cost efficient.

The deputy minister (equivalent to the permanent secretary in the United Kingdom) of each department is the client for evaluation and is responsible for evaluations being implemented in accordance with the OCG's guidelines. The deputy minister is also responsible for ensuring that adequate infrastructure is in place, that the evaluations are used internally within the department as a basis for decision making, and that they are included in relevant reports to Parliament. Reports about program performance are to be made to Parliament and on a select basis to the Treasury Board.

The departments also have their own internal audit units which are responsible for investigating and producing information about the cost efficiency of the department's internal operations. In some departments the "evaluation unit" and the "audit unit" form part of the same section under the same management. More recent initiatives have encouraged the close coordination of evaluation and audit into review units (Treasury Board Secretary 1994).

Under the 1981 policy, evaluations in individual departments were to take place cyclically and would aim to cover a specific range of activities: over a five-year period all of the department's programs were to be evaluated. This cyclic requirement has been relaxed in the 1994 policy.

Each department produced an evaluation plan which covered several years. The plans were the result of discussions within the department and with central agencies. The plan was updated annually and sent to the OCG for information. Most departments have a "senior evaluation committee" which makes decisions concerning the department's evaluation plan for the upcoming years, functions as a reference group for individual studies, and assesses and adopts any recommendations that may result from evaluations.

Canada's Present Performance-Monitoring Policy

Over time it became evident that the evaluation policy of the 1980s was not as successful as expected. Problems related to the lack of sufficient will and ability by managers of departments and agencies to utilize and exploit the opportunities available, and the limited use by central agencies and Parliament of the information provided. In 1991, the Treasury Board policy on program evaluation was revised. The revised policy called for a more strategic approach, focusing the limited resources for evaluation on priority areas (Auditor General of Canada 1993). More attention was to be paid to cross-departmental evaluations.

The OCG introduced the idea of Performance Monitoring Frameworks in February 1993. This was meant to be a tool for individual managers to structure "monitoring and reporting on the performance of their programmes, services and operations" (Office of the Comptroller General 1993) and increase the attention paid to ongoing monitoring of program performance.

The development and implementation by managers of a comprehensive strategy to monitor and report on performance was felt to be the best way to achieve the 1991 objectives. A performance-monitoring framework would normally specify:

- what are information needs to be gathered on the key aspects of program and operational performance;
- how the information will be collected, and when or how often it will be collected;
- what are the various clients' information needs; and
- when, and through what instrument, the information is going to be reported.

A good performance-monitoring framework could assist managers to:

- establish a performance-based and results-oriented management style, and make decisions that are better supported by facts and evidence (i. e. performance-based management);
- report relevant performance information to the parties to whom they are accountable and demonstrate their progress in achieving program and operational objectives efficiently and in a manner consistent with statutes and policies; and
- demonstrate that they are in control: that they know reasonably well what their program is achieving, can identify risks and solve problems in a timely manner and that their practices and procedures adequately ensure resources are spent with due regard to prudence and probity.

In 1994, the Treasury Board policy on evaluation was further revised to accommodate the shrinking analytical resources available through a focus on more encompassing "review" activities rather than evaluation or audit per se, a reemphasis on the need for a strategic application of review resources, and streamlining the guidelines for departments (Treasury Board Secretariat 1994).

The Central Unit—Function and Organization

The central unit in Canada is the Treasury Board. The Treasury Board is a committee of ministers which had two secretariats, or departments, the Treasury Board Secretariat, responsible for administration policy and personnel policy, and the Office of the Comptroller General (OCG), responsible for financial management, internal audit and evaluation.

The OCG's role was

- to define policy and standards for internal auditing, program evaluation and financial management;
- to ensure integration of the processes for budgetary and financial management with the operational processes on a program level;
- to help the departments to improve planning, reporting and management tools; and
- to promote staff development within the field of financial management, evaluation and internal auditing.

In the period 1980–84, the program evaluation branch of the OCG worked proactively to establish an infrastructure and to establish the evaluation function in the departments. This included, among other things, policy development, standards development, advice, and training of evaluators. The program evaluation branch was organized with liaison officers responsible for individual departments.

The OCG assessed and contributed to the quality of individual evaluations that were carried out in departments and agencies, and gave advice on analysis, interpretation, and use of the findings from evaluations. The OCG was also responsible for assessing how the evaluation function in departments performed and for taking appropriate corrective measures deemed necessary to improve the quality of the evaluation function.

However, it did not have the authority to direct departments to undertake specific evaluation practices. According to the auditor general, the OCG acted primarily as a facilitator and coordinator, relying on persuasion rather than specific directions (Auditor General 1993).

In June of 1993, as part of a reorganization of all departments, the OCG was disbanded as an organization and its functions merged within the Treasury Board Secretariat.

Experience of Performance Monitoring in Canada

As indicated above, most attention on performance monitoring in Canada has been on periodic program evaluation rather than on ongoing performance measurement. And these program evaluation efforts have been the subject of a relatively extensive and critical assessment from agents outside the departments and from the OCG.

In a report commissioned by the auditor general, Professor A.W. Johnson (1992) asks the following questions: "How effective are the evaluations?" and "How are they adapted to the administrative system?" Johnson suggests that the evaluations have been designed to too great an extent to be the basis for decision making within the government and departments. He feels that evaluation activity should, to a greater degree, function as an "instrument of accountability between government and parliament," but that it is extremely difficult or impossible to combine both these considerations in one single evaluation.

In keeping with its mandate, the auditor general has carried out critical assessments of the evaluations. In 1983, the auditor general concluded that progress had been made with regard to evaluation, but that the total number of evaluations and the number of evaluations in individual departments was insufficient and did not cover enough of the departments' program activities. Furthermore, the quality of the evaluations was not satisfactory, and only one evaluation report had been used in respect of the Parliament. In the early 1990s, the OCG carried out a study aimed at surveying how the program evaluations were used, and the benefits different decision makers had from program evaluations (Mayne 1994). The results, based on documentation from approximately 210 evaluations in the period 1984–89 (approximately half of the total number of evaluations in that same period), indicated that:

- approximately 20 percent of the evaluations led to considerable changes in the programs, program abandonment, or substantial reforms; and
- approximately 50 percent led to smaller program improvements, adjustments, and modifications.

The remaining evaluations only produced an increased understanding of the program and the program' s effects.

The study also shows that program evaluation plays different roles in different departments. The most prominent roles include providing:

- help for strategic planning and policy design;
- support to those responsible for improving programs; and
- a means to account for program performance and identify dollar savings.

Which role is most prominent in a department depended on, among other things:

- the specific information needs of the organization;
- the management style of the executive;
- the history of evaluation in the organization; and
- the perception of evaluation held by the principle client for evaluation, the deputy head of the organization.

From 1985–86 to 1991–92 government programs and activities covering about one-quarter of government expenditures, were evaluated. In 1991–92, $ 28.5 million was spent on program evaluation across all federal government departments.

In his 1993 annual report, the auditor general concluded that the story of program evaluations in the government of Canada is one of great potential and high expectations that have been only partly fulfilled. The report indicates that program evaluations frequently are not timely or relevant, and several large-expenditure programs have not been evaluated. Most of the evaluations are designed to meet the needs of departmental managers. The evaluations have focused on operational performance and they are less likely to challenge the existence of a program and its cost-effectiveness. The information needs of the cabinet, Parliament, and the public have not been sufficiently met. And the quality of the evaluations is uneven.

The report underlined the significance of the use of quality assessment and external review, the importance of linking program evaluation to significant decision making and budgeting, and the need for strong leadership.

The 1994 revised Treasury Board policy was in part a response to the auditor general's report. As mentioned earlier, one of its features is a stronger attempt to link together all forms of performance monitoring, and as such represents increased interest in performance measurement activity.

Assessments of the Three Country Experiences

Either or both of evaluation and performance measurement are central instruments in the public administration policy of all three nations reviewed here. Experience from the three countries in our study and from other countries as well, indicates that a combination of performance monitoring and evaluation is necessary to best fulfill the information needs of the cabinet, Parliament, managers, and public. There is also a need for adaptation to the different needs of government.

In the United Kingdom, our review shows that performance monitoring, based on an ongoing monitoring of quantitative performance indicators, came to have widespread application in the 1980s. The number of indicators in use has risen dramatically, and performance monitoring has become a key element in the Next Steps reform, in the management's salary system, and in a minister's management of the agencies under his or her jurisdiction.

The use of performance monitoring would hardly have become so widespread in the 1980s had it not been for the strong political will of the prime minister. When Margaret Thatcher came to power in 1979, public administration policy was a key campaign issue. The new prime minister's attitude to the public sector was characterized by deep-rooted distrust. Her objective was a smaller, cheaper, and more efficient public sector, which she aimed to achieve partly through privatization and partly through the introduction of management techniques such as performance management. In turn, this would make it easier to push through cost-cutting and efficiency-enhancing measures.

In many ways Canada is the opposite of the United Kingdom. In Canada, the main focus in performance monitoring has been on evaluation rather than ongoing performance measurement and the developments have not been the result of political pressure. However, the new 1994 policy in Canada underlines the use of performance indicators in the management process and suggests a move towards a more balanced approach to performance monitoring than in the past.

Norway has opted from the beginning for a combination of performance measurement and evaluation. Performance measurement is used as an instrument in operations management, while evaluation is used in strategic management and in measuring target efficiency.

In the United Kingdom and Canada, separate central units have been established to promote the development, and use of performance measurement and evaluation respectively in the public administration. Both nations actively use a formal central unit function as a means of securing support, legitimacy and backing for reform work.

The strong political pressure in the United Kingdom that came with the introduction of management techniques, including performance monitoring, is reflected in the organizational location of the central unit. When the central efficiency unit was established in 1979, the unit was placed under the jurisdiction of the Cabinet Office, with close ties to the prime minister. When the Office of the Minister for the Civil Service (OMCS) was established, it too was placed directly under the Cabinet Office. The ties with the prime minister's office were not changed in 1992 when the OMCS and the efficiency unit were merged and placed under a new office, the Office of Public Service and Science (OPPS).

One interesting feature of the organization of the central unit in the United Kingdom is that the *role as formulator of policy and implementor of public administration policy has been divided between different central unit bodies.* The ideas for central new reforms appear to have come out of the central efficiency unit, manned by a handful of selected senior individuals from private industry. On the other hand, the responsibility for implementation has been with the OMCS and then the OPPS, considerably larger units, with a larger number of staff members with a background from the public sector.

In Norway, the central-unit functions that are related to performance measurement and evaluation have been placed in organizational units that had already been established: the ministry of administration, the ministry of finance and the directorate of public management.

When we compare the United Kingdom with Norway, the most striking feature common to both countries is the lack of systematic and comprehensive central evaluation and assessment of the reform efforts. This weakens the basis for learning and the opportunity to adapt policy on the basis of experience. The synthesizing and communication of experience seems to be a central unit function that has not been given much attention in the two nations. There is little discussion of the pitfalls connected with the use of performance monitoring in the public administration. Only recently in the United Kingdom, was an assessment of the reforms undertaken by Trosa (Next Steps: Moving On 1994)—see chapter 4.

Unlike the United Kingdom and Norway, the central unit in Canada augmented by the work of the auditor general and other outside parties, has given considerable focus to charting the use and beneficial effects of evaluation. Still we have to add that also in Canada there is a general lack of in-depth analysis to enlighten the causes of failures and weaknesses. It is not until later years that we can see interesting elements of such in-depth analysis (Auditor General of Canada 1993; Mayne 1994).

In the United Kingdom, it would appear that it has been important for a prime minister so highly critical of bureaucracy to free herself from antecedents and earlier constraints. This distance (and distrust) may have been an important condition for pushing ahead with the management reforms in such a consistent manner as took place in the United Kingdom.

It would appear that exploratory, research-based evaluations have only been able to play a marginal role in the United Kingdom's extremely indicator-based approach, where the main objective has been cost reductions and productivity increases in a restricted sense. There is also evidence that Parliament rather than the British government has brought pressure to bear in order to introduce a stronger element of evaluation into public administration policy. For example, during the FMI reform it was the political discussion in Parliament that pointed the program in the direction of evaluation.

Experience from the United Kingdom would tend to suggest that a lack of adaptation and differentiation can undermine an administrative reform, although not necessarily. The PPB and the PAR program are examples of earlier reforms that died, probably due to too little adaptation. The Next Steps reform, however, which is being introduced on a broad scale with generally the same guides and principles, is still very much alive, in spite of its apparent lack of differentiation and adaptation to different objectives and needs. The lack of differentiation and adaptation probably receives far less attention, as long as political support for the reform remains strong. On the other hand, it would be interesting to explore how the substance of the Next Steps program would develop if political support for the program declined and disappeared, and the bureaucracy itself was to assume control, as happened in, for example, the PAR and PPB reforms in the 1970s.

In addition, references in the various initiatives to earlier reform experiments are limited. This is particularly true in the United Kingdom and Norway. Public administration researchers claim that this is a virtue. According to them, it is precisely this lack of evaluation and synthesizing of experiences that makes it possible to carry through new reforms unhampered with historical baggage (Brunsson 1991). In Canada, we can now discern a move towards learning and adaptation as a result of experience gained from the mistakes and flaws in previously implemented development work, but only in the limited area of program evaluation. Broader public administration reforms have not been assessed. In Norway, we see a move towards a more nuanced and research-based approach to performance measurement and evaluation (Nilsen 1994).

The implementation strategies of the three nations also have a lot in common. The trend is partial or completely full-scale implementation through political and administrative directives. This strategy bears little resemblance to an experimental approach. Canada has gone the furthest in institutionalizing the reform work with separate evaluation units in the departments and central support and monitoring units. In the United Kingdom, performance monitoring is part of a wide-ranging reform to renew and improve the efficiency of the public administration. Tasks are transferred from departments to the agencies which are to be managed with the aid of performance monitoring. In Norway, performance monitoring and evaluation is one of several instruments used together to make the public administration more manageable, efficient, and user-oriented.

In all three nations the utilization of political and administrative directives is combined with the communication of advice and information. The coupling of performance measurement and evaluation to budgeting, political decision making, and management is stressed, although success in this link is quite limited (Gray, Jenkins, and Segsworth 1994). The three nations appear to have selected somewhat different means of communicating with senior management in ministries and agencies. Canada and Norway have generally used less rigid means such as courses, guidance, and information to reach out to the managers. The United Kingdom has gone the furthest in formalizing demands on senior management. These demands take the form of performance-related contracts and bonus agreements. This measure has also been attempted in Norway, though it has seen little success.

Experiences from Canada indicate that it is extremely difficult to use evaluation as a means of controlling and sanctioning, and at the same time use evaluation as a basis for learning and for developing the organization. It would appear that the government in Canada is paying more attention to using evaluation positively in the learning and management process, while playing down the control aspect. The price of this is criticism from external review expecting evaluation to play a more control role.

Our review confirms the importance of the role of a central unit in implementing performance monitoring in a government. This is perhaps not surprising since organizations and managers on their own tend not to want to, nor feel the need to, systematically monitor and report on the performance of their programs. The experiences of the three countries shows the wide range of intervention the central unit can play depending on the historical developments, current politics, and the extent of political support.

Conclusion

Experiences from the three countries in this study indicate that a combination of program measurement and evaluation seems to be the most appropriate approach. If the development of performance monitoring proceeds too far in cultivating performance measurement, it will create a reaction and demand for supplementing the indicator-based approach with evaluations. Furthermore, the study reveals that the ability to learn from previous reform efforts is limited. Canada has done a great deal to systematize experiences. There is a similar development in Norway. In the United Kingdom, implementation of a consistent and "pure" version of an indicator-based system required first and foremost a strong political leadership and monitoring from the central unit. There are few indications of a more experimental approach in the three countries. The trend is full-scale implementation through directions, combined with the communication of advice and information from the central unit.

Note

1. The assistance of Stein Grøting and Jens Gunvaldsen in finalizing this chapter is gratefully acknowledged.

References

Arbeids- og administrasjonsdepartementet. 1992. *AADs omstillingsplan for statlig virksomhet i 90-årene.*

Administrasjonsdepartementet. 1994. *Forvaltningspolitisk redegjørelse.*

Arbeids- og administrasjonsdepartementet. 1992. *Om statens forvaltnings- og personalpolitikk.* St.meld. nr. 35 (1991–92).

Auditor General of Canada. 1993. R*eport of the Auditor General of Canada to the House of Commons Year Ending 31 March 1993.* Government Services.

Brofoss, K. 1991. "Målstyring og virksomhetsplanlegging sett fra et departement." In *Målstyring og virksomhetsplanlegging i offentlig sektor,* ed. P. Lægreid. Bergen: Alma Mater.

Brunsson, N. 1991. "Målstyring og virksomhetsplanlegging som forvaltningspolitisk strategi." In *Målstyring og virksomhetsplanlegging i offentlig sektor,* ed. P. Lægreid. Bergen: Alma Mater.

Christensen, T. 1991a. "Virksomhetsplanlegging - staffasje eller effektivt styringsverktøy?" In M*ålstyring og virksomhetsplanlegging i offentlig sektor,* ed. P. Lægreid. Bergen: Alma Mater.

Christensen, T. 1991b. V*irksomhetsplanlegging i forskning/utdanningsinstitusjoner.* Statskonsult 1991 nr. 10.

Cm. 2450 1994. N*ext Steps: Moving On.* (The Trosa Report). Cabinet Office (OPSS). London: HMSO.

Derlien, H-U. 1990. "Genesis and Structure of Evaluation Efforts in Comparative Perspective." In Pr*ogram Evaluation and the Management of Government: Patterns and Prospects Across Eight Nations,* ed. R.C. Rist. New Brunswick, N.J.: Transaction Publishers.

Dobell, R. and D. Zussman. 1981. "An Evaluation System for Government: If politics is theatre then evaluation is (mostly) art." C*anadian Public Administration* 24, no. 3.

Finansdepartementet. 1984. *Om reformer i budsjettsystemet og endringer i bevilgningsreglementet.* St.prp. nr. 52 (1984–85).

Finansdepartementet. 1985a. *Endringer i bevilgningsreglementet som trer i kraft fra 1986.* Rundskriv R–25/1985.

Finansdepartementet. 1985b. B*udsjettreformen 1986. Overgang til mer konsekvent målstyring.* Notat utarbeidet av finansavdelingen november.

Finansdepartementet. 1992a. R*esultatstyring og rapportering i statsbudsjettet for 1994.* Rundskriv R–23/1992.

Finansdepartementet. 1992b. *Statsbudsjettet (Gul Bok).*

Finansdepartementet. 1992c. *Langtidsprogrammet 1994–97.* St.meld. nr. 4 (1992–93).

Finansdepartementet. 1993. *Statsbudsjettet (Gul Bok).*

Finansdepartementet. 1994. *Statsbudsjettet (Gul Bok).*

Gray, A., B. Jenkins, and B. Segsworth. 1994. *Budgeting, Auditing, and Evaluation: Functions and Integration in Seven Governments.* New Brunswick, N.J.: Transactions Publishers.

H.M. Treasury. 1985. *Policy Work and the FMI.* Financial Management Unit.

Improving Management in Government: The Next Steps. 1988. A Report to the Prime Minister (Ibbs Report). London: HMSO.

Johnson, A. W. 1992. *Reflections on Administrative Reform in the Government of Canada 1962–1991.* Office of the Auditor General.

Kleven, T. 1993. "Det ruller og det går. Om politikeres problematiske forhold til planlegging." *Tidsskrift for samfunnsforskning* 1:31–51.

Lægreid, P. 1991. "Modernisering og målstyring i staten." In *Målstyring og virksomhetsplanlegging i offentlig sektor*, ed. P. Lægreid. Bergen: Alma Mater.

Lægreid, P. 1992. *Tendensar i utviklinga av offentleg sektor*. LOS-senteret, Notat nr. 92/37.

Making the Most of the Next Steps: The Management of Ministers' Departments and their Executive Agencies. 1991. A Report to the Prime Minister (Fraser Report). London: HMSO.

Mayne, J. 1994. "Utilizing Evaluation in Organizations: The Balancing Act." In *Can Governments Learn? Comparative Perspectives on Evaluation & Organizational Learning*, eds. F. L. Leeuw, R.C. Rist and R.C. Sonnichsen. New Brunswick, N.J.: Transaction Publishers.

Nilsen, T. H. 1991. "Virksomhetsplanlegging: Hvordan gikk det?" In *Målstyring og virksomhetsplanlegging i offentlig sektor*, ed. P. Lægreid. Bergen: Alma Mater.

Nilsen, T. H. 1994. "From management by objectives to management by results." Paper nr. 94/14 Norwegian Research Centre in Organisation and Management.

Norwegian Official Report. 1972. *Programbudsjettering*. Nr. 5.

Norwegian Official Report. 1984. *Produktivitetsfremmende reformer i statens budsjettsystem*. Nr. 23.

OECD. 1993. *Public Management Developments Survey*.

Office of the Comptroller General. 1981a. *Guide on the Program Evaluation Function*. Supply and Services.

Office of the Comptroller General. 1981b. *Principles for the Evaluation of Programs by Federal Departments and Agencies*. Supply and Services.

Office of the Comptroller General. 1993. *Performance Monitoring Frameworks*.

Olsen, J. P. 1988. *Statsstyre og institusjonsutforming*. Universitetsforlaget

Olsen, J. P. 1993a. "Et statsvitenskapelig perspektiv på offentlig sektor." In *Organisering av offentlig sektor*, ed. Lægreid og Olsen. Tano.

Olsen 1993b. Journal. Universitetsforlaget, Stat & Styring no 2.

Segsworth, R. 1989. "Policy and Program Evaluation in the Government of Canada." In *Program Evaluation and the Management of Government*, ed. R. Rist. New Brunswick, N.J.: Transaction Publishers.

Statskonsult. 1991 *Kartlegging av virksomhetsplanlegging og resultatstyring i statlige virksomheter*. Rapport nr. 16.

Steine, V. O. 1988. *Budsjettsystemer i offentlig forvaltning og erfaring med forandringer i de siste år?* Foredrag på Nordisk administrativt forbund, Reykjavik, Island.

Steine, V. O. 1991. "Hva nå? Forvaltningspolitiske utfordringer i lys av erfaringer med Den nye staten." In *Målstyring og virksomhetsplanlegging i offentlig sektor*, ed. P. Lægreid . Bergen: Alma Mater.

Treasury Board Secretariat. 1994. *Treasury Board Manual on Review, Internal Audit and Evaluation*.

3

Performance Monitoring for Budget Management: A New Role of the Budget Center

Eduardo Zapico-Goñi

Introduction

A fiscal crisis has been putting pressure for some time on the need to make immediate and substantial cuts in government spending. In most OECD (Organization for Economic Cooperation and Development) countries, financial ministers are confronting budget and spending management with firm intentions to control public expenditures. All expenditures, including programs and entitlements, have been considered as areas for such reductions. Yet the crisis continues. One of the reasons often put forward to explain the difficulties in reducing public spending is the lack of strong central leadership from the budget authority. While this may be true, the meaning of "strong" needs clarification. The qualification of "strong" is important and has implications for the role of the budget center: strong, how and for what purpose?

At the aggregate level, the control function of budgeting is now one of the highest concerns for budget authorities.[1] Budget adjustments since the 1980s have tended towards reinforcing the dominant position of the finance ministry and the budget office to control total spending. Aggregate control on spending has generally been based on: (1) tight fiscal norms, targets, and baselines to constrain budget requests; (2) multiyear financial scenarios; and (3) extending the preparation of the budget to include a new phase, the so-called pre-preparation of the budget (Schick 1986: 133).

In general, all these measures have strengthened in some fashion the finance ministries relative to spending departments. Budget negotiations take place in terms of financial ceilings. Constraining fiscal targets or norms are set before the start of the budget preparation. Total revenues and expenditures or the balance between the two are preset, in absolute terms or relative to the gross national product (GNP). The budget process begins with an extrapolation of budget trends and multiyear budget projections used to set the financial framework. Furthermore, finance ministers are surrounded by the highest-level support to resolve budget conflicts, namely inner cabinets, budget cabinets, star chambers, and so on (Tarschys 1985: 36).

However, experience from the 1980s shows that budget targets (norms) have been difficult to implement. The formal institutional strength of the budget authority during budget formulation has had difficulties in having an impact on actual spending. There often has not been a careful consideration of the reality behind spending claims. In many cases, governments discovered that past commitments already exceeded the spending totals set in the norms or the norms were formulated at an early stage of the budget process without knowing real program needs. It is not surprising that operationalizing aggregated norms into specific targets was the main obstacle (Schick 1986: 127–28). Norms were not based on a realistic assessment of what was attainable through the budget formulation and implementation process; norms were often political statements.

Since the beginning of the 1990s, similar budget norms have been suggested—for example, the Maastricht criteria of convergence for the Economic and Monetary Union in Europe: 3 percent of the gross domestic product (GDP) as a limit of public deficit and 60 percent of GDP as a limit of public debt (Italianer 1993 p. 18). Currently, complementary and more precise measures are also being proposed and/or applied with the same aim of increasing the dominant position of the central budget authority to control aggregate spending: subceilings for major spending accounts, rejecting automatic inflation premiums, reductions in entitlements, offsetting procedures or "pay-as-you-go" which oblige departments to suggest program cuts to fund other requests

(Wildavsky 1993: 28). Recent research also points in the same direction when suggesting the need for strong control during budget implementation as the necessary complement to fiscal norms and rules for discipline: maintaining the dominant position of the budget authority and limiting the possibilities to amend the draft budget or to change it during execution (Von Hagen 1992: 37ff).

The general implicit assumption of all these practical initiatives and research proposals is that firm enforcement from the budget authority to make spending departments comply with rules and norms is enough for spending control. The generally accepted roles of a strong central budget authority are the hierarchical solution of conflicts of resource allocation and firm spending guardianship or inspection of budget execution. These are important roles, but the need for the central budget office also to play a nonpreventive yet proactive steering role has traditionally been neglected. The mere tightening of constraints does not guarantee sustainable spending discipline. The problem is not just holding total spending figures but coping with forces in society which push spending above budget limits. The illusion of control felt by finance ministries during budget preparation is well-known and has been long experienced. In order to guarantee long-term spending discipline, we argue that it is not sufficient to formulate tight budgets and design rigid spending procedures if there is no financial management capacity in the budget system to meet these objectives.

In fact, the usual concern of the central budget office is to concentrate mainly on preventing decisions which produce divergent spending. Public budgets are perceived and work as tools for repressing undesirable spending behavior rather than guiding proper spending. Enforcement to comply with budgetary discipline is necessary, but positive follow-up and support might also be very important to guarantee real and sustainable spending control. We suggest that a successful long-term control on spending also depends on the existence of strong central management leadership for guiding sound strategic budgeting, able to adapt spending behavior of the whole budget system to changes in circumstances. In this line of thought, there is an increasing awareness of the need for "a comprehensive, long-term strategy if public expenditure is to be curbed effectively" (Swedish Ministry for Finance 1992), and for "establishing an expenditure management system that results in better strategic planning" (Government of Canada 1995: 1).

Sustainable fiscal discipline requires the development of overall financial management. The demand for sound spending management in the public sector is greater than ever before (OECD 1990: 9). Part of the answer to this demand is being sought by spending decentralization initiatives to encourage value for money in the behavior of public managers. The increase in the dominant position of the central budget office with respect to total spending has been accompanied with a decentralization of spending authority for line managers in departments and agencies—part of the move towards managerialism discussed in chapter 1.

This approach of course raises the shadow of Perrow's "paradox" (Perrow 1977)— decentralization without losing central power (Cothran 1993). This apparent dilemma is supposed to be solved if appropriate performance monitoring and accountability systems can guarantee line managers' spending behavior to be consistent with overall budget goals. Aiming at this, traditional detailed control on budget execution is being shifted to a more managerial one. Performance measurement is one of the essential components for the success of this shift towards budget management. There is now a widespread agreement on the need for applying the criteria of economy, efficiency, and effectiveness (3Es) for resource allocation and spending monitoring. However, it is not yet clear how the finance ministry should put these criteria into practice or, indeed, when it is appropriate and to what extent doing so in fact helps convergence with overall spending goals. A considerable number of studies on the design and quality of performance measurements have been carried out (Britan 1991: 24; Carter 1991: 85–101; Hatry 1980: 312–39; Jackson 1988: 11–15). However, relatively little has been written about the way in which performance measurements are actually being used by central budget offices in the budget process.

The aim of this chapter is to analyze how budget offices in developed western countries are approaching spending control. What roles do they and should they play from their supposedly more dominant position. The main emphasis will be on how they use performance measurement after having implemented spending decentralization. The analysis will be centered around questions such as: What is the significance of performance measurement in initiatives which have taken place since 1980 to improve budgeting? What incentives are given for the use of performance measurement? What kinds of performance measuremenst are being used for budgeting? For what, and how, are they used? What limitations have been found? What is the relevance of the currently proposed performance measurement for the budget context of today? What are the implications for the role and position of the budget office in budget management?

The following sections provide, in the first place, information on the type of budget initiatives which have been undertaken in many developed countries. Particular attention will be paid to the efforts made by budget offices in decentralizing spending and using performance measurement for improving resource allocation and spending. The main limitations of these initiatives will then be discussed. Finally, a new model of and criteria for successful performance monitoring will be proposed for the budget office to play a more relevant role for budget management today.

Current Reforms: Budget Decentralization, Performance Monitoring, and a Businesslike Spending Style

A clear shift has occurred from budget administration to budget management (see chapter 1). There might be some differences in the way in which each country has approached this shift, but most of the key concepts are common. The main aim has been to promote a new management style in public officials, to make them more concerned with, and committed to, achieving results rather than merely implementing spending procedures. This has been encouraged by providing them not only with more spending discretion but also, and simultaneously, with more responsibility for reaching agreed performance targets. The interest for more budget autonomy and performance monitoring is present in the rhetoric of many programs for improving spending: the Financial Management Initiative (FMI) in the United Kingdom; the Increased Ministerial Authority and Accountability (IMAA) and the new Expenditure Management System in Canada; the Financial Management Improvement Program (FMIP) and the Program Management and Budgeting (PMB) in Australia; triennial budgeting in Sweden; and aggregated productivity targeted budget in Denmark (Schick 1990: 26, ff). In all of them, performance monitoring is, explicitly or implicitly, considered a necessary effort to inform budgeting.

The focus on performance monitoring is not new if we take into account previous program- and performance-budget reforms. But the approach now is simpler and less oriented towards paperwork. Reforms now are focused on management concerns with what is being done and produced, and the way in which to hold managers accountable for performance, as opposed to the policy planning and analysis of program budgeting. The main aim is to promote an "entrepreneurial" style (Cothran 1993: 450). Unlike previous program budget reforms, modifying behavior is a priority. Budget format and techniques have proved not to be determining factors for improvements in budgeting. The priority is now for a more managerial spending behavior to maximize value for money.

New forms of budget organization and work style aim at running public departments and agencies as successful businesses. Although not new ideas, decentralization and budgeting by results have been the main vehicles of change to improve the functioning of central government and departments. New efforts are again being made to implement well-recognized proposals such as defining objectives, identifying responsibilities for results, and developing management, information systems and accountability. Defining a bottom-line objective for performance is one important principle of this type of initiative. For this reason, a key endeavor has been to improve budget monitoring with performance measures related to economy, efficiency, and effectiveness and to apply these criteria for budgeting and spending accountability.

These improvements require strengthening the existing financial management capacity in spending departments. Improving the quality of information on performance measurement, and developing cost-consciousness are part of the initiatives undertaken. Competence and capacity for accounting, auditing, and financial control at the agency and departmental level are conditions for financial autonomy (Sweden, Ministry for Finance 1992: 19, 29).

With different approaches depending on each country, central budget offices have played an important role in encouraging the adaptation and use of performance measures for behavioral changes in spending managers. The Treasury in the United Kingdom has set basic requirements for departments to report on performance; the Federal Finance Administration in Germany has played a very active role, but it has just been advisory, not supervisory, while the Treasury in New Zealand is more reactive to the performance measures proposed by departments (OECD 1992: 18–19).

The following initiatives and concepts are common to recent budget reforms in most developed countries:

More Flexibility on Spending Controls as an Incentive to
Improve Performance

New budget controls based on aggregate appropriations, definitions of strategic targets, and standards for performance and reporting have been proposed as less obtrusive controls which allow decentralizing of day-to-day spending decisions. This initiative is supposed to provide the right incentive for sound financial management by making officials more responsible for spending performance. Performance measurement is to be used as a basis for budget control. Decentralization initiatives were oriented to substitute performance measurement and monitoring for traditional spending controls from central budget units. A common declared intention has been to reduce, as much as possible, the application of rules and hierarchical authority in relations between the budget office, spending departments, and agencies (OECD 1989: 4).

More specifically, the initiatives for reducing rigidity in spending behavior are:

- relaxing central controls to move away from obsolete, detailed controls on inputs, compliance with general rules, and formal uniform procedures;
- broader budget frameworks while simultaneously tightening aggregated expenditure control;
- the possibility of keeping savings realized beyond the central targets, as opposed to the traditional practice of automatic reappropriation to the center of all budget credits remaining unspent by agencies;
- increased flexibility in the timing of expenditures;
- the possibility of reallocation of funds between programs or activities; and
- using the revenue generated for pricing for public services.

Most of these budget control modifications have been implemented in advanced reforms with the aim of increasing autonomy and responsibility of spending officials for performance.

Budget Negotiations for Productive Performance

A budget process is now officially treated as a formal negotiation to reach a "contract" or an agreement in which resources and spending autonomy are provided in exchange for promises to achieve performance targets. Central budget offices request the submission of performance-targets documents, and the signature of budget agreements, often with a triennial perspective. This is the case of Memoranda of Understandings in Canada, the Management Plan in the United Kingdom, and the in-depth budget request in Sweden (Gray, Jenkins, and Segsworth 1993: 48, 109, 146).

The allocation of resources is intended to align with the level of performance reached by managers. Performance measurement is a fundamental element of this budget reform. Performance measurement facilitates more effective decision making by changing the pattern of budget discussions between the finance ministry and spending ministries, and between spending ministries and subordinate agencies. Ideally, contract budgeting aims to provide full correlation with resource allocation and performance. "In theory, . . . the linkage should be direct and explicit. Incremental resources would be provided for incremental performance." (OECD 1988: 7).

Although no country is trying to use performance measurement as the sole basis for budgeting, performance is an important element to be considered in resource allocation (the Netherlands, Sweden) or to encourage the best use of resources during budget implementation (Canada, Australia, the United States, the United Kingdom). In any case, budget officials are supposed to take advantage of performance data (the traditional 3Es) as one factor in resource allocation (OECD 1992: 32). For example, in Sweden, one of the countries more advanced in this field, the triennial budget procedure requires the submission of progress reports assessing performance achievements. Reports are made by agencies themselves and audited by the Swedish National Audit Office (Sweden. Ministry for Finance 1993: 5, ff.).

This new approach to budgeting means a qualitative change in the role to be played by the central budget office. It is clear that "contracts" for budgeting-by-results and decentralization implies skills and a capacity for strategy development, target-setting, performance measurement, and reporting from spending agencies. The question which now arises is: assuming that agencies can cope with these conditions, what is the role of the central budget office? One part of the answer has already been given. In the beginning, budget officials should actively facilitate managerial innovations such as measuring performance. Once performance measurement matures, the budget office should play a more circumscribed role (Schick 1990: 33), probably to postevaluation, coordination, and so on. However, what if agencies are uncertain about the objectives they should seek and the performance criteria of success? In cases where organizational or contextual factors give rise to this uncertainty, what role should the budget office play? We suggest this is an increasing problem in public management today and the last section of this chapter deals with this dilemma. But first let us analyze the effects of these reforms to date.

Preliminary Assessments of Budget Reforms

There has not been in-depth evaluation of whether these budgeting reforms have had the expected results of increasing efficient and effective spending behavior in government. However, relevant information is available signaling limited impact. Evidence is both empirical (limited scope of the performance indicators used and weak connections between performance measurement and evaluation with budgeting) and theoretical (mismatch between the business management model and public budgeting).

Limited Scope of Performance Measurement

The limited scope of most performance measurement systems does not allow for the assessment of the actual benefits achieved for citizens and program effectiveness. In general, the type of measures used have related to efficiency and productivity (OECD 1990: 12). The emphasis of most budget reforms has fallen on administrative costs and operational activities. Only slow progress has been made in developing information on the management of effectiveness of policies and spending programs. It has been recognized that agencies have had difficulties in measuring performance and in designing appropriate monitoring systems (Flynn et al. 1988: 35ff).

There has not been adequate information put in place on management performance which would be capable of guaranteeing that, once spending and service delivery is decentralized, the central units of ministerial departments and the finance ministry would be able to keep track of what was happening to public funds. The inadequacy of measures currently in use is recognized in several countries advanced in this field, such as Canada, the United Kingdom, and Australia (Schick 1990). Often, it has been believed impossible to measure and quantify key outputs and outcomes. In two of the most advanced countries, some measurement weaknesses are well-recognized. In the United Kingdom, in general, the difficulty in measuring performance has meant that, after decentralization, the indicators chosen have allowed the center to apply a form of "back-seat driving" rather than the expected "hands-off" control (Carter 1989: 131, 138). In Sweden, formulating appropriate criteria to measure results has been more difficult than expected in some areas (Sweden, Ministry of Finance 1992).

Weak Connections between Performance Measurement and/or Evaluation with Budgeting

The link between resource allocation and performance measurement and/or evaluation has proved to be very difficult to apply in most countries at different levels of government. "The evidence from different national experiences (United States, United Kingdom, Canada, Germany, Spain, Sweden, Finland) indicates that even where the need for this function (regular and integrated feedback from auditing and evaluation into budgeting) is recognized its realization is infrequent" (Gray, Jenkins, and Segsworth 1993: 191). Studies by the General Accounting Office (1993) and the Congressional Budget Office (1993) in the United States focused on cases of excellence at various levels of government found similar results as the international comparative studies mentioned above. The studies found little evidence of significant influence of performance measurement on resource allocation.

Several countries—Sweden, the Netherlands, the United Kingdom—do have information on performance systematically available during the budget process. There are some cases of reasonable connections between operational efficiency and resource allocation, but initiatives to link resources and outcomes are scarce. "The relationship of performance measurement to resource allocation is unsettled" (OECD 1993: 11). In the United Kingdom, the Treasury requests spending departments to support their budget bids with measurement of performance achievements. However, the scope of performance measurement in use is limited to operational performance (as Trosa discusses in chapter 4). Spending departments are frequently not willing to monitor or evaluate program effectiveness (Gray, Jenkins, and Segsworth 1993: 49, 50). Still, performance measurement is seen as necessary and important to promote a budget-management culture in government.

As suggested, one reason for the failure to link budget and performance is the weak development of performance measurement. Another important reason, however, has been neglected or has not been paid sufficient attention. There is a built-in paradox in public budgeting facing the budget office and spending managers: most budget holders have known that efficient performance and saving public resources will mean less budget credits for the following year. Traditionally, the more savings they make during a fiscal year, the less money their programs are allocated next year. Spending managers' behavior anticipates these decisions of the central budget office, if necessary creating financial data to be reported to the center, so as not to damage their own budget.

The probable reaction of spending managers to the demands for efficiency to reallocate resources is one of suspicion and mistrust. Even if financial management reform in some countries proposes that performance measurement be used by line managers when spending their budget and not by budget officers when allocating resources, budget office decisions when implementing contract budgeting will be perceived as rewards or penalties. To improve the spending culture and behavior in departments, it is necessary that the budget office plays a qualitatively different role as will be discussed in the following section. Some initiatives to improve budgeting might reduce this mistrust. Flexible budget control and budget agreements on medium-term resource stability may help. But, of course, the higher the guarantee of future budget funds, the lower the incentive to make budget agreements. The convergence of budget and performance monitoring depends on several conditions that might well be part of a new role of the budget office.

Mismatch between the Business Management Model and Public Budgeting

Applying private-sector, business-management techniques and competitive, market-like, solutions to government might be possible and useful in some cases but not always. Most initiatives for budget adjustment have assumed that the problem of government is either its size (hence cuts in aggregate spending, privatization) or its inefficient performance (hence decentralization, budgeting-by-results). The concern here is the lack of appropriateness of these adjustments and reform initiatives for current government problems.

For many observers, spending decentralization, performance monitoring, and competing for resources sound like a panacea. However, the effects are not as positive or as relevant as expected. Spending keeps on growing. Decentralization and performance measurement are necessary but just as a point of departure. As soon as obsolete and obstructive detailed spending controls are abolished, it is vital that other control systems are *already* working. Independent behavior and fragmentation might follow decentralization and performance competition for resources, if special efforts to promote budget coordination are not made. Since the impact of all these initiatives to stop the growth of spending has been weak, there is increasing recognition that it is necessary to analyze the context, the problems, and the model used for improving public budget management. Given the lack of impact of private-sector management techniques on public spending control, new solutions have to be found to answer specific problems of budget management in government.

However, there is a noticeably weak capacity in most countries for learning from and developing the managerial model used in their reforms. No country has evaluated in depth the impact on government efficiency and effectiveness due to these budgeting reforms. "Evaluation of reform efforts remains largely ad hoc and inadequate in most countries because of problems of measurement and sensitivities to the political dimension" (OECD 1993: 9). A few countries have taken some steps: developing systematic methods for monitoring, reporting on progress, creating steering committees, developing procedures for close cooperation between the finance ministry and spending departments, and developing appropriate methodology for evaluation.

Australia has undertaken a comprehensive evaluation of its public sector reform initiatives (Australia, Task Force on Management Improvement 1992). The discussion about implementing performance measurement in the United Kingdom presented by Trosa in chapter 4 is based on research on the impact of their reforms done for the Cabinet Office (United Kingdom, Cabinet Office 1994). In Canada, as reported by Nilsen in chapter 2, the Office of the Comptroller General has assessed the effects of its program-evaluation efforts which has been complemented by an audit on government evaluation done by the parliamentary auditor general of Canada (1993). In this respect, the role of audit and accounting agencies to evaluate financial management reform should not be neglected. Their evaluations might be very helpful as incentives for the redesign and development of the initiatives (OECD 1990: 16). One of the main obstacles for more systematic evaluation of improvements in financial management has been the absence of reliable and relevant performance measures to learn about the impact of increasing spending autonomy and accountability of line managers.

One of the conditions needed in the budget context for the success of performance measurement is to have "a certain stability of resources" (OECD 1993: 5). Scientific literature on control in nonprofit organizations anticipated these kinds of difficulties (Hofstede 1981: 193). While the traditional performance model based on the 3Es is useful in a context of stability and certainty, we argue that it may be inappropriate or at least insufficient for the type of tasks performed by many public organizations, especially by central departments and highly professionalized public organizations, and in general for budget management under uncertainty.

Initiatives focused on efficiency and competition for budget resources, such as the Financial Management Initiative in the United Kingdom, will realize some savings. However, given the current public budget context of instability, significant budget resources will be wasted on outdated projects efficiently run but solving old problems. This is likely to occur with budget initiatives mainly focused on improving productivity, taking for granted the continuity of policy objectives and institutional arrangements. Furthermore, budgetary reforms in the past have typically proposed a "once-and-for-all" change. What is required today is not an initiative to make one specific change but to increase the capacity of government to adapt its budget behavior to a permanent situation of unpredictable change (Metcalfe and Richards 1990: 210). If the central budget office wants to control spending, it needs to increase the adaptability of budget behavior and the budget model used, related performance measurements, and criteria of success to the ongoing changes in circumstances. Otherwise, the budget incentives and accountability systems will encourage dysfunctional spending. The next section proposes a new conceptual framework to guide the adaptation of the role of the central budget office for budgeting in the uncertain financial management situation governments find themselves in today. In times of uncertainty, the strength of the budget authority should be based on flexible strategic leadership rather than attempting rigid enforcement on spending.

Adapting the Role of the Central Budget Organization and Performance Criteria to the Current Context

Today, government spending is more than ever surrounded by uncertainty and decreasing availability of resources. This budget situation was identified long ago as characterizing budgeting in underdeveloped countries (Wildavsky 1975: 9). The behavior of finance ministries in these countries was identified as "repetitive budgeting." Many budgeting and planning changes take place after the budget has been approved. Rather than adapting spending behavior, modifying the budget data becomes the usual response. Budget estimates lose meaning because of frequent overspending. Furthermore, incessant competitive lobbying for resources makes interministerial relations disintegrate: departments defend their own interests without paying attention to consequences for overall government finances (Wildavsky 1975: 163).

This situation and budget behavior reaction have been reproduced in the last years in OECD countries. Wildavsky himself explains this by introducing the "spending culture" as a new variable. As he put it: "Why would their (Western countries') spending budget have to be redone several times a year?" His answer is political values or preferences. The level of spending today is a function of the political culture (values) of yesterday (Wildavsky 1988: 672 et seq.). This means that spending control in Western countries has failed because governments and their constituents have wanted to spend more. According to this argument, the lack of budget discipline can be explained by spending behavior which defends one's own national way of life, or own particular interest. This is very relevant to understanding why there is a lack of spending discipline and, more importantly, how much the budget authority should focus its efforts on building collective support for budget adjustments.

An important step forward in this direction is provided by Metcalfe's suggestion that under instability and scarcity of resources, the central

unit should build capacity for adaptation into the budget system—
"flexibility budgeting" (Metcalfe and Richards 1990). In this context,
sustainable spending discipline requires a qualitatively different approach to the type of budget reforms undertaken by OECD countries
since the 1980s. If problems were predictable and policy know-how to
solve them were available, the budget office could limit itself to initiatives which focus on efficiency in order to guarantee spending discipline—"efficiency budgeting" in Metcalfe's terminology. This would
require pressure on spending departments to increase responsibility for
productivity and cost reductions. Standardization (performance measurement) and specialization (decentralization) become the responses
to fiscal stress from the spending side. The behavior of the central
budget office is top-down: budget cuts, arbitration of conflicts, pressures on spending departments to define objectives, and commitment
to productivity increases. These are the types of budget initiatives
taken in the 1980s which were analyzed in the previous section. However, the financial management context since the 1980s has combined
both scarcity and uncertainty. This is a different context that requires
flexibility more than efficiency for sustainable spending control.

In this context, augmenting the power of the central budget office to
play its traditional role by using direct and firm control on spending
behavior or making further efforts to increase productivity and establish norms and standards of performance may create undesired rigidity
and encourage further interdepartmental conflicts. Instead, the central
budget office should take the responsibility for the development of the
strategic capacity of the whole budgetary system. This demands a
permanent capacity for redesigning and developing the framework for
the budget process. The budget authority not only should play a legislative and police-like role in setting norms and standards, monitoring
compliance, and applying sanctions, but also should provide strategic
leadership for adaptation. Given the situation of change and uncertainty, strategic budgetary guidance is needed to guarantee long-last-
ing spending discipline. Figure 3.1 shows the main components of the
new role to be played by the central budget office for developing
"flexibility budgeting," as compared to the one proposed in current
budget reforms in OECD countries. New criteria of success (performance measures), future anticipation (dealing with uncertainty), budget roles (interaction among participants), and budget feedback systems (accountability) are the main elements and are discussed below.

FIGURE 3.1
A New Role for Central Budget Offices

	Traditional Budget Office Role	Budget Office Role Under Uncertainty
Criteria of Successful Performance:	maximization/optimization of performance (economy, efficiency, effectiveness)	adaptation (diagnosis, design, development)
Uncertainty Reduction:	planning/programming, and budgeting for results	strategic management of budgeting (achieving budget adaptability)
Interaction With Other Budget Participants:	bilateral, competitive bargaining and arbitration	building trust through multilateral cooperative bargaining
Accountability:	negative enforcement by inspection	positive orientation learning

Performance Monitoring under Instability

The usual proposal to evaluate performance in governments uses the 3Es: economy, efficiency, and effectiveness. Traditional budgeting has emphasized procedural regularity in using resources. Today's budget performance is perceived more in the framework of producing public services and is concerned with results, obtaining things (value) by using public resources (for money). The hidden assumption here is that policies and objectives are fixed standards according to which budget performance is measured. But today, spending programs are formulated within a framework of rapid and unexpected socioeconomic change. The ideal budget performance cannot be represented by economic, efficient, and effective behavior according to fixed budget targets but rather as the capacity to find budget responses to new challenges. The capacities of the budget actors should match the need for change and adapting government to new unexpected problems. Performance monitoring needs to cover these new criteria if budget rigidity is to be avoided.

The 3Es do not capture the most relevant components of appropriate budget management in times of rapid change. The capacity and skill to formulate strategies for budget adaptation and to carry out change need to be considered when assessing the budget performance of spending managers. Budget monitoring and evaluation based on the 3Es are valuable in situations where we can anticipate what actions determine what outcomes, such as for routine and repetitive operations. In the course of time, know-how is developed and outcomes become more predictable.

However, in situations where objectives cannot be well measured or results cannot be predicted, performance cannot be "controlled." As Hofstede argues, cybernetic control is only possible in the case of mechanical procedures or highly operative activities which involve almost completely automated work, with clear objectives and the application of technology (Hofstede 1981: 199). However, although unpredictable activities cannot be controlled, they can be managed. Activities and organizations in which it is not possible to apply control based on the 3Es are precisely those which demand a higher quality of management performance: ability to readjust resources and activities, improvising responses to match and cope with unanticipated challenges.

Since the 3Es are mainly appropriate for assessing the results of operational tasks or policies under certainty, a new approach and a new role of the central budget office is needed to measure and assess performance in a context of instability. Metcalfe (1993) proposes the use of 3Ds, referring to the capacity for:

- *Diagnosis*: an adequate definition of the new problems management is confronting and consideration of the main interests of stakeholders.
- *Design*: an appropriate strategy for solving these problems. Building structures and strategies internally coherent and consistent with the problems they are trying to solve.
- *Development*: a capacity for solving implementation problems and managing change as a learning process.

These concepts are further developed in chapter 11.

What should matter to the finance ministry in times of change and uncertainty is not how efficient or effective each manager has been in achieving their individual budget goals, but the overall budget flexibility or ability to redefine budget problems and the capacity for appropriate reaction. This approach is strategic in nature and is oriented to the long term. And it relates well to the process of budget decentralization. The 3Ds approach is based on using relevant criteria to measure performance and can be applied for evaluating central budget offices when they are decentralizing spending authority.

Central budget offices are now delegating spending responsibility, but do they have the capacity and skill to manage the whole decentralized system? Now that they have more time to coordinate interdepartmental action, do they know how to do it? A capacity for budget innovation at the center of government is crucial for strategic leadership and keeping track of, and for anticipating and promoting, adaptive budgetary learning within the spending departments' financial management practices. This requires other changes in the role to be played by the finance ministry for budget flexibility.

Strategic Management of Spending vs. Planning and Programming

Traditionally, budget reform for the finance ministry has meant the introduction of planning and program budgeting. Multiyear projections of spending, comprehensive calculation of costs and benefits, and reallocation of resources to more productive activities represent the rational alternative to incrementalism. However, budgeting depends both on technical calculations and human behavior. Traditional prescriptions for budget reform have focused their attention on the former to the detriment of the latter. But today the concern is not so much to answer the famous question of V.O. Key: "On what basis shall it be decided to allocate x dollars to activity A instead of activity B," as quoted by W.E. Klay. In situations of uncertainty, instead of maximizing or optimizing utility, the concern is for budget adaptability to the changing environment (Klay 1991: 273). Spending behavior precedes calculations, targets, and formats for budget change. In the last decades, with the help of informatics, finance ministries have introduced and consolidated sophisticated econometric models which have allowed long-range forecasting. The exercise is predominantly one of mathematical extrapolation of economic variables. Nevertheless, concern is increasing about continuous overspending above anticipated estimates.

The proposal here is that in times of change and uncertainty the finance ministry should guide the improvement of strategic budgeting capacities of departments and agencies rather than just planning and programming spending. If the finance ministry wants to control spending, it cannot limit its role just to projecting figures and enforcing

FIGURE 3.2
Characteristics of Program vs. Strategic Budgeting

Planning and Program Budgeting (stability)	Strategic Management and Budgeting (uncertainty)
Agents	
• planning staff	• line and planning staff
Anticipation of the Future	
• long-term spending forecasting by linear extrapolation • comprehensive analysis • quantitative calculation (economic/demographic) • objectivity and continuity assumptions	• process of spending behavior adaptation • speculative and selective analysis • qualitative perception (sociopolitical) • judgment and discontinuity assumptions
Budget Direction/Decision Criteria	
• specific goals and objectives • marginal utility of spending (3Es)	• vision and orientation • leadership judgement
Control and Monitoring	
• budgeting by objectives • performance indicators (3Es) • objective follow-up • accountability for compliance	• building commitment • awareness of resistance to implementation of spending strategies • evaluation for learning • creating a strategic spending culture

norms and procedures to monitor the formal compliance of spending departments. The finance ministry has to provide overall strategic leadership for budgeting and has to facilitate financial-management development in departments (see figure 3.2). Although budgeting and strategic management are usually perceived as two processes which are very difficult to merge properly, they may indeed complement each other. They can be compatible and mutually supporting processes (Hallamachi and Boydston 1991: 315).

In contrast with program budgeting, strategic budget leadership involves anticipation, provision of budget direction, and the provision of mechanisms for budget control, monitoring, and development (Klay 1991: 273).

Anticipation. Planning and program spending have traditionally involved preparing documents or forms useful for verifying whether reality corresponds with the anticipated budget figures, rather than the other way around. Budgeting has been often perceived as a neutral and technical exercise that begins and finishes with the extrapolation of financial figures and the formulation of a document that specifies in detail all decisions to be made and operations to be undertaken. Strategic management sees anticipating the future more as "a pattern in stream of actions" (Mintzberg and Brian 1991: 13). Budget flexibility demands that this stream of spending behavior be consistent within the ongoing context. This means a continuing effort towards anticipating and influencing changes in the environment. Anticipating the future is perceived as a process in which there is awareness of possible discontinuities in trends. Anticipation does not mean just figuring out the future financial aggregates by forecasting and quantitatively extrapolating economic and demographic trends, but also carrying out future-oriented qualitative research, such as scanning the environment and relevant budget documentation, pooling opinions, and so on, to identify emerging financial problems and opportunities. This requires: considering the implications on the budget of sociocultural factors, doing qualitative research, and gathering information on new variables which have no historical precedent. All these efforts to anticipate the future cannot be made by experts in planning and budgeting alone but jointly with line managers, either at the center of government and/or at the center of spending departments.

Providing budget direction and leadership. Contrary to the assumptions of program budgeting, budget direction does not necessarily imply specifying all the goals of spending programs. Budget leadership does not require that objectives be listed, ranked, and quantified. Doing so may generate negative behavior and resistance. Today, direction is perceived as being synonymous with vision or pathfinding. Budgetary guidance generates positive coordination and motivation. A leader's perception on how to adapt budget behavior or decision style is a more appropriate decision criteria than maximizing the marginal utility (3Es) of spending.

Providing mechanisms for budget control, monitoring, and development. Anticipating change and providing strategic vision is not enough for budget flexibility. Just as important is the capacity of the finance ministry and spending departments to execute the budget as approved in order to reach desired results. Management by objectives, budget for results, performance standards, and so on are usually presented as preconditions for appropriate follow-up. But they have proved to be insufficient outside situations of stability and certainty.

Budgetary adjustment is not just a technical exercise. Budget adaptation is first of all a behavioral process. There is a need for participation and for creating compromise for change. The more unstructured the budget context is—multiple stake holders, conflicting relations, major modifications rather than incremental—the higher will be the need to understand budget implementation as a participatory and adaptive process (Berman 1980: 214). The capacity to respond to changing conditions, especially with scarcity of resources, requires not only appropriate authoritative institutions, norms, and procedures, but also commitment and an organizational culture open to the consideration of change.

Creating a "strategic spending culture" is essential for flexibility budgeting. This means accepting change not as a dysfunctional but as a normal state of evolution, confronting spending conflicts and resistance to budgetary change, having and applying long-term values, deciding according to long-term rather than immediate results, and accepting risk and experimentation (Klay 1991: 280). A further condition for adaptability is having coherence between the strategy chosen and the monitoring systems in place. Information, evaluation, and accountability systems should provide appropriate feedback for learning and development, not just information on the mechanical implementation of the strategy.

But perhaps the main feature of public budget discipline is that it requires interorganizational commitment. Traditional prescriptions to build commitment have mainly focused on its internal aspect (intraorganizational commitment). Today, budget officials from the finance ministry have to confront the challenge of building commitment outside their organization. This is more the case in federal and regionalized countries: they have to obtain the commitment of officials from other departments or other levels of government to adapt their spending behavior. Negotiation, persuasion, coalition-building, boundary, and networking management roles may be more effective in this situation than merely applying a hierarchical top-down approach with departments that in fact do not recognize the authority of the finance ministry. This demands substantial training for budget officials in these techniques, traditionally neglected. Developing negotiating skills is a must for budget officials to be able to control spending.

Managing Budget Negotiations: Building Trust and Cooperation

Setting norms, enforcing procedures and priorities, and arbitrating conflicts on competing demands for resources are traditional roles of a budget office. They are all mainly top-down. To guarantee budget coordination, especially in unstable times, they need to be complemented by well-functioning horizontal budget communication and information systems aimed at voluntary compliance. Budgetary discipline requires that priorities and directives be well-transmitted, accepted, and internalized by budgetary actors. Building trust and cooperation is another of the major challenges and roles of central units to achieve flexibility budgeting.

Most of the political science research on budgeting assumes that the budget process entails bargaining over conflicting goals or interests. Budget actors are perceived as guardians and advocates with naturally opposing roles (Wildavsky 1975: 4). Their interests are supposed to be always and necessarily antagonistic. Budgeting is considered a negotiation exercise to satisfy budget actors competing for resources. The assumption is that whatever one gets, the others lose. Behavior during budget negotiations is supposed to be purely distributive with step-by-step concessions and compromises from supposedly clear opening positions. The search for joint program action during the budget procedure has been traditionally neglected. Positions are focused on defeating the counterpart. Winning together is rarely, if ever, considered.

However, budget negotiations might be also seen as an opportunity for reducing unnecessary uncertainty. This means considering budgeting beyond a simple exchange of resources. Negotiating in a complex budgetary context means that initial positions are not properly known until well after negotiations have begun. Enhancing cooperation requires preventing future budget conflict, developing and sharing financial and program information, searching for feasible spending decisions, and developing common perceptions of spending priorities and values (Winham 1977: 97). This is not an appeal to goodwill but to considering budget negotiations as a management problem. This requires the finance ministry to play an active role at subaggregate levels to encourage open discussion on interdepartmental initiatives during budget formulation.

Essentially, budget negotiations are "social negotiations." These negotiations involve the special interaction of two or more social organi-

FIGURE 3.3
Building Trust Within Budget Negotiations

(a) *Distribution* of Resources (competition)
(b) *Integration* of Complementary Spending Values and Interests (cooperation)
(c) *Restructuring* the Rules of the Budgetary Game
(d) *Internal Preparation* of Budget Requests in Departments

zations (Walton and McKersie 1965: 5, ff). Budget "social negotiations" have the following characteristics:

- the technical components of budget negotiations are combined with human dimensions such as attitudes, feelings, values, expectations on rewards, and/or penalties;
- the agreement to allocate resources only represents one step within the negotiating relationship, a relationship which exists throughout the entire budget cycle, and is subject to further modifications during the execution of the budget;
- the budget negotiations are repeated successively and in a concatenated manner every year;
- politicians and officials directly participating in the negotiations represent groups or organizations whose members are interested in the outcome. The members of these groups exercise multiple and not necessarily compatible pressures on their representatives; and
- the agenda of the budgetary negotiations is usually focused on confrontation among individual interests, however, these are always defended within a broader collective framework: economic crisis, public deficit, unemployment, etc.

To avoid having confrontation dominate the budget negotiations, all components of the budget negotiations should be taken into consideration and encouraged: (a) distribution of resources (competition), (b) integration of values and interests in spending (cooperation), (c) restructuring of the rules of the budget game, and (d) the internal preparation of negotiating positions in each group (figure 3.3).

Building a proper mix of competition and cooperation:(a) and (b). Central budget offices should not be limited to imposing norms and rules to constrain requests for resources, framing competitive discussion, and solving conflicts through arbitration on resource distribution. Their effort could also focus on promoting positive attitudes in budgetary negotiations among advocates of spending (interchange of information, consultation, search for the identification of common policy interests, joint action, etc.), and between guardians and advocates to internalize collective overall objectives (such as, the deficit). The former will relieve the center of cross-fire confrontations. Both the former and the latter will facilitate the budget process being used as an opportunity for annual strategic policy-making (Wamsley and Hedblom 1983: 355ff).

Attention should be paid during the budget formulation to identifying spending interdependencies and lines of cooperation among interministerial programs. This requires joint definition of the problem and coordinated resource allocation for its solution, and is an important component of budget negotiation to be encouraged especially in times of uncertainty. Joint interministerial action during budget negotiations could be used to identify strategic synergies, either positive or negative (Ansoff 1965, chapter 6). The encouragement of budget behavior based on trust and cooperation could improve the effectiveness of public policy (positive synergy) and avoid spending which is substantially unnecessary or useless (negative synergy). Building trust and common budgetary values could be a powerful way to avoid substantial misspending because of unnecessary overlap or ineffectiveness due to lack of policy coordination.

Budgeting is not necessarily a completely competitive exercise. In many areas, the policy objectives of various ministries are not in conflict or their effectiveness depends on coordinated action rather than on increasing resources. Furthermore, communication and consultation among departments during the budget procedure may have very positive indirect consequences: they may relieve the finance ministry of multiple uncoordinated pressures for spending with a similar or compatible goal, and they make more transparent the financial effort of a policy providing an overall picture of resources allocated to the various departments with common goals.

To encourage cooperation in the budgetary process, the central budget unit has to build budget commitment. Current financial-management decentralization initiatives aim to increase productivity by encouraging competition among departments to pursue their individual goals regardless of the impact on the spending behavior of others. This encourages a search for efficiency within individual departments. The long-term strategic implications of interdepartmental cooperation have been mainly neglected. Many spending cuts today in one policy, may cause an immediate or future increase in spending in the same or in other policies. "Not to spend in certain instances is false economy" (Metcalfe and Richards 1990: 96).

Given the dependence on the same source of resources and the increasing diversity of interests and criteria for evaluating spending, the tension between departments is an unavoidable and an essential part of actual budget life. However, the problem is not the existence of conflict but neglecting its existence. Lack of recognition of conflicts leads to distortions, such as misuse of information, lack of consultation beyond compliance with rules, and less interaction. To the extent that complementary tasks and potential benefits are made more transparent and interdependencies become clearer under the mediation of the central budget office, those units in conflict will be more disposed to resolving the problems jointly (Walton and Dutton 1969: 73). The evaluation systems, criteria of success and, in general, incentives that explicitly or tacitly are being used by the ministry of finance are of crucial importance in bringing this about.

All of this does not mean, however, that competitive bargaining is completely undesirable. Both competition and cooperation are useful for flexibility budgeting. Each of them is simultaneously a challenge and an opportunity for central budget offices in the budget process. Maintaining a balance between these two components of budget negotiations, namely the competition for resources and cooperation in policies, should be one of the main concerns of the budget authority. The proper mix is related to the other two ways in which budget negotiations can also be improved: by restructuring the rules of the budgetary game, and by improving intradepartmental financial management for budget negotiation.

Restructuring the rules of the budgetary game: (c). The role of the center is to create an appropriate mix in which cooperation and competition are adapted to the budget context. The finance ministry should facilitate the adaptation of the relative weight of these components according to its capacity to control spending growth. From small signals to major reforms, the finance ministry can modify attitudes towards spending. In essence, restructuring the game requires budgetary actors to negotiate on how to negotiate for resource allocation, and how to reach consensus on what rules to apply. The question here is not a top-down vs. bottom-up budgeting approach but that of reaching an appropriate equilibrium of both approaches that guarantees cooperation under discipline. There is no ideal budget competition/cooperation mix. The one put into practice should fit the structure of real power distribution.

Improving internal financial management: (d). A second way in which the central budget unit can improve the functioning of budget negotiation is by encouraging more effective internal preparation at the departmental level. Finance ministries cannot guarantee that targets and rules for convergence will be implemented by spending departments as formulated by the center unless they are previously negotiated and accepted. Proper negotiations guarantee that relevant interests will be taken into account (incorporated or compensated) when defining budgetary policy.

This means that spending ministries cannot efficiently negotiate with the finance ministry without prior integration of departmental interests. The interests of the main actors in each department and their constituents and stakeholders should be effectively incorporated in negotiating the budget position if overspending and resistance to implementation is to be avoided. Representatives negotiating with the finance ministry or with other departments should defend positions which respond to well-integrated internal budget interests. The quality of internal sectoral policy advice for resource allocation is an important factor for preparing budget negotiations. In Australia, as Nicholson points out in chapter 8, the department of finance annually reviews the budget process including the quality of advice to each minister involved in budget deliberations. Successful flexibility budgeting requires good communication and consultation among the main actors and effective interaction mechanisms across the entire budgetary network, intra- and interdepartmental. Budget strategy and hierarchical budget arbitration cannot be effectively applied unless information and communication systems, and horizontal voluntary interaction, are consolidated and performing well during the budget formulation.

Redesigning Accountability Institutions and Encouraging Learning[2]

The final aspect of the new role for the budget office deals with accountability. The traditional aim of financial control is to fight fraud. As Metcalfe suggests, this aim should be complemented by the more positive aim of encouraging the desired overall budget performance (Metcalfe and Richards 1990). Because of recent spending decentralization trends, initiatives to improve financial accountability systems need to be reinforced to ensure that delegated spending authority is being applied properly and results have reached anticipated standards. This reinforcement does not mean just increasing the capacity to identify culpability or to enforce punishment.

To be successful in improving accountability, it is necessary to change the commonly held but false assumption that accountability and spending performance are inherently in conflict. Accountability is usually reduced to issuing and applying legal and financial regulations to constrain the efficient performance of public servants. Although difficult to achieve, a well-designed accountability system may encourage good spending results without damaging public service ethics. There need be no trade-off between accountability and performance, as Mayne discusses in chapter 6. What is needed is to overcome the widespread negative view of accountability. This applies to both those in charge of running budget accountability institutions and to budget holders. The objective of financial control should not only be to prevent irregularities in the use of public resources but also to motivate desired behavior.

A positive perception of accountability might encourage desired budget decisions rather than just prevent undesired ones. The two faces of the budgetary accountability coin should be taken into account: the constraining aspect of checking poor spending performance or the misuse of power (accountability institutions reacting intermittently and negatively to correct unacceptable budget nondiscipline), and the guiding approach which requires the provision of a proactive and continuous feedback by setting values and norms from which policy and standards are derived (Metcalfe and Richards 1990: 44, ff). Figure 3.4 illustrates two views of accountability.

Budget reforms since the 1980s prescribe budget targets and performance standards, but solving the deficiencies of current accountability institutions is not just a question of finding ideal criteria (performance measures) for success. The effectiveness of accountability systems has been diluted to mere answerability, making it only necessary to justify and explain what has been done and to respond to questions raised by Parliament. There is usually no assessment against standards or expectations, nor the application of sanctions or rewards. One of the difficulties lies in recognizing and capturing the multiple and conflicting pressures coming from different groups (managers, professionals, clients, peers, constituencies, etc.) claiming a need for modifications to

FIGURE 3.4
Redesigning Accountability

Accountability Characteristic	Traditional Accountability	New Accountability
Perception:	emphasis on the negative function	positive guidance for sound performance
Scope:	inspection for compliance	learning
Timing:	intermittent	continuous
Role of Center:	reactive	proactive
Objective:	maintenance of status quo	adaptation

spending targets. Ideally, priorities need to be established according to the relevance of such groups—as sources of power legitimation—to construct a framework of performance reference that synthesizes all relevant criteria of success. Appropriate accountability regimes should take into account and be coherent with the existing mix of sources of influence.

Accountability and budget performance assessment in the public sector should also be oriented towards adapting spending values and beliefs rather than just applying rational criteria (such as the 3Es) and enforcing compliance. Negative accountability should be compensated with positively oriented assessments and organizational learning. Inspection and rigid control on undesired spending do not guarantee improvement in spending performance. On the contrary, at a certain point accountability can actually begin to encourage dysfunctional behavior ("creative" accounting, biased or fictitious budgeting, concealing information, nonproductive internal competition, etc.). In contrast, positive accountability facilitates the internalization of sound performance values and provides guidance for sound spending behavior.

In short, another role of the finance ministry in flexibility budgeting should be to facilitate the balanced functioning of spending accountability. This means avoiding monopolizing accountability efforts on inspection and negative performance in which the only concern of the finance ministry is to keep the control and stability of the budget system. The traditional accountability system only functions when reacting to nondisciplined budget behavior. A new accountability approach which is more proactive and continuous needs to be developed if capacity to change is considered a priority. The finance ministry and the financial management unit in spending departments should encourage flexibility budgeting by explicitly or tacitly rewarding, or not punishing, adaptive behavior, that is, taking risks and experimentation. A positive perception of accountability as guidance rather than inspection is more appropriate in a context of instability. Overemphasis on inspection of nondesired budget behavior means blockage and incapacity to adapt. A continuous guiding role played by the central budget offices facilitates adaptation.

Conclusions

Current reforms for sound financial management need performance measurement for monitoring spending discipline. Spending decentralization and "contract budgeting" require the development of performance measurement if central budget offices want to avoid abdicating control on spending discipline and to encourage compliance with overall budget objectives. Performance measurement is also necessary to avoid arbitrary or opportunistic cuts. Budget authority considers the setting of targets and performance measurement as preconditions to obtaining budget resources and more autonomy for spending.

Although performance measurement is an old idea, the new approach for its implementation nevertheless deserves recognition. "Contract budgeting" is a relevant incentive for spending managers to design and use proper performance measures. The acknowledgment that performance measures are for managers and not for budget officials also reduces resistance for further improvements. However, progress made so far with performance measures has been very limited. The main achievements have been with monitoring productivity and operational performance.

Some limitations have been found in most countries, such as the narrow scope of performance measures and the weak connections between performance monitoring, evaluation, and budgeting. Strengthening this link will require more effort than anticipated. The triennial budget experience is a good example that opens up new possibilities for the budget office to reorient its time and resources towards further integration of budget participants. The production and use of performance measurement for budgeting depends in fact on the interest and openness of the main participants to cooperate. The reliability of budget performance information depends on the mutual perception of budget officials, financial controllers, and spending managers. To encourage budgeting on the bases of performance monitoring and evaluation requires their integration from the organizational, informational, and social point of view (Gray, Jenkins, and Segsworth 1993: 193ff). Besides technical requirements, the integration of budget participants demands an important dose of cooperation. Searching for common interests and building trust has been identified as one of the important new roles of the budget office.

Previous research provides evidence that traditional performance measurement (3Es) can work in a stable budgetary context, under conditions of predictability. However, these conditions do not represent some important difficulties of public budgeting today, such as instability, the different interests of the main budget actors, and the growing interdependence among actors. Budgeting has been traditionally focused on preventing or correcting deviant budget behavior by enforcing fiscal rules and norms. Central budget offices usually have not provided strategic management guidance for sound spending except by extrapolating budget figures and fiscal scenarios. Strong central institutions are expected to play only a role of guardianship and arbitration.

However, in the long term, the problem of budgetary control is the lack of leadership for budget adaptation. Most decisions for budget discipline are based on spending cuts in the next-year budget preparation. But the capacity to adapt budget behavior to economic crisis remains weak. While a general framework of budget norms and procedures for budgetary discipline is useful to prevent deviations, the hidden face of budgeting as a strategic tool should be reconsidered as a complementary approach. Just tightening constraints does not guarantee progress towards sustainable budgetary discipline. Central budget offices have to provide guidance for sound financial management behavior consistent with the budget context. Flexibility budgeting and its implications on the role of the budget office have been analyzed and proposed as a complement to contract budgeting and traditional performance measurement.

There is a need for performance measurement and evaluation to capture changing conditions affecting spending management. If radical, quick, and unanticipated change affect the spending performance of managers, then spending monitoring and evaluation systems should encourage adaptation. Performance measures or criteria of success should reward the capacity for responding to change. Contract budgeting and performance measurement in most countries have focused on cost reduction and productivity. There has been a quantitative and productivity bias in performance monitoring encouraging efficient but rigid spending behavior. Qualitative measures and new criteria for success are necessary today. The 3Ds suggested, in line with "flexibility budget," as criteria for successful performance—capacity for *diagnosis*, *design*, and *development*—are a more qualitative approach than the 3Es. They need to be supported by evaluation along with monitoring, but they more fully capture the capacity for budget adaptation.

In a complex budgetary context, declining resources and uncertainty provoke repetitive budgeting—frequent and erratic adjustments of budgetary figures. Interdepartmental struggles, interdependence, and difficult communication demand a new budget management role for the central budget office. In this situation, it is necessary that the central budget office dedicates resources and efforts to building trust and cooperation among main budget actors (budgeters, auditors, evaluators, managers, etc.). The finance ministry has to take responsibility for budget flexibility. Beyond setting budget norms, rules, and operating standards of performance, central budget offices should lead financial-management development at an interorganizational level. To achieve this, the budget center has to play a new role quite different from the traditional one. Four main components of this new role have been identified and analyzed:

1. Redefining successful budget performance in terms of the adaptability of spending behavior to changes in the environment;
2. Encouraging the coherence of budgeting with strategic management;
3. Building trust through cooperative bargaining in the budget process; and
4. Redesigning accountability institutions for organizational learning.

The role of the central budget office needs to be developed beyond the traditional bureaucratic model based on a hierarchical authority of the finance ministry and also beyond the managerial model based on decentralization and specialization. While there is no ideal budget system—it has to be adapted to each financial context—we have argued for a model which requires the budget office to lead overall strategic initiatives for the proactive anticipation of future budget conditions.

Notes

1. This paper makes no distinction between finance ministries and budget offices, referred to collectively as the budget authority.
2. This section is based on Metcalfe and Richards (1990).

References

Ansoff, H. I. 1965. *Corporate Strategy*. New York: McGraw Hill.

Berman, P. 1980. "Thinking about Programmed and Adaptive Implementation: Matching Strategies to Situations." In *Why Policies Succeed or Fail*, ed. H. M. Ingram and D. E. Mann. Newbury Park, Cal.: Sage.

Britan, G. 1991. *Measuring Performance for Federal Agencies: Issues and Options for Performance Indicators* (Draft Report). Washington, D.C.: Government Accounting Office.

Auditor General of Canada. 1993. *Report of the Auditor General of Canada to the House of Commons Year Ending 31 March 1993*.

Cabinet Office. 1994. *Next Steps: Moving On* (The Trosa Report). (Cm 2450). London: HMSO.

Carter, N. 1989. "Performance Indicators: Backseat Driving or Hands off Control ?" *Policy and Politics* XVII, no. 2: 131–38.

Carter, N. 1991. "Learning to Measure Performance: The Use of Indicators in Organizations." *Public Administration* 69: 85–101.

Congressional Budget Office. 1993. *Using Performance Measures in the Federal Budget Process*. Washington, D.C.: Government Printing Office.

Cothran, D. 1993. "Entrepreneurial Budgeting: An Emerging Reform?" *Public Administration Review* 53, no. 5:445–54.

Flynn, A., A. Gray, et al. 1988. "Making Indicators Perform." *Public Money and Management* VIII, no. 4: 35–41.

General Accounting Office. 1993. *Performance Budgeting: State Experiences and Implications for the Federal Government*. Washington, D.C.: Government Accounting Office.

Government of Canada. 1995. *The Expenditure Management System of the Government of Canada*. Treasury Board.

Gray, A, Bill Jenkins, and B. Segsworth. 1993. *Budgeting, Auditing, and Evaluation*. New Brunswick, N.J.: Transaction Publishers.

Hallamachi, A. and R. Boydston. 1991. "Strategic Management with Annual and Multi-year Operating Budget." *Public Budgeting and Financial Management* 3, no. 2: 293–317.

Hatry, H. 1980. "Performance Measurement Principles and Techniques—An Overview for Local Government." *Public Productivity Review*. IV, no. 4: 312–39.

Hofstede, G. 1981. "Management Control of Public and Not-For-Profit Activities." *Accounting Organizations and Society* 6, no. 3: 193–211.

Italianer, A. 1993. "Mastering Maastricht." In *Economic and Monetary Union: Implications for National Policy-Makers*, ed. K. Gretschmann. European Institute of Public Administration.

Jackson, P. 1988. "The Management of Performance in the Public Sector." *Public Money and Management* Winter: 11–15.

Klay, W. 1991. "Strategic Management, Policy Analysis and Budgeting." *Public Budgeting and Financial Management* 3, no. 2: 273–92.

Landau, M. and R. Stout, Jr. 1979. "To Manage is Not to Control: Or the Folly of Type II Errors." *Public Administration Review*, March/April: 148–56.

Metcalfe, L. and S. Richard. 1990. *Improving Public Management*, 2nd ed. Newbury Park, Cal.: Sage.

Metcalfe, L. 1993. "Public Management: From Imitation to Implementation." In *Modern Government*, ed. J. Kooiman. Newbury Park, Cal.: Sage 173–89.

Ministry for Finance. 1992. *Regulation and Management in the Central Government Administration and Financial Preconditions for Government Agencies*. Sweden:

Ministry for Finance. 1993. *Management of Government Administration*. Sweden:

Mintzberg, H. and J. Brian. 1991. *The Strategy Process*. Englewood Cliffs, N.J.: Prentice Hall International.

OECD. 1988. *Measuring Performance and Allocating Resources*. CT-PUMA/3.1/88.3.

OECD. 1989. *Incentives in Budgetary Systems: from Experiments to Structural Changes*. PUMA.

OECD. 1990. *Public Management Developments*. PUMA.

OECD. 1992. *Performance Measurement in Public Sector*. PUMA/PAC (91) 4.

OECD. 1993. *Public Management Developments, Survey 1993*.

Perrow, C. 1977. "The Bureaucratic Paradox: The Efficient Organization Centralizes in order to Decentralize." *Organizational Dynamics*, Spring, AMACOM.

Schick, A. 1986. "Macro-Budgetary Adaptations to Fiscal Stress in Industrialized Democracies." *Public Administration Review*, March-April: 124–34.

Schick, A. 1990. "Budgeting for Results: Recent Developments in Five Industrialized Countries." *Public Administration Review* January-February: 26–34.

Tarschys, D. 1985. "Curbing Public Expenditure: Current Trends." *Journal of Public Policy* 5 (February): 23–67.

Task Force on Management Improvement. 1992. *The Australian Public Service Reformed—An Evaluation of a Decade of Public Sector Reform*. Australian Government Publishing Service.

von Hagen, J. 1992. *Budgeting Procedures and Fiscal Performance in the European Communities*. Economic Papers, no. 96: October. Commission of the European Communities.

Wamsley, G. and K. Hedblom. 1983. "Budgeting: Strategic Instrument or Mindless Ritual?" In *Handbook of Organization Management*, ed. W. B. Eddy. New York: M. Dekker.

Walton, R. and J. Dutton. 1969."The Management of Interdepartmental Conflict: A Modern Review." *Administrative Science Quarterly* 14, no. 1: 73–84.

Walton, R. and R. McKersie. 1965. *A Behavioural Theory of Labour Relations: An Analysis of a Social Interaction System*. New York: McGraw-Hill.

Wildavsky, A. 1975. *Budgeting: A Comparative Theory of Budgetary Processes*. New York: Little Brown & Co.

Wildavsky, A. 1988. "A Cultural Theory of Budgeting." *International Journal of Public Administration* 11, no. 6: 651–77.

Wildavsky, A. 1993. "Norms and Rules to Facilitate Convergence on Budget Balance." *Public Administration Review* 53, no. 1: 28–30.

Winham, G. 1977. "Negotiations as a Management Process." *World Politics* 30, no. 1: 87–114.

4

Public Sector Reform Strategy:
A Giant Leap or a Small Step?

Sylvie Trosa

This chapter will examine the issue of implementing public sector reform through the two examples of the United Kingdom and France. It will focus on the target- (objective) setting process and its supporting performance-monitoring system as a relevant illustration of the main implementation problems faced in the modernization of a public service.

A basic aim of public sector reform efforts in both countries could be described as goal-achievement models: setting and controlling targets is considered as being the only way to ensure more autonomy within civil service and to motivate staff in order to achieve better results. The targets are also the basis of quasi-performance contracts either between discrete units of administration and the centers of the departments or between individual managers and their hierarchy.

However, France and the United Kingdom can appear as two opposite models in terms of how to reach this reform aim:

- France has emphasized the need to give more recognition to the work of civil servants and to implement changes gradually and through consensus of the departments and their staff.
- The United Kingdom has focused its efforts on the citizens and the need for civil servants to become accountable. Its strategy is to implement the changes as quickly as possible and for departments know that they are obliged to follow the new principles.

The French approach is incremental, bottom-up and public-service employee oriented; the British approach is top-down, aiming more at a big bang than little steps, and is customer-driven.

This difference is particularly noticeable when examining target setting. The purposes are not the same in both countries. Targets in the United Kingdom are supposed to achieve better value for money and accountability for public scrutiny. Targets in France aim at resource allocation within departments and are supposed to help decision making at a decentralized level. The emphasis on the target-setting process differs also. France focuses on the means of implementation. The United Kingdom is preoccupied mainly by the nature and the level of targets.

This chapter will try to show how on the same issue, two radically different approaches can be developed by two countries and how the approaches could be considered more as complementary than opposite.

The Target-Setting Process in the United Kingdom

The Next Steps Initiative

In 1993, the author was asked to undertake an evaluation of the British public-service reform by examining twenty-five agencies (Next Steps: Moving On 1994). The research looks at the experience of British agencies since 1988 and is based on an analysis of the agencies' framework documents, Cabinet Office and Treasury notes, and interviews with staff from central departments, centers of departments and agency chief executives. Performance measures in the United Kingdom are closely related to the target-setting process. As a result, this study considers at the same time the effectiveness of the target-setting process, the performance measures, and the quality of indicators.

The United Kingdom has had the same experience as other countries in trying to implement performance monitoring: performance measures had been implemented since the 1970s but without great success. The reasons were several: the performance measures were not related enough to previously defined targets, and they did not assess all aspects of the activity of an agency, being concentrated on productivity measures but not on measures of quality or effectiveness. The autonomy attributed to agencies was not consequent enough to motivate staff for better financial management (National Audit Office 1989).

Since the Next Steps reform (Improving Management in Government: The Next Steps 1988), performance measures have been only one dimension of a global, coherent approach. Agencies are autonomous and are to manage within agreed targets. Performance measures are the way to check if the targets have been achieved. Thus, the emphasis is more on targets, the performance measures are only a technical way to assess the effectiveness of targets.[1]

To understand the Next Steps reform it is necessary to reiterate the ideas that were at the origin of the reform:

95 percent of civil servants work in service delivery (Improving Management in Government: The Next Steps 1988)

Many services do not need direct, day-to-day ministerial involvement and are largely discrete. While the government may have a duty to specify the service, provide the resources, and monitor the delivery of the service and remain ultimately accountable, management and delivery of the service are best done according to the needs of the particular job and not to the needs of a monolithic civil service and at arms length from ministers on a "customer/contractor" relationship. (Kemp)

Real improvements depend on individuals being held personally responsible for results. A sense of ownership and personal identification with the product is essential to getting better performance. (Goldsworthy 1991)

The Efficiency Unit suggested that an Agency offered the most practical way of organizing work to take into account these realities. They defined an Agency as a discrete area of work with a single, named individual, a Chief Executive, in charge, with personal responsibility to the Minister for day-to-day management. An agency is focused and structured around the job to be done. (Goldsworthy 1991)

The main ideas of Next Steps are the following:

- It is necessary to put more emphasis on service delivery.
- A clear distinction between policy functions and service delivery should be an aim.
- Personal responsibility of senior executives is the catalyst for better performance.
- Corporate identity of professional organizations is the best motivator for the staff.

The three main features of a U.K. agency are:

- a clear identity asserted through a framework document;

- an organization centered on a precise role/function; and
- a way to guarantee internal devolution within departments.

There is no official blueprint for agencies. Some agencies are composed of twenty people, others of 60,000. Some agencies have purely service delivery functions, others also have regulatory responsibilities or are in charge of delivering policy advice. Experience, however, shows that there are still some guidelines which apply:

- An agency should be a coherent management unit, that can have clear identifiable aims.
- An organization should only become an agency if the agency status means significant improvements.
- Before creating an agency, the question of whether it should or should not remain within the civil service should be solved.
- Each agency is provided with a formal framework document, signed by the minister, assessing the responsibilities of all parties of the reform, setting the ministerial objectives and the flexibilities the agency can use.

We examined some of these features:

1.   One Agency: One profession.

An agency in the United Kingdom is structured around a precise role, which helps to increase the sense of corporate identy (and thereby the motivation for efficiency). Agencies are supposed to be functional organizations, and not deal with too many separate professions. In some cases, the establishment of an agency has resulted in the amalgamation of several divisions whose functions were closely related, in other cases divisions have been split because their functions were not coherent. All this makes the target-setting exercise easier (it is more difficult to have aggregate targets for very different jobs and kinds of services provided).

2.   The Agency: A way to ensure devolution.

Our inquiry showed that without the impetus of the Cabinet Office and the Next Steps reform, departments would never have been willing to undertake significant devolution. There are two indications of this assertion: first, there had not been any consequent effort towards devolution before Next Steps; and second, a lot of tension still exists concerning the level of autonomy within departments but now agencies can use their framework documents to defend their freedoms.

3. The Agency: The sense of corporate identity as a motivator for the staff.

Examination of the progress of the Next Steps reform shows that the sense of corporate identity has been a crucial catalyst for productivity improvement: it has motivated staff. The following question: "Would the changes have occurred without the Next Steps initiative?" was part of the inquiry. The general answer was that, even if from a technical viewpoint all management improvements would have been possible without the Next Steps reform, the major outcome from Next Steps was the sense of professionalism and new identity which was created. Next Steps has even been described by Peter Kemp as mainly a symbolic operation. The ideas of Next Steps are not very different from the Fulton's proposals in 1968. The difference is a high level political commitment, a clear marketing of the reform and a new attention to the executive divisions through use of the word "agencies." Staff members are proud to work in their agencies.

Why are Targets Set in the United Kingdom?

Targets are clearly meant to be able to prove efficiency gains. This is the result of the general political context in the United Kingdom where civil service was considered as being nonproductive. It is also a necessity for agencies: Next Steps has made it clear that every agency could be privatized; therefore agencies have a real incentive to try and show their best results. "The setting of genuine indicators of agency performance is a mandatory requirement for establishing an Agency" (Goldsworthy 1991: 7). The Treasury, too, has declared that the level of autonomy of each agency would vary according to the targets achieved. And it has effectively worked that way: the level of autonomy is tailored by the Treasury to the perceived efficiency of the agency.

Targets are also a means for increased accountability. The Treasury and Civil Service Committee of the House of Commons (TCSC) since 1988 has been very concerned that the Next Steps reform does not diminish the quality of information due to Members of Parliament and that management requirements do not become a shelter for agencies to avoid giving public explanations. Therefore, the targets of each agency are discussed by the TCSC and officially are even supposed to be changed only with its agreement. Practically this is, of course, too heavy a burden and some targets are changed through an agreement between the minister, the chief executive and the permanent secretary, but sooner or later they still inform TCSC.

To avoid any uncertainty in future we recommend that any change either to an Agency's framework or to its annual targets should be announced in a written answer. (Treasury and Civil Service Committee. Eighth Report 1990: xxxvi)

The Way Targets are Set

1.   A top-down procedure.

Targets are supposed to be set by ministers in each department, the procedure is top-down. The stated reason is that in a hierarchical system the minister is primarily accountable for the results. Therefore he or she has the responsibility to set targets. The TCSC (1990: xv) has commented:

> We are pleased to note that Next Steps has brought this clarity to the decision making process and that the responsibility for the choice of targets and for the allocation of resources to achieve the desired ends is clearly attributed to ministers.

This might seem surprising, because the minister is not only responsible for the objectives and the goals of public policies but also for their translation into operational targets, which might seem more naturally to fall in the hands of the chief executives. Nevertheless all official papers emphasize that targets are the province of the ministers. The explanation may be the desire to remind the agencies that they are under the hierarchy of the department. Another explanation is that agencies are supposed to be only concerned with executing operations and not be part of the policy making. As Goldsworthy (1991: 5) has said, "The Efficiency unit believed that the answer was to separate the executive functions of government from the policy-making role, and to break down further the monolithic, centrally-controlled management structure."

In practice, our research showed that things do not proceed that way. Ministers do define their priorities but the agencies, which have the information on all implementation problems, propose a range of targets, which are then negotiated with the center of the department and the minister. And indeed, the central departments now tend to agree with the idea that there should be feedback from the implementation problems to the policy proposals, and a positive link between the advice of the agencies and the general views of the departments.[2] But even if the proposals come from agencies, the Next Steps principles insist on the importance of the fact that targets have to be either set or approved by ministers.

The Treasury and Civil Service Committee of the House of Commons emphasized (1990) that the corporate plans of the agencies should make a clearer distinction between the targets related to the priorities of the ministers and the targets used for internal management, in order to clarify the levels of accountability. The newer documents tend to follow this approach.

2.   Targets as quantifiable and objective measures.

The second characteristic of British targets is that they have to be as often as possible measurable in the most objective way (H.M. Treasury 1992). The reason is that performance against targets should inform decision making: that is, poor performance should have consequences on budget allocations or on the performance-related pay of chief executives. Decisions can only be based on performance against targets if the measures produce automatic, quantified answers. There should be no scope for human judgment or any subjective interpretation. The advantage of this viewpoint is to emphasis simple, measurable targets and indicators. The disadvantage of this viewpoint is the difficulty of any form of shared interpretation (for example between centers of departments and agencies, or between different hierarchical layers) of the results.

Nevertheless, our inquiry showed that agencies are quite conscious that any target can have unforeseen negative side-effects and that interpretation of results against targets should always include analysis with staff on what the impact of every target or indicator is. (For example, has a target been reached by decreasing quality? Is an increase in production the result of higher productivity or of better economical factors?) This viewpoint is not shared by all centers of departments which prefer having automatic techniques for controlling agencies: it is easier to justify decisions based on quantitative indicators than to explain more qualitative judgments, especially when the department is unsure about its own authority.

The Nature of Targets and Measures

Analysis made by the Next Steps team of the targets set up by framework documents shows that 21 percent of the targets are efficiency targets, relating inputs to a level of outputs. The Treasury guide (1992) says:

> At its simplest, an efficiency gain is counted as an increase in volume or quality of output for the same level of input, or a decrease in input for the same level of output. However efficiency gains may accrue from other sources. For example, economy savings may count, provided these are as a result of management action, and not windfall gains.

Efficiency gains are generally measured in terms of a percentage usually of direct running costs. For example, the Royal Air Force maintenance group targets of "reduce the cost per unit of output by 2.5 percent" could be represented as "efficiency gains of 2.5 percent."

The apparently low amount of efficiency targets can be explained by the fact that at an early stage agencies set economy targets, that is, targets not related to a level of output (for example, reduce by 5 percent the ratio of labor costs). The problem with this kind of target is that one is never sure that there has not been any substitution between factors of production, in which case the overall productivity would not have changed.

Among the 426 key targets in the framework documents for 1991–92 (for one hundred agencies):

- 15 percent are unit cost/return on asset targets;
- 21 percent are efficiency targets (generally from 1.5 to 2.5 percent a year); and
- 10 percent are economy targets.

All other targets are either effectiveness, quality, or improvement targets.

Consider two examples, one of a trading fund,[3] Companies House, and of an agency which is not a trading fund, the employment service. As we see below, the most interesting aspect of targets is the year-over-year comparison.

These examples show that target setting is a continuous process of rectifying, correcting errors, and interpreting situations. Some targets are at first set too high or too low, some are not precise enough and

TABLE 4.1
Companies House
(The agency that registers all private companies in United Kingdom.)

Performance Indicator	Target	Achieved
1990–91		
Companies that have filed all accounts and annual returns	83%	81.6%
Document processing time in days	18	7
Increase in output per member of staff	12%	17%
Decrease in unit costs in real terms	7%	2% (because of an unpredictable downturn in workload)
1991–92		
Documents available within five days of receipt	100%	52.6%
Compliance rate for annual returns	85%	89%
Searches for customers within two hours	100%	99.8%
Reduction in unit costs in real terms	1%	2%
1992–93		
Documents available within five days of receipt	100%	38.7% (the average processing time was 7.2 days)
Compliance rate for accounts and annual returns	85%	85%
Searches for customers, within two hours	100%	99.2%
Reduction in unit costs, in real terms annually	2%	2.2%

Employment Service
(This example shows only a part of the targets.)

Performance Indicator	1990–91 Target	Achieved	1991–92 Target	Achieved
Placing number of unemployed into jobs	1.65 million	1.4 million	1.3 million	1.332 million
Placing long-term unemployed into jobs (1990–91)	275,000	208.000	indicator changed	indicator changed
Percentage of total unemployed placings for long-term unemployed (1991–92)	n/a	n/a	16%	19%
Long-term unemployed to be contracted every six months (1990–91)	100%	100%	indicator changed	indicator changed
Long-term unemployed contracted and offered an interview every six months (1991–92)	n/a	n/	100%	97%
Efficiency savings	13.6 million	13.6 million	19.2 million	15.2 million

get more precise or more demanding with time. Some targets can be abandoned from one year to another because they are no longer relevant, others can be added. A good or a bad result does not mean anything without the analysis of its causes.

However, a problem is that the United Kingdom central departments are not always aware of these uncertainties and tend to consider targets as absolute data without taking into account their evolution and the context agencies are operating in. Therefore, the new version of the Next Steps' annual review edited by the Cabinet Office publishes the results of the targets with a qualitative analysis explaining why they are or are not achieved.

Issues in the Target-Setting Process

A number of issues arise about the target-setting process:

- Is the current balance between the different types targets (i.e. efficiency and quality) adequate?
- How is it possible to check that the level of targets is demanding enough?
- Do targets reflect the core part of the activities of an agency? Do the targets, as they are set, actually permit a better understanding of the extent to which the agencies have accomplished their aims?
- Targets are made public and their results may be controversial. Does this situation lead to better targets or simply to targets intended to primarily give a good image of the activity?

1.   The balance between the different types of targets.

All Agencies should have a handful of robust and meaningful top level output targets which measure financial performance, efficiency and quality of customer service, over and above whatever subsidiary performance indicators are required for the Agency's internal management purposes. (Making the Most of Next Steps 1991)

Many agencies now have a whole range of targets, covering efficiency, quality, and effectiveness. This process is still being completed in a number of cases for a number of reasons.

Targets have been set primarily in the areas where agencies were previously able to measure their performance, either for technical reasons when information systems existed or for pragmatic causes, certain activities being more easy to measure than others (e.g. benefits agency, child support agency). In these cases, the perhaps more logical process of setting targets first and then building the measurement systems is reversed, targets are inferred from the measurement possibilities and their limits, and not the contrary. The consequence can be that activities which are more difficult to measure are left without any kind of target (for example policy advise or research activities). There are two solutions which have been followed by some agencies: either build quantitative measures in spite of the difficulties for those activities but being conscious of their limits, or accept more qualitative indicators as a part of the performance measures.

An adequate balance between the different kinds of targets requires that the wishes of the centers of departments and of the central administrations about their priorities are clear. For example, if the emphasis is only on productivity, agencies might consider that financial targets are the most relevant and concentrate their energy on those. Indeed, this is commonly thought to be the case, with agencies assuming that the Treasury is more interested in productivity targets. In that case, quality targets can be neglected or be limited to very simple delay and accuracy targets. All agencies assert that they do not know what kind of trade-off between raising the quality and making efficiency savings they are allowed to do. The central departments vigorously deny this by declaring that it is an internal management problem of the agencies. The agencies are nevertheless sensitive to a general feeling that the first aim is to save money.

The debate about the level of choice between efficiency and quality is technically and politically difficult. It requires a good knowledge of the needs of the different clients of the agency and a climate of confidence between the agency and the central departments. When the examination of the possible levels of services has not been undertaken with enough depth or when the agency has not been able to raise those questions with the center of the department, the corporate plans can contain a series of targets which are more a catalog than real choices between objectives and available resources.

It is clear that the question of the hierarchy of the targets has not been not raised when corporate plans have too many targets: all fields are covered but it is not possible to know which are the priorities and which targets are contradictory. Numerous studies have emphasized the difficulty of clarifying objectives when the essence of political work is to handle complex compromises that do not always allow transparency (Meny and Thoenig 1990). Without denying this fact, the lack of clarity of the priorities in some U.K. agencies seems to be more the result of insufficient strategic planning, either because they had no time, or because they did not feel it was expected from them and had no obvious incentive for strategic planning.

2.   The level of targets.

Central departments and centers of departments look for targets set at a demanding level: targets proposed by agencies are sometimes judged to be too high or too low by central departments. This is partly the result of the fact that in every public sector reform there is a discrepancy between some agencies that have a long tradition of performance measurement and qualified staff and others that just started their information systems and have few management staff. Launching audits to check if the agencies are setting targets at the right level can only be an exceptional way of working. Several solutions to setting the right level of target have been found in the United Kingdom.

A negotiated procedure of setting targets. Targets are discussed between the agency, the center of the department, and the central departments. This pragmatic approach does not seem to create difficulties because the responsibility for the target setting is shared between various players, having different interests. Centers of departments and central departments tend always to be more demanding than agencies.

The development of benchmarking. The more realistic way to appreciate the level of targets is to be able to compare the measures with similar bodies either in the private or public sector or at an international level. The central departments have launched a study on benchmarking. But agencies themselves have developed benchmarking tools to be able to better plead their proposals. For example, an agency dealing with historical patrimony which could not reach its targets because of a decline in the number of visitors, could prove that similar private organizations had had the same problem. The British Patent Office knows the targets of the other European patent offices.

3.   The targets and aims of the agency.

This question is in a sense the opposite of the previous one: in the same way that targets cannot be simply deduced from the existing performance measures, measures and indicators themselves need to be considered in a work context and cannot be deduced mechanically from general objectives.

To take an example: an agency in charge of delivering drivers' licenses seems to be a very easy case. The aim will be to deliver as many licenses as quickly as possible and the indicator will be the number and the speed of the delivery. But in practice, there is a contradiction between delivering the licenses quickly and checking that they are delivered to those entitled to a license. There are also several clients with conflicting interests: the drivers, the car manufacturers, the insurance companies, and the police. Setting the targets and the indicators in that case needs to go through the complete analysis of the clients, their interests, and the possible contradictions between objectives. Most of the time these kinds of issues cannot be foreseen and are discovered through practice.

The original intention of the Next Steps reform was that the debate about the agency's aims should be settled during the initial examination of options, which were to determine before launching an agency whether it should remain in the public sector and what its mission is. It was then expected that the targets should follow naturally: if the aims are clear, there should not be any problem in setting the targets and the indicators. In practice this does not work as the aim of the agency will inevitably change over time and through experience, thereby impacting on the targets. Target setting, after a few years of practice, appears less than a purely deductive process beginning with the aims and ending with indicators, and more of an iterative approach where aims are confronted with implementation issues.

The British experience shows that there are probably three different kinds of approaches which should not be confused:

- the setting of strategic aims and targets which can be done at the highest level of the departments;
- the measures of performance which tend to be comprehensive and require a good knowledge of the work processes and adequate information systems; and
- the definition of indicators of objectives, which require a process involving staff to know what are the most adequate criteria of the success of the activities.

These three topics are logically related, but it appears difficult to simply deduct one from the other. Each of them requires a specific analysis and process.

4. Are performance measures only output measures?

The British experience has focused on output targets for several reasons:

- Output targets can be more readily measured, outcome targets cannot always be (the impact of an economical policy can need several years to be assessed).
- Agencies can more easily be held accountable for output targets but not for outcome targets, because most of the time several factors are affecting the outcome results.

This focus on output measures suggests that target setting and performance measurement in the United Kingdom are primarily meant to assess accountability, which is not necessarily the case in other countries.[4]

The advantage of output measures is to clarify the issue of accountability, the disadvantage is that the assessment of performance is not always complemented by an evaluation of the outcomes. Carter and Greer (1993) remark "It should be pointed out, however, that this focus on Performance Indicators represents a very narrow understanding of performance evaluation. Nowhere in Next Steps or the Citizen's Charter is there any attempt to develop alternative mechanisms of performance evaluation." The first principle of Next Steps was to dissociate completely the issue of performance measurement and of evaluation: outputs are under the responsibility of the agency which has only an executive role, while outcomes are set by ministers who are accountable for the objectives and the long-term results.

There are several limitations to this approach:

Targets are not related enough to the core activity or the aims of the agency. "The welter of performance measures and indicators provided are often poorly related to departmental aims and objectives ... key policies frequently have no indicators relating to them included in departmental reports." (Treasury and Civil Service Committee. Seventh Report 1991)

Knowledge of the outcomes can be necessary to adapt and modify the management of the agencies. To take an example: one agency has among others a target to reduce infractions by the professional body with which they are concerned. The output target is to increase the number of pursuits but the agency does not know if actually it is pursuing 10 or 90 percent of the infractions. If it is 90 percent, its management probably does not need to be changed; if it is 10 percent the question of the quality of management or of the adequacy of the target is raised. In this case, performance measure is really useful, even for internal management, only if combined with an evaluation of the outcome. That is the reason why some agencies have proposed to set not only output but outcome targets (such as to decrease the number of road accidents due to the lack of security norms). (Transport Research Laboratory 1993)

5.   The publicity of targets.

The issue of the publicity of targets is difficult: if targets are not made public, the incentive for the whole reform will be weak, because a main sanction of not reaching the targets is the publicity made about these failures and the debate in parliamentary committees. The Next Steps principles emphasize that one major benefit of the reform is the increased transparency of the activities of the public sector. But at the same time the emphasis on publicity can distort the quality of targets: agencies can feel encouraged to set easier targets that they can reach with 100 percent success. On the other hand, ministers may wish to set the toughest targets for reasons of public opinion even if the agency is not able to implement them successfully. There have been several cases where everybody knew that some financial targets of the agency were impossible to achieve (child support agency) but the minister still insisted on keeping them for political reasons. On quality targets, debate continues on whether the target should be to reach 100 percent of quality because it would not be acceptable to admit in advance a certain percentage of errors or whether the targets should be more realistic allowing for a certain error rate. (Her Majesty's Stationary Office has been severely judged by Central departments and some MP's because it admitted not to be able to achieve a 100 percent quality target.)

In every case, the British experience shows that the process of making the results public needs to be used in a culture of tolerance, trying more to help agencies to perform better than to judge or condemn them, otherwise there will be two types of targets: the real, achievable targets and the official, public targets.

6.   How are performance measures used?

The main use of performance measures in the United Kingdom is accountability: the chief executive is accountable to the minister for reaching the targets. This accountability does not imply necessarily any formal consequence such as changing a chief executive or precise sanctions when the activity of the agency is considered as being unsatisfactory. It is more about public blame and tough discussions in Parliament.

The question has been raised whether performance measures could be the basis of budget allocations. For example, if an agency does not reach its targets, should there be some sort of sanction such as decreased resources? This question has no official answer. In practice, sanctions on budget allocations are not used because there is a real danger of impacting on the user who is not responsible for the failure in meeting the targets. Often the Treasury prefers to increase the control or to diminish the level of flexibilities on an agency which is failing. The sanctions are effective mainly on managers and staff: chief executives cannot benefit from their performance-related pay unless they exceed the targets of the agency. When the targets are not achieved, staff are not entitled to bonus schemes.

It becomes clear that performance measures do not lead to automatic decisions. They are more the starting point for discussions than the only tool for decision making.

Conclusions on the U.K. Experience

The main results of the target setting process in the United Kingdom is that now each agency

- has to enter into a debate about its aims and the ways it uses to achieve these aims;
- has to be able to measure its results; and
- has to be able to show improvement over time.

The evolution in the United Kingdom about the target setting process from their initial model has been:

- to accept that assessment of the target achievements can involve some interpretation and human judgment;
- to endorse more qualitative measures; and
- to recommend that published targets should be accompanied by a full explanation of their meaning.

The Target-Setting Process in France

In France, state-provided services are seldom organized by function (that is offering just one product or involving just one profession or skill). Most public services are organized territorially. Nearly all ministries have one center of the department with a number of local agencies in every "département" and/or region. Only 5 percent of public servants work in the centers of the departments and 95 percent work in the local agencies belonging to the central government, mainly in the local "départements" which are the basic territorial structure of the country. There are ninety-five "départements." France has a double structure at the local level, with elected local authorities on one side and local agencies of the government under the authority of the prefect[5] on the other side. This tight network of state agencies has been created since the eighteenth century in order to guarantee the national unity of the country. France is very centralized in its national rules but very decentralized in its organization.

The public sector reform launched in 1989 aims to set up what is called "centres de responsabilité," that is responsibility centers, in the local agencies of the state. The philosophy of the reform has been summarized in a declaration of the prime minister (with legal binding value), the Circulaire of the 29 February 1989, called Circulaire Rocard. The philosophy is the same as in the British case: it is about enabling more autonomy in management as a counterpart for increased responsibility and a better knowledge of the results. The difference with most Anglo-Saxon countries is that France wants to keep a strong national framework of common rules. No French government would accept the diveu ity of pay and personnel arrangements existing in the United Kingdom. The flexibilities available for agencies are defined in an uniform way for all agencies. Personnel rules remain centrally controlled, because public servants are grouped within "corps" with a written status, that is, public servants are recruited between twenty and twenty-five years of age through a national exam that gives them a certain level and then trained by the government (at least three years for level B and A). Promotion is also through exam and there are quotas from one level to another. This explains why these rules will remain national as long as this system exists.

France has opted for modernization at a steady, learn-as-you-go pace, rather than forced, rapid, comprehensive reform. The Circulaire of Michel Rocard (1989) sets objectives but it lays down no timetable. The selection of responsibility centers is left to the discretion of whichever department the center is attached to. The underlying implementation ideas are:

- that volunteers can be relied on to encourage the less enthusiastic to keep up with developments; and
- to allow for the fact that departments will have reached different levels of maturity in management control, giving the less experienced enough time to catch up.

This idea of a gradual pace as a learning aid derives from the fact that French senior civil servants have analyzed the causes of their past failures,[6] especially with the Planning, Programming, and Budgetary System (PPBS): the ideal of management of the 1970s aspired to be very rational and technically perfect (how to have measures which describe most adequately the facts) but it was too top-down without asking the local services, which are responsible for effective implementation, what they thought about these models and without taking enough time to convince them to be active in the process of change. Therefore the changes remained limited to high level managers and did not go deeply into the culture of the services.

Therefore, the new principles of modernization are oriented towards a more bottom-up and negotiated approach. The emphasis is less on trying to define perfect targets than on knowing how it is possible to embed the change in the culture of staff.

Why are Targets Set in France?

There are several reasons:

1. To make better choices with scarce resources.

The economic reason behind target setting is important: when the state has to deal with decreasing budgets, it needs criteria for the allocation of money, and one of them is performance. But this principle is not applied everywhere. It is more used at a local than at a national level and for little, comparable units rather than for whole departments. It is effective at a decentralized level because it

- allows organizations to benchmark similar units having the same objectives and constraints; and

- is not necessary to make choices between very general and unrelated objectives.

At a national level, budget allocation means that one must choose, for example, between education and defence. To the contrary, at a local level one can compare several agencies doing the same job or having the same mission. At a national level one has to deal with more general aims, which makes choices difficult: motives for allocating resources have more to do with political reasons than with performance.

Performance measures are used at a local level when it is possible to compare similar units, without interfering with public policy choices.

2.   To increase the legitimacy of the public service.

In France, the budget issue, however, was not the central worry. Most decisive was the legitimacy crisis of the state, which could be observed through the increasing doubts about its efficiency, and complaints of users about the quality of the services provided. The assumption (Declaration of Michel Rocard 1989) is that a state which is able to demonstrate its performance is therefore more legitimate: this assumes public opinion is aware of the quality of the services offered to the citizens. The interesting point in this crisis of legitimacy is that the movement of modernization is no more the privilege of the so-called production agencies (which can measure their products more easily than regulation bodies) but it tends to be an effort even of the more classical parts of the government, such as the police.

The issue of increasing the legitimacy of the public service is also related to the words used to justify the necessity of the public-sector reform. The experience of the past years showed that a certain honesty in the words used to explain why modernization is a priority, is a prerequisite of success for changes. Different kinds of mistakes have been made: the first one was to promote exclusively the advantages for civil servants of performance measures (especially in the first period of the socialist government between 1982 and 1986). Staff members were not told clearly what were their duties, for example, being accountable for products, their cost, or their utility. Staff did not believe in such false "consensus." The second error was to frighten them by the prospective of privatization and to be ambiguous about the fact that their efforts were supposed to contribute to public-sector reform. This has been the tendency of the right-wing government during the period 1986 to 1988. Now there are no major differences between political parties at least about what is said on public-sector reform.

Another issue was to convince staff that performance measures are not intended to control and punish them but to help decision making. This is not always easy because performance has something to do with accountability, for example, to be responsible for the decisions that have been taken. The general feeling now is that responsibility should be more of a collective culture rather than the idea of incriminating a particular civil servant (Rapport du Conseil Scientifique de l'Evaluation 1992).

> 3. To clarify responsibilities and create a better dialog between political authority and public service.

The third reason for the development of performance measures has been to enhance the relationship between the political level and the administration (Association des Service Publics 1994). Managing better, having more information on the cost of the decisions, and developing different tactics to implementation are techniques that provide the public service with arguments to defend its approach, because it can provide objective data to the minister. To take an example: if a minister asks a department to increase its effort for the protection of the environment, this department will not be able to ask for more staff or discuss the way of implementing this decision if it has no information about what its staff is doing, what its efficiency and workload are, how previous experiences in that field were managed, and so on. And French agencies discovered when they launched the process of modernization that, in most cases, the chief executives did not know the real tasks of their staff members, how much time they spent on each activity, and what were precisely the resources allocated to each objective or function. This became clear when several departments launched zero-based budget studies in their agencies (France, Ministère de l'Equipement 1989). Performance measurement is, then, a prerequisite to discuss the feasibility of new objectives. Management is not considered as reducing the role of politics but as allowing a more open and transparent discussion between political and managerial level.

France does not have the same tradition as the Anglo-Saxon countries concerning the relationship between politicians and civil servants. The so-called Westminster model often assumes a clearcut delineation between policy functions and implementation. French civil servants are supposed to be independent: even when they are fired by a minister they belong to statutory bodies, "les corps," and remain at the same level within the civil service. But, contrary to the British tradition, it is common for civil servants to work within ministers' teams that have a political role but also to contribute to the effective management of a department. On the other hand, a significant number (at least 50 percent and often more) of ministers are civil servants (they can remain civil servants), so there can be some confusion of tasks and persons. Therefore, the management reform process is an attempt to clarify responsibilities.

4. To constrain the centers of the departments.

The fourth reason to set targets is to organize pressure on the centers of departments in order to force them to change their working methods. This strategy is derived from a pragmatic view. The experience of the 1970s showed that it was too difficult to introduce performance measures from the top because there are too many products at the general level of a department and it requires too sophisticated information systems. Therefore, it seems more appropriate to start performance measures in little units, whose products are easy to identify and only afterwards to determine which measures need to be aggregated at a global level. This means that a certain number of measures will remain at a local level for the sole purpose of helping decision making but will never come to the center of the department. (To compare with the model of the 1970s: engineers defined all possible products at a global level and all information had to be aggregated [Crozier and Petitbon 1993]).

Another reason for this strategy is more tactical: if local agencies start with performance measures, they will pressure the centers of departments to do the same.

As a result, the main motto of performance measure is negotiation: the targets are defined between the centers of departments and the chief executives on the basis of the proposals of agencies; they are written in a contract, signed by the minister or the general director by delegation of his minister, and last three years with a revision every year. These contracts are based on plans called " plans objectifs/ moyens" (Vallemont 1991) where the agency relates its priorities with the resources necessary to fulfil them. The agency is also supposed to know the unit costs of certain, especially important, products.

France has taken the explicit viewpoint that the government can only change if local agencies are sufficiently empowered to be able to exercise pressure on the centers of departments, obliging them to concentrate on the definition of policy objectives and abandoning day-to-day management (the assumption being that centers of departments do not change by their own will because they do not have any interest to do so).

This analysis is exactly the same as the U.K. approach (Making the Most of Next Steps, 1991). Underlying this process has been a concern that targets cannot only come from the top (which is too remote and too constrained) or solely from the bottom (which is lacking global data on economical, technological, or strategic issues), but that they have to be the result of an iterative approach between both. In fact this dialogue is very demanding for the central units because it changes completely their role: they are no longer producing rules about how to manage or deliver routine support services but they have to analyze and respond to local rational planning derived from strategic thinking. Being able to answer more strategic requests implies that centers of departments should become stronger in providing policy advice and their ability to set long-term objectives.

Results management increases the power of the executive agencies, by giving them instruments to program, forecast, and measure. This approach means that the same effort has to be done for the central departments, in particular by giving them expertise in forecasting public policies and objectives, which is not always the case. In a lot of European countries, the decrease in resources has had the result of cutting staff in central policy divisions.

Currently, in most departments in France the reform is embedded in the practices of local agencies, but the evolution of the centers of the departments is not yet achieved. This constitutes another common point with the United Kingdom, as the author previously identified, "The relationship with centers of departments: My main conclusion is that there exists a considerable cultural gap on both sides with chief executives often believing that departments' management is a bureaucratic obstacle, and departments viewing agencies as little fortresses following their aims regardless" (Next Steps: Moving On 1994: 6). The difficulty of a strategy of empowering the periphery against the center is that the maturity of the agencies in management issues grows quicker than the cultural change in the center, creating a series of tensions and conflicts. If the gap between both is growing, the whole reform can be jeopardized, either because agencies are discouraged or because centers of departments fight against the reform.

Both in France and in the United Kingdom, one cannot yet assess whether the reforms have reached a point of no return and will be self-sustaining.

The Way Targets are Set

French departments try to meet several challenges in setting targets:

- To make a clear distinction between central compulsory indicators and the indicators under the autonomous responsibility of the agencies;
- To be unambiguous about the goals of public policies;
- To define an adequate balance between testing and extending performance measures;
- To tailor the targets to the culture of each organization; and
- To complete performance measures with interpretation and evaluation.

1. Making a clear difference between compulsory indicators and autonomous decision making.

A bottom-up approach. The lessons drawn from the PPBS experience tended to emphasize a bottom-up approach: the agencies are now free within general frameworks defined by departments to choose the best way to monitor their modernization (Rocard 1989). The frameworks only define the principles which should be followed (such as to involve the users in the quality of the service on a permanent basis) and some specific prior objectives (for example, raise the number of training days to six per year for each agent). Nevertheless, the chief executives are completely free to choose the best way to reach these principles and there is no compulsory management method imposed by the center (such as total quality management, zero-based budget, etc.).

But this freedom in managing is only possible if, before starting the reform, the government defines what should be compulsory for each agency (for example, to measure certain defined costs) and what should remain under the sole responsibility of the agency. Staff and agencies have to know on which basis they will be judged, which is only possible if they know for which targets they are accountable. The assumption is that agencies and staff cannot be held accountable for all targets: they are accountable primarily for a handful of robust targets and the others remain under the management responsibility of the agency.[7] It is a question of clarity (too many targets means unclear priorities) and of finding the right balance between autonomy and accountability. Some departments have achieved this clarification, others have not.

In the past, when the French government decided to launch a reform it proceeded in two ways: either everything (tools and objectives) was imposed (which does not take in account the necessities of the ownership of the changes by staff) or there was no blueprint at all and the agencies had to find their own way without any help (in which case it becomes hard to benchmark and to generalize the experiences). The approach now in France is to be very precise on what is under the responsibility of the center and what is relevant for the decision making of the agency. The government can oblige agencies to calculate the costs of products judged as especially important or to follow a few indicators which are relevant for the whole ministry, but in this case the data asked must be simple and not too numerous (not requiring agencies to follow a hundred indicators as happened before). For example, the Department of Transport required its agencies to calculate the resources required for each product for each client (this can be done in one year, because there are only three main clients and three main products), but all the other data and indicators had to be chosen by each agency and not aggregated at a national level.[8]

Differentiate accountability and decision-making indicators. Local management indicators do not have to be aggregated or centralized because their first purpose is to help local services to organize themselves. In practice, if one puts in the same system the compulsory information needed for accountability and the information needed by staff to improve their work, the result is a complex, useless system of dozens of indicators. For example, the same Department of Transport in the 1970s used more than 400 measures to allocate resources. There are now less than forty national compulsory indicators or measures (France, Ministère de l'Equipement 1992).

In order to avoid any kind of confusion of responsibilities there are two kinds of indicators: accountability indicators about unit costs, delays of certain sensitive products; and decision-helping indicators which are built on the basis of a completely specific, local approach. To take an example: the national indicator for building authorizations is the speed of delivery, the local indicator might be the quality of the explanation in case of a refusal because the mayors of a specific region have asked for more explicit documents.

The national measures or indicators are related to the means necessary for achieving a required level of output, for example how many machines per hour for each kind of road. The local measures are less output indicators than indicators of improvements, that are closely related to the objectives. If, for example, an agency has drawn the conclusion that internal communication is lacking, the objective will be to increase the knowledge of the decisions of the management committee by the staff and to give more opportunities to staff to tell their viewpoint. The indicators can be the number of readers of the internal review, the number of papers prepared by the staff, the rapidity of issuing the review, and so forth.

Departments have also become aware that if they asked for compulsory indicators, they had to provide information and explanations to the agencies which had gathered data. One solution is to provide this information by showing the results of all services in similar situations in order to allow them to compare themselves, as a benchmarking exercise.

To summarize: there are three levels of indicators, two imposed and one free. The two imposed are first, a few indicators responding to national or central priorities or to the needs of accountability (like knowing the cost of removing the snow every day in every part of the country) and second, a few indicators describing the workload of the service (e.g., unemployment, numbers of the population, specific problems, etc.). The third type of indicator which is not compulsory but discussed with the center, are the indicators related to the objectives and the plans defined at a local level. In fact, the underlying problem is that most of the time the central administration does not know where to set the delineation between what is just imposed and what needs coordination, advice and control.

2. Objectives first?

One of the most frequent questions raised in the local experiences the author had (as head of the evaluation branch of the department of Equipment) was whether to begin with the definition of the objectives or with the measure of performance or the establishment of indicators.

Based on the French experience, there does not seem to be a general answer. The information necessary for the definition of objectives is sometimes cogent enough to start the management process with the statement of the objectives, based on information about clients and users, and a strategic view of the important choices faced. In that case, the main challenge is to create a consensus about objectives. On the other hand, when information is lacking (no strategic view of the future, little knowledge of what the agencies are really doing) it is useful to use methods like strategic analysis as a step towards objectives, or to begin with a debate on the factors of success of the activities in order to define the purposes of the organization. Thus, it has not always been possible to say "objectives first." Going through indicators and diagnosis has sometimes been an important way to clarify the objectives.

It seems necessary to make a difference between the goals and the methods used. The method has to be tailored to every specific context: management will know when it is better to start with objectives, indicators, or the diagnosis, and how to balance them. Nevertheless, goals are supposed to be unambiguous. Evaluation studies conducted in agencies all lead to the conclusion that it is not possible to motivate an organization very long without giving it a clear understanding of its priorities. As an example: the modernization of police in France since 1985, based on an agreement between better working conditions and more performance measures, has met difficulties because staff did not clearly perceive what the goals of the police were: were they to repress, to be closer to the population, to prevent crime?

3. Define the right balance and rhythm between testing and extending performance measures to all agencies.

An innovation is that the French government tries to test changes in a few agencies before making general rules or issuing blueprints. These are the recommendations of the committee for the devolution of administrations (1993) and relates to the fact that France is a country whose tradition relies on written, general rules. It is seldom possible to initiate changes without modifying legal or administrative rules. Experimenting in that case is trying new solutions before issuing a blueprint for everyone. Nevertheless, testing is considered a good method as long as it is an honest exercise whose purpose is to analyze the results as a transition for wider changes and not just to show best, but isolated, practice.

In France before 1985, the government used to act in two ways, either deciding on a general reform without testing it, that is without having an idea of the concrete problems in implementing the reform,[9] or testing on a few organizations but without any perspective on generalization so that a few years later the experimental service organizations were discouraged, because they were too isolated from the mainstream action.[10]

Now the government has decided that all reforms should be launched only after having tested their principles in a few agencies. Nevertheless, all agencies are allowed to join the reform if they feel ready for it and centers of departments are required to analyze what should be extended and what should not. To take an example, when the agencies of the Department of Transport began to set up their performance measures in 1991, they were left free to choose the most adequate measures and indicators but at the same time the center of the department launched a working group to explore which measures and indicators could be extended to some or all agencies. Even in a country less constrained by written rules such as Australia, the issue of finding the right balance between letting people test their own solutions and generalizing them to everyone still exists.[11]

4. Tailor the targets to the culture of each organization.

Understanding the values. The main reason to proceed in an incremental way is that targets have to be tailored to the values and the culture of each organization.[12] Changes in public sector management are paradoxical: improvements mean that to a certain extent the culture of the public service is modified, but, at the same time, if the new objectives appear to be too remote from the prevailing culture, staff will tend to consider management as a new artificial fad or worse as a denial of the quality of their work.[13] In any case, the lessons drawn by French managers from the 1970s is that at least any management initiative should be preceded by an effort to understand the core values of the different layers of staff . The culture (the values, the way of working, the type of hierarchical relationships) can be very different from one agency to another (Thoenig 1993). The problem is that there is often not enough energy devoted to this issue: everybody feels they can define the culture of an organization and there is a very real danger of falling into clichés. There are very precise sociological techniques which should be used to identify a culture (i.e., what are the groups within an organization, their interests, their constraints and resources, their strategy).

For example, before starting the changes, agencies now launch studies to find out what are the interests of the different groups among staff members, so that they can understand who are their supporters and who will not help and why. This might seem very far from the technical problems of setting up performance measures, but the French viewpoint is that performance measures only work if they appear to be helpful to staff and managers, which implies a strategy to build up alliances, to convince the reluctant, and to use adequate incentives.

A very important condition for change is to explain why it is required and how it will be useful: very often the will of staff to change is taken as obvious. In fact, it is not obvious, because some employees are happy to work as they have always worked or do not want to change at all. Furthermore, the interests of more senior staff are not the same as the interests of lower level staff. In this case, it is necessary to have very precise argumentation, different for each group of staff, explaining why change is needed and what are the benefits for their own work.

Embed a sense of ownership of the reform. This point also refers to resources which assist the change: mostly training, but also modernization of the conditions of work (computers, process of working, etc). Several staff inquiries performed in agencies showed that staff members were not so much expecting increments in salaries as better working conditions. Some failed experiences in implementing performance measures also showed that change implied that managers devote more time to monitoring the reform process: change does not happen without taking the time for explanation and discussion. Furthermore, work on performance issues can be seen as an abstract exercise, so it is important that managers are able to prove that things are effectively changing. This is also justified because very often people are not convinced by the new principles of management as long as they have not experienced them by themselves. Therefore, the French government has considerably increased its training efforts (now 3.5 percent of the wages). All training is henceforth supposed to be what we call "action-training," that is, training accompanied by a real modernization project, where the trainees put into practice what they have learned.

The same paradox, of finding the right balance between voluntary and top-driven change, applies to the issue of the speed of the changes.

If the rhythm is too slow, the energy can be diluted. If the rhythm is too quick, there is a danger of a lack of ownership of the reform by staff. The experience of most agencies shows that achieving a good definition of objectives and targets, which are not too general, takes two or three years . This can be helped by experts, coming either from the private sector or from the administration but only to give advice and to conduct surveys. The costs were paid partly by the centers of departments and partly by a special budget newly created in central departments to help modernization. Often central departments wanted to go too fast or did not use experts enough to help the innovating agencies.

If performance measures are not part of day-to-day work, staff will provide the centers of departments with a lot of information, not useful either for them (because they do not feel concerned) or for the department (because the information system will be provided with at best approximate data).

Know the problems before the solutions. Another condition of success appears to be able to have an adequate link between the tools and methods suggested by the centers and the operating environment an agency has to deal with. Very often official papers emphasize that agencies are free to choose their own solutions but de facto everyone knows that certain approaches are more accepted by central departments than others. The issue is to avoid a current failure in many management reforms of giving the impression that generic tools can be applied to any situation (total quality management, zero-based budgeting, etc.). The best solution to avoid this is to give the agency enough time to undertake a good analysis of the problems it has to deal with: what, in this particular situation, is the specific problem to solve? Managers often jump to solutions before spending time on understanding the problems (Crozier 1991). Doing this often takes more time than expected because the first reaction of the top managers (without any preliminary work) is to describe the problems with universal and abstract words (such as the necessity to improve human resource management, to better communicate, and to increase quality).

A major problem of performance measurement is to translate general public-policy objectives into operational quantified targets. There is often a gap between the general aims and the quantitative measures, probably because most of the time there has not been enough energy invested to investigate and analyze the problems. The logical path is more and more often :

- knowing the public-policy goals being sought;
- defining how to implement them and therefore first know the problems met during this or past implementations; and
- set performance targets.

5. To complete performance measures with interpretation and evaluation.

French managers have noticed that the reluctance of the staff towards target setting comes from the intuitive knowledge that no indicator is accurate or perfect, and often has undesired side-effects: every indicator has unforeseen consequences (such as increasing the quantity of products by decreasing the quality). Therefore, the emphasis is now less on having perfect measures or indicators than on having regular and accepted mechanisms allowing an interpretation of the results of indicators and correcting them if necessary. An indicator can be imprecise if there is an accepted and negotiated procedure of discussing the results, between agencies and the staff in charge of the control.

Furthermore, evaluation has to accompany the use of indicators, because performance measures give information on how an organization acts and its products but is never sufficient to assess why the agency could not meet the public policy's objectives. The answer to this type of question often requires different types of inquiries, statistical, but also sociological. Performance measurement is the necessary basis of evaluation but is not sufficient for it. We noticed in the French experience that staff members are asking for evaluation because they want to know, especially when their outputs are measured, if their activity is useful and for whom. The demand for evaluation even comes more from staff in over-the-counter activities or bottom-line managers because they are very eager to have feedback from clients and users. This is not without creating difficulties: as the expectations for evaluation are greater at bottom-line levels than in the center, it is more complex to motivate agencies to evaluate public policies or budgets at a central level.

Evaluation is also a means to get staff and their clients closer by launching customers' inquiries. The departments where performance monitoring has succeeded are the departments which managed to create closer relationships between staff and their clients or users. Several reasons can be given: if the modernization helps an agency to modify its relationships with its partners, it is almost certain that the changes can last and survive even if the most important managers have gone (because the partners and the clients will have adopted different ways of working together). Peoples' attitudes have changed but furthermore the relationship in which they are working has necessarily been improved. Sociologists have showed that the relationship with users is often more motivating for the staff than the traditional hierarchical system. On the other hand, an exclusively inward-looking reform is not likely to succeed. An evaluation of the corporate plans of the Department of Transport showed that the most effective and lasting plans were the plans which tried to build up new relationships with clients and users (Ministère de l'Equipement 1989).

Comparison of the French and the British Performance-Measurement and Target-Setting Process

The Purposes of Performance Measures

The common feature between both France and the United Kingdom is that performance monitoring is intended to make possible a more autonomous management of agencies: without any performance-measurement system, central departments cannot assess whether the targets are met or whether the autonomy is misused. The aim is to modify a control based on inputs and to establish a control based on outputs. In both countries, the development of performance measures has been presented by the Treasury as a prerequisite of the devolution of competencies.

There is, nevertheless, a major difference. France has emphasized performance measure as a tool for helping decision making for managers, while the United Kingdom has pursued the needs of accountability. The difference can be mainly explained by the constitutional system: accountability to the Parliament has been of crucial importance in the United Kingdom, and it has not been in France where the Parliament has no tradition of controlling the work of the administration.

Another reason is that the U.K. reform has taken the citizen as a starting point: civil servants are publicly accountable for their results. Through the Citizen's Charter (1991) the citizen is entitled to know what level of services is provided. In France, the assumption of the reform was that the changes could not take place by considering citizens and civil servants as antagonistic, but on the contrary, by motivating and empowering the civil service.

Are the practical consequences of this difference in philosophy very important? Any national target-setting experience will lead to a difference between centrally imposed targets and indicators meant for accountability, and targets and indicators necessary to help managers to manage better. The first category is public, centrally aggregated, and controlled; the second category is autonomous, not always public, and central levels know the result only for information and comparison and not for control. However, the difference between the processes of the two countries tends to decrease with time.

The United Kingdom remains more concerned with the needs of adequate control, whereas France emphasizes the time and the ownership necessary for changes. Both systems can have advantages and disadvantages: the U.K. system has given agencies more financial and personnel flexibilities than in the French case, is clearer about the requirements for accountability, and is more control oriented. British official papers seldom use the word control and the central departments would deny the element of controlling. It does not change the fact that every year a tough discussion about targets to assess whether they are robust, demanding, and adequate enough takes place. The French system has given agencies more time to experiment with reform and has invested more on training and communication. On the other hand, France has been more ambiguous about the kinds of indicators or targets which are considered as compulsory.

The unresolved issue on comparing both countries is whether it would be possible to launch a reform as comprehensive and rapid as the British have done, but giving at the same time more freedom to agencies to find their own way of defining their strategy and convincing their staff.

The Strategy of Implementing Performance Measures

France has paid a lot of attention to the way performance measures should be implemented and especially to the problem of how to convince staff to accept performance monitoring. Official papers describe the implementation methods, covering such aspects as:

- when it is relevant to begin the process with the objectives or the indicators;
- the methods which can be used to define or know the expectations of clients (strategic analysis, etc. . . .), the central departments have published case studies in order to help agencies, and small teams have been created in the centers of departments to help agencies build their management tools;
- the ways to discuss indicators with staff, which aspects should be participative or should not; and
- the possibilities for training.

In the United Kingdom, the emphasis is more on the definition of the targets: What is a good target? How does one assess its quality? The way to implement targets is left free: agencies are supposed to find the best way to do it. They have not been given significant help or advice on implementation issues, neither by the centers of the departments nor by central departments. The reasons are the following:

The will to change very quickly. Some agencies had less than one year to set targets, even though a process of setting targets based on the strengths and weaknesses of an agency through customers' surveys, was implemented. Target setting, even shared with staff, needs more than a few months of work. Some surveys launched in agencies among the staff show that often staff members considered that targets have been imposed without consultation and debate. This problem could still be corrected in coming years.

The new philosophy of nonprescriptive centers. Central units are not to prescribe any blueprint on agencies. This idea has gone so far that it sometimes even excludes advising agencies (in France, special budgets have been created just to help advise agencies). The result is that there is an important diversity in the way agencies have set targets: some have followed a process very similar to the French one, launching studies, audits, and consulting with staff about targets. Most of the time, this occurs in the case of large agencies with a large number of staff which need internal unity to succeed (such as the employment service) or of agencies having previous experience in management (such as the land registry). Other agencies have been forced to set up targets without having had the time either to think sufficiently about their goals or to develop them from the bottom-up rather than in an exclusively top-down manner.

The disadvantage in the French case of giving agencies more time is that only some of the agencies have a full set of targets, whereas British agencies now have all efficiency, economy, and quality targets.

The Use of Targets and Indicators

The U.K. experience had an initial aim of being able to make decisions based on performance measures. This is now partly the case: the performance-related pay of management staff and the group-bonus schemes are dependent on exceeding targets. When an agency is not able to achieve its targets, the amount of flexibilities allowed in its framework document can be revised. The policy of user fees can also be related to performance measures: if an agency is able to demonstrate that an increase of fees will make its action more effective (for example by enabling the delivery of more sophisticated services which in the medium term will attract more users), it can propose this change to the minister and the Treasury.

In France, the Treasury has never accepted the idea that decisions could be based on performance measures, at least not at a national level. Rather, the Treasury thinks that budget choices are the result of political considerations which have only a remote relationship with performance. It may also be the case that the Treasury does not want to make its own criteria of choice explicit or public.

In spite of these differences, both countries have to face common issues:

- How is it possible to take performance measures into account in budget allocations without having negative impact on the service users?
- How is it possible to have objective criteria for budget allocation while knowing at the same time that every indicator typically has unforeseen negative consequences?

The relationship between performance measures and decision making seems more easy at a local level where one has decentralized, comparable units. In these cases, there is not a choice between different goals and any negative impacts due to allocation based on the indicators can be rectified in a very flexible and rapid way, unlike the case at the level of very large organizations or departments.

Issues for the Future in the United Kingdom and in France

The need to achieve a certain level of generalization of the reform process. Performance measurement has to reach a certain level of widespread use to be able to change a national system. In the departments where a lot of services have become agencies, the pressure on the center is effective and has obliged the center to change, to withdraw from day-to-day management and make a greater effort on a more precise definition of the key public-policy objectives. In other cases, the agencies remain very isolated in the department and their action is hindered by the fact that the central services have not changed their way of managing. To take an example: an agency is supposed to have a global running cost budget, but when it asks for its budget each year after the vote of the finance law, the real management of this budget, the redistribution of money, remains split between different central services not working together. The consequence is that the agency cannot obtain a real global budget of its own.

The issue is to be able simultaneously to provide enough time to deal with the different degrees of maturity of services and to go fast enough so that the innovators do not feel isolated.

The necessity to find a credible link between the reforms and employ professional skills in order to convince the staff. The general question asked of any new modernization process is: Are the changes really deep or only a new management fashion? Of course it is very hard to answer that question. A lot of civil servants were very dubious about the modernization initiative because they did not see any relationship with their work and their professional skills: it was a supplementary burden to what they had normally to do. Furthermore, some factors of success are not implemented well enough:

- incentives for good managing services or sanctions (performance-related pay or group-bonus schemes remain too rare); and
- the allocation of resources is only marginally related to performance (it depends on the quality of the relationship between each department and the Treasury).

There is still not any clear incentive for modernization which deals with the key organizational issue of budgets.

In an ideal society it would be possible to bring together the strengths of the different public-sector reform initiatives: the rapidity of the

British method and the French emphasis on ownership and well-embedding the changes, the clarity and simplicity of the British targets and the French evaluation of the outcomes, the British experience of defining the different types of targets and the French effort to tailor the targets to the individual organizational culture.

Notes

1. The definition of the concepts are the following: objectives are the general aims of the public policies; targets are operational objectives which can be quantified or checked; measures are quantitative data; indicators are the signs which show if a target is reached or not when it is not possible to quantify it exactly, they are also called "proxies." An objective can be to reduce unemployment in the United Kingdom; the target will be to find a job for 20,000 people; the indicator will be the time needed to find a job (assuming that the quickest one finds a job, the more likely he is to remain employed).
2. Richard Mottram, Permanent Secretary, Next Steps team, in answer to the TCSC, 1993.
3. A trading fund is a financial technique meant to insure commercial type accounts in an agency. Trading funds can carry over from year to year all their running costs and keep their revenues. They all have accrual accounting. An agency can only become a trading fund if more than 50 percent of its revenues come from external receipts.
4. Organization for Economic Cooperation and Development (OECD) 1994, "Performance Management in Government: Performance Measurement and Results-Oriented Management." Occasional Paper no. 3. Paris.
5. The *prefect* is the general delegate of the French government in each local area (département). He is in charge of coordinating the activities of all local offices of national ministeries.
6. This has been particularly the case for the department of equipment (roads, social housing, transport, environment) that has been one of the pioneers of PPBS in the seventies. See Vallemont (1989).
7. It depends of course on what accountability is. If accountability is the duty to provide information and explanations, French agencies are accountable for all their targets. If accountability means to be judged and that this judgement can impact on career or resources, agencies are primarily accountable for the government's targets.
8. This has been called "operation CLAIRE," Ministère de l'equipement (1987).
9. Total quality management was introduced in 1985 following this model.
10. The department of education has always been very well known for its "pilot schools." The innovations have never spread to the whole department.
11. Pointed out in a speech by Steve Sedgwick, Secretary, Department of Finance. Lakeside Hotel, Canberra, 14 July, 1994.
12. As stated in the Chatres des services publics (1993): "The public sector reform will succeed only because the civil servants accept its objectives."
13. A French sociologist, Philippe d'Iribarne (1993), has studied the relationship between management techniques and national cultures and demonstrated that some techniques are doomed to fail because they are contradictory with some national

values. For example, Japanese techniques never worked in France because they refer to a strong sense of community that is not in the French anarchist, individualistic tradition.

References

Association des Service Publics.1994. *L'Etat moderne et l'administration*. Librarie générale de droit et de juriprudence.

Cabinet Office. 1994. *Next Steps: Moving On*. (The Trosa Report). (Cm 2450) London: HMSO.

Carter, N. and P. Greer. 1993. "Evaluating Agencies: the Next Steps and Performance Indicators." Pu*blic Administration*. 71 Autumn: 407—16.

Committee for the devolution of administrations.1993. *Recommendations pour la conduite de la deconcentration*. 17 juin.

Comptroller and Auditor General. 1989. *The Next Steps Initiative*. London: HMSO.

Crozier, M. 1991. *L'entreprise a l'écoute*. Éditions d'organisation.

Crozier, P. and F. Petitbon. 1993. *Le fonctionnaire au quotidien*. Éditions d'organisation.

d'Iribarne, P. 1993. *La Logique de l'honneur*. Paris: Seuil.

Declaration of Michel Rocard, P. M. 1990. *Rencontres nationales du service Public*. Journal Officiel.

Goldsworthy, D. 1991. *Setting Up Next Steps*. London: HMSO.

H.M. Treasury 1992. *A Guide for Setting Targets and Measuring Performance*. London: HMSO.

Improving Management in Government: The Next Steps. A Report to the Prime Minister (Ibbs Report, 1988). London: HMSO.

Kemp, P. Personal communication.

Making the Most of Next Steps: The Management of Ministers' Departments and their Executive Agencies . A Report to the Prime Minister (Fraser Report, 1991). London: HMSO.

Meny, Y. and J. C. Thoenig. 1990. *Politiques publiques*. Paris: Presses Universitaires de France.

Ministère de l'Equipement. 1989. *L'analyse strategique*. Les cahiers du management (internal review). France.

Ministère de l'Equipement. 1989. *Les projects de service*. Les cahiers du management (internal review). France.

Ministère de l'Equipement. 1992. *Rencontres de l'Equipement* (internal paper). France.

Rapport du Conseil Scientifique de l'Evaluation. 1992. Paris: Documentation francaise.

Rocard, M. 1989. *La circulaire du 29 fevrier*. Journal Officiel.

The Citizen's Charter. 1991. (Cm 1599). London: HMSO.

Thoenig, J. C. and P. Gibert. 1993. "La gestion publique: entre amnesie l'apprentissage et l'amnesie." *Politiques et Management Public* 11, no. 1: 3–21.

Transport Research Laboratory. 1993. *Framework Document*.

Treasury and Civil Service Committee. 1990. *Progress in the Next Steps Initiative*. Eighth Report. (HC 481). London: HMSO.

Treasury and Civil Service Committee. 1991. *The Next Steps Initiative*. Seventh Report. (HC496). London: HMSO.

Vallemont, S. 1989. "Le projet de progrés et de modernisation de l'administration de l'Equipement." *Politiques et Management Public* 7, no. 3: 167–77.

Vallemont, S. 1991. *Moderniser l'administration*. Paris: Nathan.

5

Performance-Monitoring Systems: A Basis for Decisions?

Rolf Sandahl

Introduction

Many people regard the creation of better results-information systems as one of the most important factors in the transformation of the public sector from a system controlled by regulations into one more oriented towards results (see chapter 1). In Sweden, as in many other countries, a great deal of time and considerable resources have been devoted recently to improving these systems. One reason for this is that governments expect a correlation between these systems and budget savings or redistribution of resources between spheres of activity.

This is not to imply that systems of follow-up and evaluation did not previously exist in Sweden. Indeed, this aspect of Swedish public administration is probably fairly well covered from an international perspective. The new element has been the desire of government to give its agencies an enhanced role as producers of results information. And this new role was to be a permanent, continuous affair. Bearing in mind the nature of the Swedish system of public administration, this enhanced role is not illogical.

In Sweden, there is a clear distinction, both conceptually and organizationally, between ministries and agencies, reflecting the principle that politics and administration are essentially separate matters. Another, more drastic, way of putting it would be to say that Swedish government agencies in principle enjoy the same degree of autonomy as the courts. Implementation of parliamentary or governmental decisions is the responsibility of the agencies themselves. In their day-to-day work, agencies are comparatively autonomous vis-à-vis the ministries. Specifically, the government may not, in principle, intervene in the processing of individual cases.

By international standards, Swedish ministries are also very small, rarely employing more than 200 people. The agencies, on the other hand, are numerous and vary widely in size. A few number their employees in the thousands. In a further group of seventy to eighty agencies, the number of staff range from one to several hundred. Lastly, there are more than a thousand agencies with only a few personnel, in some cases no more than a handful. Many agencies are also subdivided into regional and local offices.

Considering the number of agencies, their powers, and independence in relation to the ministries, and the fact that they are the bodies which implement policy decisions, it was not unreasonable to encourage agencies to become producers of results information. This idea was not new, however. Like many other countries, Sweden had earlier experimented with program budgeting, where the development and production of results information constituted an important part of the reform. It had little success, however. Factors favoring a more successful outcome this time around were those linked to changing external circumstances, such as the deteriorating economic situation, which might be thought to add urgency to incentives to find a solution for more effective government spending.

One of the questions we shall be attempting to answer in this chapter relates to the nature of the data yielded by new information systems operating in the public sector. Another question concerns the relationship between these and other systems designed to produce results data. Yet a further question is concerned with the part all these information systems—new and existing—play in the political decision-making process. Is there a connection between results information and decision making?

We shall be attempting to provide a more subtly defined and more realistic picture of these follow-up and evaluation systems than those purveyed either by the optimists, determined to see in these systems "solutions" to the public debt problem, or by the pessimists, who "have seen it all before."

Let us begin with a brief description of those results-oriented follow-up and evaluation systems which have long been in place in the public sector. This will enable us to gain a better perspective on the new information systems which have been developed.

The Swedish System of Public Inquiries and Policy Commissions

Ad Hoc Policy Commissions

Traditionally, appointed ad hoc policy commissions have played a great part in preparing the ground for many decisions. The commissions have been important for providing briefing and background material both with respect to fundamental policy decisions and in connection with the day-to-day fine calibration of the approaches available in various spheres of activity. A commission system resembling the one existing today had already begun to take form in the seventeenth century.

Today, the Swedish commission system is quite comprehensive in scope. There are few countries which employ specially appointed commissions to the same extent in the preparation of proposed reforms. Finland, which partially shares the same administrative tradition as Sweden, is perhaps the nearest equivalent. The Swedish commission system has played a central role in the preparation of political decisions during the whole of this century (Meijer 1956: 8; DsSB 1984). It celebrated its greatest triumphs, however, in the 1960s and 1970s with over 300 commissions working annually. In recent years, almost 200 different commissions have been at work annually (Petersson 1988; The Swedish Agency for Administrative Development 1991).

A Meeting Place for Stakeholders . . .

If we consider developments over a comparatively long period of time, practically every question of any significance has been examined by a commission. The commissions involved often contain representatives of the political parties and stakeholders, such as trade unions, the employers associations, organizations for students, teachers, consumers, environmental interests, and so on. This means that a number of different interested parties are briefed using the same factual material and are able to influence which material is considered relevant in assessing the matter at issue. Considering this, the committee system is seen as playing an important role within the democratic process in Sweden (DsSB, 1984: 3).

. . . and Expertise

The Swedish policy-commission system can also be regarded as a major channel for introducing knowledge of the current state of research in various fields of activity into the political decision-making process.[1] For instance, during the period 1955–89, at least one scientist was involved in about one-quarter of the commissions (Johansson 1992: 64–65).

Within the framework of the system of public official inquiries in Sweden we find in various research reports and statements of expert opinion quite a few examples of what we have more recently designated as evaluations, even when we go back to the 1950s and the 1960s, or indeed even earlier. They are often to be found under such headings as "previous experience," "the current situation," and so on. A scientific approach to the assessment of the effects of various measures of public intervention can therefore by no means be considered a radically new departure.

The picture we have given of the commission system supports the contention that this system permitted Sweden to introduce the ex post assessment of effects probably before this was done in many other countries.

The Referral System—Another Channel for Stakeholders and Expertise

Any description of the commission system would not be complete without an account of the Swedish system of political referral (*remissystemet*). The various reports produced by the commissions are referred to a large number of interested parties—official and nonofficial organizations both public and private—for consideration and comment. These comprise agencies, research bodies, interested pressure groups, and so on. Agencies such as the Swedish National Audit Office also play a significant part in this respect.

These review bodies often devote a significant amount of energy to developing critical opinions concerning the work of the various commissions. This is not merely a way of establishing a polite mode of intercourse between different sections of the political system, and between central government and other parts of society. It is also a way of "fine-combing" the expertise available in society with respect to the matters being analyzed. Frequently, the analyses of the commissions have been supplemented by new knowledge in precisely this way.

New Channels for Expertise and Research

It was not until the early years of the 1960s that evaluation came to be viewed as an activity which might continuously provide politicians and other decision makers with the briefing materials required for reassessments. An example may be given to illustrate this. After the introduction of the compulsory nine-year comprehensive school system in 1962, the Swedish Board of Education was given the responsibility of continuously monitoring the development of the system and thereby evaluating it. The intention was that the evaluations would provide the factual basis for successive revisions of the school system's general curricula (Franke-Wikberg and Lundgren 1980: 17).

But the school system was not the only sector where it was intended to bring evaluation activities into the decision-making process on a more continuous basis. As early as the 1960s, many discussions were conducted concerning the effects of various instruments of social and consumer policy with a view to enabling the most disadvantaged groups to obtain real benefits from them.

Thus, an interest in questions of evaluation was developing in several different policy areas, as part of what we may call an intrasectoral development process. This led to the creation of research bodies in a number of sectors, such as construction, crime prevention, energy, regional policy, and so on, with evaluation as one of their principal tasks. Parallel to evaluation gaining a foothold within several specific policy areas, a more general or suprasectoral grasp of the questions involved was maturing.

But alongside these more sectorally oriented evaluation tasks entrusted to certain agencies, it may be stated that every agency has a particular responsibility for producing information about the results of its own activities.

Performance Information for the Budgetary Process

One process in which monitoring information about results has been required of agencies, at least in formal terms, has long been the budgetary process, that is, the regular, official process in which the agencies make their annual request to the government for new appropriations for their activities, followed by the discussions within the government and Parliament. In practice, however, these discussions have usually been more concerned with the financial framework for the activities than with the activities themselves.

This was the budgetary process it was hoped to change. The center of gravity was to move from input control to output control. After the initial decision in 1988, this revised process involved the replacement of the customary annual budget request by a variety of budget documents (Sandahl 1993). One of these was an extended (in-depth) budget request. In the initial years of the reform, a properly drawn-up account of results attained over the immediately preceding five-year period and a detailed plan of proposed results for the forthcoming three-year period was requested. The agencies were required to submit this request every third year. However, this did not mean that all agencies should submit their in-depth budget requests at the same time. This would defeat the whole idea of attempting to improve planning practices. Instead, one third of the agencies presented their triennial requests each year.

In recent years, a more flexible attitude has been adopted in connection with this document, since "the administrative classification of the agencies into three budgetary cycles makes it more difficult to bring about a system of management by results that is flexible and appropriate to the activities in question." Even should the planning period be extended, however, each particular activity, regardless of its size, is to be subject to reassessment every sixth year. This means that the output and effects of the activities in question are to be evaluated in relation to their operational goals and to overall policy objectives (Budget Bill, 1992: 64).

In the intervening years, when agencies are not required to present in-depth budget requests, there are two other documents that will be submitted. One is a simplified budget request. For most agencies this document will serve a limited purpose: it will enable them to rectify earlier decisions, provided the request is restricted to certain technical and financial adjustments and does not entail a reappraisal of the approved direction for the current three-year period.

The second of the two documents is a performance-based follow-up report. The main purpose of this document is to show what has been achieved during the year in terms of activities. The difference between this report and the in-depth assessment lies in rather less emphasis being put on effectiveness analyses (the in-depth budget requests in fact also include both an analysis of resources and an analysis of external conditions). The effects dealt with are those easily captured, that is, they express correlations and not necessarily causal correlations.

On the whole, an in-depth budget request should be more concerned with evaluation, while, as its name implies, a performance-based follow-up report should contain a relatively greater proportion of follow-up (monitoring) data.

While there has been a slight easing of the emphasis on the in-depth budget request, the emphasis on the annual report has correspondingly increased. Government representatives have declared that the annual report should "be given greater prominence and should also be regarded as the natural report-back document for results analyses." In the future it should also be the "annual report which, in compliance with a special request by the Government, contains an account of in-depth results analyses, in addition to the current report-back material contained in the document each year in the results accounts. Accounts of more comprehensive effects analyses may instead be given in special reports." (Budget Bill 1992: 65).

Why was this shift made to view the annual report as the natural document for reporting back? If the purpose was to obtain factual material of high quality for the reassessment of priorities, would not the in-depth budget request really be preferable, given that the whole aim of that document was to give concrete form to a more analytical evaluation effort?

One explanation may well be that expectations concerning the information from the in-depth budget request—and fundamental reassessments are in fact mentioned in the arguments for introducing the reform—were too optimistic. This kind of information, which usually requires a breadth of perspective and an objectivity either lacking in agencies or inappropriate for their purposes, must be generated by other sources, such as the traditional system of government commissions described above. In this respect it may not be too much to speak of a failure of theory: the ideas underlying or the expectations vested in this document were based on mistaken assumptions as to the nature of reality.

But might it perhaps be the case that not even materials produced by the traditional commission system would be adequate for making decisions involving fundamental reassessments? Let us discuss the extent to which information about results is utilized in various decision-making situations.

Does Information About Results Influence Policy Decisions?

Which Decisions?

The decisions in question are made either at the agency level or at the government or parliament level. At the latter level, we have distinguished between two types of decision-making process. One is the more regular and recurrent budget process, through which resources are allocated to agencies. The other one is the ad hoc decision-making processes outside the framework of the current budget process. These include fundamental reassessments of the scope and orientation of central government activities in given areas, including perhaps even the issue of their very existence.

But there are of course no firmly delimited boundaries between what we refer to as fundamental reassessments and more everyday ones. We may speak of a range or continuum. At one end of the scale, we will find decisions which most people would quite intuitively perceive as dramatic changes of direction, as fundamental reassessments. At the other end of the scale there will be the minor adjustments carried out by agencies in the daily course of their normal activities. The purpose of the new budget process is to include questions more oriented towards reassessment.

Further reflection, however, will persuade most people that it is not feasible to commission an agency to question its own existence. Issues involving fundamental reassessments are not appropriate for agencies to deal with. Issues of this kind, and this may be seen as one of the reasons for the reduced emphasis on the in-depth budget request, must therefore be dealt with by other bodies, such as policy commissions, as they were in the past. In this perspective, we may speak of a failure of theory.

The Impact of Commissions and Evaluations

But, as we suggested above, this does not mean that this kind of ad hoc commission has the superior perspective. The situation is rather the reverse. In a dissertation, published in the spring of 1992 on the Swedish commission system during the period 1955–89, Johansson (1992) reaches the conclusion that the greater part of the knowledge accumulated within the commission system is not regarded as relating to fundamental premises for various central government endeavors, but rather to issues having relevance to the choice of technical solutions within the framework of certain major postulates.

The dissertation examines three policy areas, studying among other things the effect of the accumulation and dissemination of knowledge within the framework of the various commissions on political positions.

Johansson makes no distinction between evaluation and other kinds of analysis. It is, however, not unreasonable to interpret a significant part of the accumulation and dissemination of knowledge discussed in the dissertation as evaluation. A considerable number of the analyses submitted to the commissions in the three policy areas have been concerned with ex post conditions after various central government interventions.

In one of these areas, the Swedish system of financing higher education, Johansson asserts that the Social Democratic party then in power changed its position as a result of studies commissioned by the special commission investigating the social framework of education in the early 1960s. What these analyses revealed, to the surprise of contemporary observers, was that imbalances in the recruitment of students from different social backgrounds were primarily found in the transition from compulsory schooling to upper secondary studies. More significant effects would therefore be produced by investing in measures permitting children from working-class homes to continue their studies after compulsory school, than by influencing the economic situation of university students. This led to the shelving of the original idea entertained by the Social Democrats of introducing nonrepayable maintenance grants.

However, this is the only instance among the cases studied of a change of position on a central issue resulting from the provision of new factual and theoretical material demonstrating that an earlier position was based on erroneous assumptions. Furthermore, the commission investigating systems of financing study some twenty years later (1985–87) does not provide a single example of anyone drastically changing his or her point of view on the basis of information emerging from the various inquiries.

The material at our disposal would therefore seem to indicate that the knowledge acquired through the mediation of the commission system only leads to the rejection of basic assumptions in exceptional cases. Unfortunately, our knowledge of other kinds of evaluations and other spheres of activity is severely limited, due to the lack of studies.

However, indirect indications, too, seem to confirm this finding. In studies of policy formation in different areas, such as housing policy, energy policy, crime prevention, and so on, newly acquired knowledge resulting from individual evaluations is almost never referred to as a major explanation for changes of any significance.

We would not, however, wish to exclude the possibility of long-term learning effects. In the first place, it is conceivable that a number of evaluations of the policies pursued within a given policy area may result over time in the question being placed on the political agenda in a way that it would otherwise not have been. It becomes an issue on which politicians are obliged to take action. Second, it is possible that in the long term certain kinds of knowledge may influence judgments as to whether various regulatory measures are operating as intended. A conceivable but as yet not particularly well-substantiated hypothesis might be formulated in the following terms: a whole series of studies undertaken in the 1980s with respect to the effects of different regulatory measures in the energy sector may have influenced politicians in the 1990s in their judgment of what it may or may not be feasible to achieve with the help of various regulations in, for instance, relation to the environment.

Why is the Impact so Limited?

One reason for the difficulty of individual evaluations to deal with fundamental reassessments of various areas of policy may perhaps be the fact that society is growing more complex. It is not possible, as it formerly was, to speak of reassessing individual sectors. It is not only the case that many areas are now more integrated with one another than they used to be, but the traditional sectors are also made up of a number of different constituents. The housing sector, for instance, includes elements such as land policy, housing finance policy, and housing design policy. The cultural sector includes such policy areas as music, theaters, and museums. It is no insignificant task to reassess all these constituent elements. The mere fact that fundamental reassessments occur so seldom, at intervals of a decade or sometimes even more, means that the general progress of society may well suffice for reassessment of a policy area, perhaps without even a formal evaluation of the policies pursued there. Policy areas are becoming more and more integrated with one another. At the same time, this entails limiting the scope of evaluations in terms of both time and subject matter if they are to provide conclusions of the slightest accuracy or relevance. As a result, these will only be able to provide a partial contribution to the information political decision makers will need to process before making fundamental policy decisions.

But if fundamental reassessments are not, as a rule, based on results information, then what factors do determine policy decisions? It is said that politicians deal in intentions rather than effects. They are primarily concerned with what is going to be accomplished rather than what exactly has been achieved, hardly an environment conducive to a productive discussion of an evaluative analysis (Tarshys 1986).

This may sound very discouraging to an evaluator, but it should not be forgotten that, to a great extent, political decision making is about political parties wishing to realize their intentions. Fundamental policy shifts can therefore be said to be caused by a fundamental shift in values. Decision makers may, for instance, no longer regard influencing the orientation of the cultural consumption of individuals or the development of energy use as tasks for central government, to take examples from spheres of activity affected by central government intervention in Sweden.

In this view, of course, it would be quite irrelevant to base any decision on a series of results analyses. As a consequence, attitudes to the future of central government policy will be regarded as quite unaffected by such analyses. Even if such analyses were to demonstrate that central government policies had significantly contributed to the attainment of desired goals, the policies would nonetheless be earmarked for termination—it is quite simply not seen as the task of central government to influence developments in the areas in question (Furubo and Sandahl 1993).

We might logically expect to observe the same lack of interest in evaluation in times of unfavorable economic circumstances. Even if a fundamental shift in values were not involved, one may, at least in principle, imagine decision makers reasoning as follows: "Well, even though it may be consonant with our values to set ourselves the goal of altering the cultural consumption of individuals in a certain way, and although these same values also permit us to make use of economic stimuli to achieve this goal, we can't afford it." Thus, even if the measures used were effective, central government involvement would have to cease.

This latter case is naturally of great interest, as it is exactly the situation many countries face, including Sweden. Even if the policies pursued in various spheres have proved successful to the extent that the measures implemented have contributed to the fulfillment of stated goals, it is, nonetheless, the view of many politicians that we in many cases cannot afford to continue with them (Swedish National Audit Office 1994).

Neither should we forget that the more changeable society becomes, giving rise to completely novel situations, the less utility there will probably be in results information, since this information will increasingly consist of historical data.

But it is naturally impossible for policy to be dictated in every situation exclusively by value judgments, for behind these guidelines there may be found an accumulation of factual material. We might also be able to say that the further down the hierarchical chain we proceed, that is, to the agencies whose task it is to carry out the policies decided upon, the less scope there will be for value judgments. It is not possible to question the politically determined orientation of policy, even if in certain cases there is some independence in the choice of means. Between all these "big" decisions, however, there are the continuous day-to-day issues of policy.

The Impact of Follow-up Information

If we now consider the information generated in the new budgetary process, it belongs in the context of day-to-day issues of policy execution rather than large-scale reassessments. The information in the annual reports, for instance, may even be said to be most useful at agency level, since it is production-oriented, that is to say, the results are principally reported in output terms, and with a high degree of detail.

The ministries have not always found this material to be of great utility. One may naturally ask whether this is due to the agencies or the ministries which are the commissioners and recipients of this information. If we consider the part played by the ministries in this process, it may be claimed that all the analyses available indicate that the ministries are something of a weak link in results-based management. Analyses of both the agency-specific directives and the spending authorizations mentioned above show that the ministries find it hard to delimit their information requirements. There is a clear tendency to ask such sweeping questions that the choice of results information to be produced is in reality delegated to the agencies. It also transpires that goals—particularly goals concerning results—are formulated in such general terms that it is impossible to use them as follow-up or evaluation criteria.

But there is currently a very high level of awareness of this relatively weak ministerial role. It has led to more comprehensive training efforts for ministerial staff in Sweden than at any previous time. The National Audit Office has a key role with respect to annual reports, not just as a review body but also in terms of giving support to ministries when it is a matter of defining the information required to make an assessment of agency activities.

The fact remains, however, that the Swedish system of political administration, with small ministries and many independent agencies, means that specialist knowledge—one of the key factors if relevant information is to be ordered—is to be found in the agencies. This is one of the reasons why the ministries have been content to demand in general terms that the agencies report on what they have achieved rather than to order specific results information. We should not forget, however, that ministry officials constitute an essential part of the political system, and are regulated to a high degree by political signals. This quite naturally delays the more long-term impartial and issue-oriented exchange of ideas between ministries and agencies which is necessary if the process is to develop.

If the initial aim was to obtain valuable management information, it must be admitted that it has now assumed the character of control information. And this may be regarded as a natural development, partly in view of the relative weakness of the ministries as orderers of information which makes the performance-based follow-up report the "natural" reporting-back document rather than the in-depth budget request, and partly because the emphasis on the annual report arose after responsibility for developing the budgetary process passed from the ministry of public administration to the ministry of finance. It is not unreasonable to assume that the ministry of finance will, in the first instance, be interested in being able to check where the money has gone, especially in a period when the issue of the budget deficit is a pressing, everyday concern. At the same time the ministry of finance also realizes that large-scale savings are accomplished on a different basis from that constituted by the information provided by agencies.

Even if the original purpose of using results information from agencies to provide the basis for various policy priorities has not been achieved, which might, to a certain degree, be characterized as a failure of theory, it does not mean that the information obtained is of no use. Placing demands on agencies has the long-term goal of creating a mindset of promoting results and planning. The general picture is that such a mindset is considerably more in evidence at agency level now, as is also an interest in these issues. What is more, many agencies conduct operations oriented towards production, and in this respect the results information demanded is highly relevant. It may therefore be said that the follow-up and evaluation systems created within the framework of the budget process primarily have the agencies themselves as their users. In many cases, of course, it will also be of use to both the government and Parliament, as has emerged from survey interviews. This applies to both annual reports and in-depth budget requests. In due course, it may be possible to adapt these documents for use by both the government and Parliament.

Neither should we forget that many agencies have other follow-up systems and produce materials other than annual reports and in-depth budget requests. These other materials concern factors which may be essential for decisions to be made at the government and the parliament levels. At the same time, members of the public must be allowed the democratic right to find out how their tax contributions are managed. They should be able to ascertain the results of agencies' performance without undue effort, with a view to making their own assessment should they so wish. Part of the underlying data on which to base such an assessment is available from these information systems.

Marginalism: A Problem?

If we now accept that many decisions are made outside the current budget process and are based on materials other than those produced by agencies, one may well ask whether the problem so often encountered in the literature in the West, namely that the budgetary process is merely concerned with marginalism, is in fact a real problem, at least if we confine our attention to Sweden. The basic decision-making material in the budget process has improved, but in general the budget process "covers the same things as before." Or to put it another way: marginalism still characterizes the budget process.

On the other hand, it would be unwise to think that the current budget process could replace major ad hoc reassessments. It seems a little wide of the mark to criticize the budget process for not having done this. It may be the case that marginalism is less of a problem in the context of the Swedish budget process precisely because there exist fairly good mechanisms for undertaking ad hoc reassessments. We have described the role played in this connection by the commissions system. In it we have created a channel for introducing current research and what we now call results information into the political process. The current budget process is not, therefore, a good arena for the consideration of comprehensive changes, since it is not possible to continuously reassess everything. Agency operations must have stability (The Swedish Agency for Administrative Development 1993: 98). On the other hand, a good deal of results information in close proximity to the agencies is becoming increasingly available, little or none of which existed previously.

There are a number of points to be made in this connection, however. One, made earlier, is that a major review of the current budget process is not possible, simply for reasons of time. This is not to say that changes—such as those involving the transfer of resources from one area to another—are unfeasible within individual sectors. In the traffic safety area, for instance, one might well consider reassigning resources from traffic-safety information activities to traffic-safety research. This could be done without affecting the overall budgetary framework for the sector in any way. In other words, the budget allocation remains unchanged from year to year, although funds may be reallocated within that sector. Various kinds of results information are often used as a basis for these changes. The connection will be tenuous if the view is taken that information about results does not affect budgetary decisions and attention is focused on the overall budget framework. No assessment of the significance of this type of information can be wholly valid without an evaluation of the ways in which it affects the activity in question. For example, an evaluation can show that an activity is working well, with increased resource investment in that area as a result. Equally, it may find evidence of poor performance. However, the conclusion usually drawn in cases where unsatisfactory results are indicated is either that not enough was invested to begin with, or that the resources should be transferred to another type of activity.

What we are saying is that results information in itself has little or nothing to do with the decisions made on the basis of these data. When considering assertions to the effect that the connection between evaluation and budgetary decisions is at best tenuous, a clear distinction should be made: is this a reference to the overall budget framework or to more discrete aspects of the budget, relating to individual activities. The answer to the question: "What is the connection between evaluation and budgeting decisions?" will depend on the particular perspective adopted. What we have attempted to establish here is that major changes at the aggregate budget level are based on political considerations rather than information about results, while priority shifts within a given budgetary framework may very well be based on results information.

Summary

In this chapter, we have tried to demonstrate that there are a number of different systems for generating results information in the Swedish public sector. No single information system will be able to provide, and this may perhaps appear self-evident, all the information needed to make decisions at various levels. We have tried to relate the type of information produced within the framework of the new budgetary process to other information systems. This has enabled us to establish that this information is primarily of use at the operative level, that is at the agency level, and that the original concept of reassessment has not really worked out as was anticipated. This does not mean that the information lacks value at the policy-making level, but a lot of decisions of major significance are made on grounds other than those provided by the results information presented by individual agencies. In itself this is not strange, as policy making is naturally about realizing political intentions, and in this process it is quite simply the case that different criteria, that, for example, value or reality judgments, are used to evaluate the same facts.

Note

1. With the exception of Foyer, (1969), "The Social Sciences in Royal Commissions in Sweden" in *Scandinavian Political Studies* 4: 183–203, there have been few studies of this function of the system. However, Premfors, 1983, "Governmental Commissions in Sweden," *American Behavioral Scientist* 26, no. 5: 623–42, is able to confirm the significance of social research in the commissions. The publication of Johansson, 1992, means there is a study now available which to a certain extent discusses this function within the commission system. In his essay, (1992) "Seven Observations on Evaluations in the Swedish Political System" (in *Program and Policy Evaluation in Comparative Perspective*, ed. John Mayne & Ross Conner, London & New York: Elsevier) Evert Vedung provides an overview of some of the features of Swedish commissions under the enlightening heading "The Stakeholder Model in Practise: Ad hoc Policy Commissions." One of the features of the commission system pointed out by Vedung is that their results are always published, providing "testimony to the remarkable openness of the Swedish State policy-making system."

References

Budget Bill. 1992. 1991–92: vol. 150.

DsSB 1984. *Memorandum of the Swedish system of official commissions*. Statsrådsberedningen, vol. 1.

Foyer, L. 1969. "The Social Sciences in Royal Commissions in Sweden." *Scandinavian Political Studies*. 4: 183–203.

Franke-Wikberg, S. and U. Lundgren. 1980. *Att värdera utbildning*. Stockholm: Wahlström & Widstrand.

Furubo, J-E. and R. Sandahl. 1993. *Does the Result Matter*. Swedish National Audit Office.

Johansson, J. 1992. *Det statliga kommittéväsendet—Kunskap, kontroll, konsensus*. Edsbruk: Akademitryck AB.

Meijer, H. 1956. *Kommittépolitik och kommittéarbete*. Lund, Sweden: Gleerup.

Petersson, O. 1988. *Maktens nätverk*. Stockholm: Carlssons.

Premfors, R. 1983. "Governmental Commissions in Sweden." *American Behavioral Scientist*, 26, no. 5: 623–42.

Sandahl, R. 1993. "Connected or Separated? Budgeting, Auditing and Evaluation in Sweden." In Bu*dgeting, Auditing, & Evaluation. Functions and Integration in Seven Governments*, eds. Gray, Jenkins, and Segsworth. New Brunswick, NJ: Transaction Publishers.

Swedish National Audit Office. 1994. *Information för omprövning*. En studie av beslutsunderlagets kvalitet och användning.

Tarshys, D. 1986. "För döva öron? Politikern och utvärderaren." In *Utvärdering av offentlig politik*, ed. Palmlund. Stockholm: Liber.

The Swedish Agency for Administrative Development. 1991. Draft version of a paper about the Swedish Commissions, 1991-03-01.

The Swedish Agency for Administrative Development. 1993. *Utvecklad Styrnings-dialog*, 20.

Vedung, E. 1992. "Seven Observations on Evaluations in the Swedish Political System." In *Program and Policy Evaluation in Comparative Perpective*, ed. John Mayne and Ross Conner. London: Elsevier.

6

Accountability for Program Performance: A Key to Effective Performance Monitoring and Reporting

John Mayne

As we saw earlier in chapter 1, public-sector reform initiatives frequently reference the importance of performance monitoring. And over the past twenty years, we have learned quite a lot about measuring the performance of government programs and services. Yet success is still often elusive, as other chapters in this book illustrate.

In part we are dealing with quite a complex activity—the measurement of public-sector performance and its use in a political environment. There are no simple answers or we would have succeeded long ago. In this chapter, we examine one critical but frequently weak link in organizational use of performance information, namely the reporting of performance information and its use in accountability. On the one hand, rhetoric on reporting of actual performance is frequently weak or absent, suggesting to many that the demand for performance information is symbolic. And on the other hand, meaningful accountability—which might make use of performance information—while always part of the aim of public-sector reform, is acknowledged by many to be the weakest component of public sector reform initiatives.

We suggest that reforming public administration requires reforming the concept of accountability in the public sector. We further suggest that essential to this reform of accountability is the need for practical performance measures and reporting.

We first address the question of the role of accountability in the new public management and suggest the need for a new perspective on accountability. We then discuss the link with performance monitoring and argue that accountability and performance monitoring/reporting are mutually supportive. We conclude by discussing principles for effective performance reporting.

Accountability: The Weak Link in Public-Sector Reform

Public-sector reform efforts have proven weak in one area in particular, an area essential also for effective performance monitoring: that of closing the accountability loop. Public-sector reform almost always calls for enhanced or increased accountability, but is usually either vague on accountability by whom, for what, and how, or offers only a very traditional and ultimately self-defeating view of accountability. In a review of several articles on managerial reforms, Aucoin (1990b: 201–2) notes that " the issue of 'accountability' . . . is the major issue raised by these reforms."
The Canadian experience mirrors that of other countries:

> The missing link all along has been effective accountability for the use of authorities for which people have been entrusted. . . . As Public Service 2000 simplifies the Public Service's administration, and more and more stress is placed on a results-oriented and client-sensitive culture, the importance of effective accountability is going to become correspondingly greater. (Government of Canada 1990: 89)

Yet it is clear that effective accountability is essential for successful public-sector reform. Without the closing of the accountability loop, many of the directions of public-sector reform are at best unworkable, and more likely will lead to mismanagement and a loss of control. Indeed, a key issue in the new public management, is how to reconcile the desires of elected officials to remain and even enhance their control over the public service, in Aucoin's (1990a: 115) words, "to reestablish the primacy of representative government over bureaucracy" with the direction of public-sector reform. As managers are given more flexibility and empowerment to manage public funds, we should expect a greater degree of accountability for the outcomes achieved. "Increased public accountability on part of management cannot be escaped without diminishing good politics" (Aucoin 1990b: 204).

Accomplishment Accountability: A Positive Force for Reform

Traditionally, accountability has been viewed as something done to someone. People are held accountable and blame is melted out for failures. Accountability is control, and conjures up the "more traditional concepts of accountability, notably due process, probity, stewardship. In other words, ethical behaviour" (Holmes 1992: 481). Accountability in this view is a rather negative force, something any sensible manager seeks to avoid if possible since no good is likely to come from it. And in an environment where success is staying out of trouble and following the correct administrative procedures, this traditional accountability, besides being an annoyance, is probably seen as of secondary importance to those managers trying to accomplish some public-sector objectives. Most would agree that some amount of regularity accountability is needed, but are quite content to leave it all to the auditors to handle.

The problem is that the "holding people to account for correct procedures" mindset of accountability appears antithetical to public-sector reform based on a results, empowerment, and service-oriented public sector.

There is, however, an alternative perspective on accountability that is not only quite consistent with public-sector reform but acts as a catalyst to reform. What is needed to complete the accountability loop in a reformed public service, is the incentive to demonstrate what results have been accomplished. The key is to make this *demonstration* the essence of the accountability regime. Accomplishment accountability is the credible demonstration of what one has achieved that is of significance and value. To be of value implies that performance is reported on in the context of preestablished expectations of what was to be accomplished.

A recent paper from the Organization for Economic Cooperation and Development (OECD) points out the shift occurring from regularity to performance accountability (1992). And a recent evaluation of the Australian public-sector reform experience comments on "a perceived tendency of various review bodies (and the public) to interpret accountability primarily in the negative sense of: to hold to account or punish failure." It goes on to compare accountability as "blame apportionment" vs. as "answering for" actions and as an essential link to future planning (Task Force on Management Improvement 1992: 506–7).

We suggest that public-sector managers would welcome the occasion to demonstrate to their superiors, their clients, and the public what their programs are achieving, and where achievements are less than expected, not to shy away from explaining what went wrong and what they are doing to improve things in the future. Such demonstration might be done internal to the organization. But it is just such demonstration to the public which is also needed for a service-oriented public service to become a reality.

Barzelay (1992: 127–28) makes the point this way:

> [T]he most effective way to hold employees accountable is to make them feel accountable. This route to accountability is attractive, in part, because employees want to be accountable. They want to be accountable because it is the only way for them, as for us all, to be important.

He goes on to argue that we feel important when we are having an impact (are accomplishing something) and when we are being paid attention to.

Thus a reform-minded accountability regime would be one that provided the opportunity for managers (and ministers) to demonstrate to appropriate persons and bodies what has been accomplished in relation to what is expected with the resources and authorities entrusted to them. And, of course, it is reasonable to expect that public servants and ministers getting and using public money have such an obligation to answer on what they have accomplished. In this regime, "being in control" means:

- knowing what you are supposed to achieve;
- knowing in a timely manner the results that have been achieved;
- being able to credibly demonstrate what was achieved;
- constantly striving for more cost-effective ways of achieving the results; and
- being able to show that you acted wisely on this knowledge, i.e., that the decisions and actions you took were reasonable in light of what happened.[1]

Accomplishment accountability based on this positive act of demonstrating performance puts accountability in the hands of managers and would be a further incentive to pursue reform initiatives (and indeed to manage better). It allows managers to demonstrate that they are in control. Furthermore, it makes sense. "The ethic of constantly seeking more cost effective outcomes is worthy of at least equal bill-ing with the more traditional concepts of accountability." (Holmes 1992: 481). We are not suggesting that probity and prudence can be neglected but that accomplishment accountability is what is essential for effective public-service reform.

Several things are required for an effective accomplishment accountability regime, such as a management regime which demands accountability and pays attention to the information.[2] In addition, the following requirements are of interest here:

- a clear understanding and agreement (preferably in writing, if only as an aide-memoire) of what is to be accomplished and what authorities and resources are being conferred;
- enlightened and informed judgment to effectively hold someone to account for their actions; and, of course,
- credible performance information of what actually has occurred.

Accomplishment accountability is directly or indirectly called for by most public-sector reform initiatives. It suggests that the accountability should not be seen as "blame apportionment" or reporting on compliance with procedures but rather as a useful and essential management process for

- *understanding* the performance of programs, services, and operations;
- *agreeing* on performance expectations;
- *improving* performance through supportive assessment and corrective action aimed at creating a continuous learning environment; and
- *demonstrating* to others, including the public, the levels of public-sector performance attained.

A Requirement for Accomplishment Accountability

With this revised concept of accountability, we *can* close the accountability loop so often left open or incomplete in a logical and consistent manner: pursue accomplishment accountability and get a buy-in from managers. Make the demonstration of what has been accomplished the responsibility of managers, that is, managing should include an individual responsibility for accounting for performance. Requiring managers to demonstrate what they have accomplished will be seen as an opportunity for all but the most recalcitrant managers. A requirement for accountability becomes a responsibility to account for performance. It also provides a smart manager in this age of frequent challenges to programs with evidence on what value has been obtained for the public resources spent.

And, of course, requiring the demonstration of performance provides just the realistic and practical demand for performance information that is needed to foster effective performance monitoring. To manage well and be able to give a credible demonstration of their performance, managers would need good performance information: "Thus, performance measurement reinforces efforts towards modernization and enables an organization to demonstrate its results and their value to politicians, customers and the public" (OECD 1994: 19).

We have been silent on to whom the demonstration of performance is to be done. This will vary among jurisdictions. But be it internal accounting, formal accounting between government and Parliament, or an accounting to the public, the same principles can apply.

To date, most public accounting for performance has involved governments reporting to legislative bodies. Both Canada and Australia, for example, have established formal means for this annual reporting.

But there is an additional element at work. It has been argued that a form of accountability reporting directly to the public will be established in a service-oriented public service. Carter and Greer (1993: 416) suggest that the Citizen's Charter in the United Kingdom will lead to a "broader form of accountability; not just to the Department and to Parliament but also to consumers and service users." The public is likely to see it as such. The Economist argues that "Now accountability is also to customers through the Citizen's Charter" (The Economist 1993: 57). Many countries are establishing and publishing service standards to inform service users of what services are available and the level of service delivery they can expect to receive. In many cases this includes a requirement to publish service delivery performance against the standards, so as to directly inform clients how well they are doing.

In a parliamentary system, this "accountability" might more accurately be described as a reporting relationship, since formally, public servants are only accountable to the public through ministers and Parliament. However described, the intent is that managers assume a responsibility to demonstrate to their publics what services and benefits are being delivered.

An enlightened administration might require just such accounting from its managers. In Norway in 1982, a Plan of Action for a User-

Minded Public Service was begun which emphasized that "organizing contact with the public is a management responsibility" (Eriksen 1987). In Canada, the government's policy on review (evaluation internal audit and performance monitoring) requires managers "to account for performance and to inform clients of the level, quality and cost of services provided," and the service standard initiative requires the publishing of performance against standards (Treasury Board of Canada 1995).

The Auditor General of Australia has stressed the need for effective public reporting:

> Taxpayers have a right to know:
> * the real goals of government programs,
> * how effective these programs are in achieving those goals,
> * what unintended effects result from the programs, and have a right to expect the government to put effective measures in place to do this. (Taylor 1992: 460)

Making public service managers responsible for demonstrating to their ministers, governing bodies, and their public clients what is being accomplished would close the loop on public-sector reform. It would ensure a responsive public service. It would also ensure that performance monitoring would become an integral element of good management in the new public-sector management.

Building Common Performance Expectations

The motivation to establish realistic and challenging performance expectations is often the weakest part of an accountability regime. To be most effective, the process involves consultation, discussion, and probably debate over just what is expected to result from the resources and authorities provided. Agreement of expectations implies a shared vision of what is to be accomplished and what will be viewed as success. Whether or not it includes detailed performance targets depends on the nature of the accountability regime being established. Typically, the higher up one is in an accountability chain, the more performance expectations are stated in terms of broader results rather than quantitative output targets, and less direct control exists in accomplishing the agreed performance expectations. Where long-term outcomes are part of the accountability agreement, lower-level performance indicators are usually provided to show progress towards the desired outcomes.

Further, in the public sector we must allow for multiple and perhaps conflicting objectives. Working towards agreements on performance expectations in a constructive fashion may result in the resolution of this multiple objectives problem. If not, agreement can still be reached on specific expectations for the several objectives being sought. Performance monitoring will provide evidence on the extent to which these differing goals are being attained. In light of this information, decision makers may choose to modify one or more of the objectives.

The value of agreeing on performance expectations was highlighted by the recent review of administrative reform in the United Kingdom:

> Departments and Agencies were more likely to express satisfaction with their working relationship where the [performance] targets were clear and realistic and were accepted by both parties. (Efficiency Unit 1991: 13)

Settings targets is a good message for those who want to be sure their efforts are taken seriously and their work is meaningful.

Effective External Performance Reporting

Most governments have limited experience in reporting performance. Certainly, much reporting of performance is not effective communication. In the United Kingdom, for example, the Treasury and Civil Service Committee (1991, x-xi) commented that "the welter of performance measures and indicators are often poorly related to departmental aims and objectives."

In this light, some of the lessons learned from performance measurement are relevant. Effective performance reporting has two main principles.[3]

1. It must be of significance and value for those to whom the reporting is being done.

"Significant" means it makes a difference to decisions. This implies in most cases that the performance information will be presented in relation to expectations previously established. Gaps between what is expected to be reported on and what is actually reported on will guarantee loss of credibility. This often is the result when rather than reporting on whether outcome objectives are being achieved, the amount of activity carried out in relation to the objective is reported on.

2. It must be credible not only to those being reported to, but also, since the information in most reporting situations is widely available, it must be defensible to challenge.

Credibility implies transparency, relevance, reliability, and timeliness. We feel credibility ought to be manifest in the information itself. However, and perhaps more realistically, many argue that credibility is greatly enhanced with an independent check on the information produced. Thus, for example, auditors general are increasingly providing quality checks on performance information provided to parliaments.

Good External Performance Reporting Practices

Within these two basic principles of effective performance reporting, a number of other good practices derived from performance measurement experience can be briefly mentioned.

Comparative Information

In most cases, performance information needs comparative information to be meaningful and credible. "Good" performance is in relation to something. Knowing what level of performance was expected is one way to set up a comparison. Valid and accepted performance benchmarks provide a baseline to use. A valid time series is another way to show performance variations over time and to establish a comparison base. Effective performance reporting should encourage and make easy comparisons among programs or over time. This builds credibility.

Reporting Strategy

To be most effective, a well thought-out reporting strategy needs to be developed to determine which aspects of performance should be reported when, to whom, and how often. In any organization, reporting on performance will and should occur at all levels. Performance reporting is done for several purposes: demonstrating performance, affecting operational management, and as input into strategic decisions. Clearly a key element of the strategy is to have the right kind of information reported at the right time, that is, when decisions are being made and accounting is required.

Annual reporting of all aspects of performance is usually not practical or even meaningful. It is not practical because of the prohibitive cost involved in such comprehensive reporting each year. It may not be meaningful, because some performance results only manifest themselves over a period of time. Other performance information useful for day-to-day management may be outdated soon after it is produced. What is likely needed is annual reporting of certain performance measures and a more in-depth reporting on other aspects of performance periodically. In this way, over a period of time—perhaps three to five years—a full reporting of performance is accomplished in the most cost-effective way.[4]

A cost-effective strategy might be to report annually on a select number of key measures of performance which give a reasonable idea of overall performance. Some of these key measures will be good measures of aspects of performance while others may be rather simple indicators or proximates of aspects of performance (such as key outputs which are assumed to produce the desired outcomes). Then on a periodic basis (perhaps every three to five years), more in-depth evaluations can check the robustness of the presumed link between these outputs and the desired outcomes.

Explanatory Information

Reporting of performance information requires adequate accompanying explanatory information. The Office of the Comptroller General (1991) suggests that:

> Meaningful reports of [performance] require you to interpret the results. Simple numbers . . . say very little and may be misleading. Good performance indicators require:
> * comparability with other indicators (over time, with other services, etc.) and
> * a contextual discussion about the environment and an interpretive analysis of the significance of the indicator, and whether it continues to be valid.

Raaum (1992: 24) suggests that three types of explanatory information may be needed:

> * Background information about the program . . . [which] provides a context for analyzing what has been accomplished.

- An explanation of what performance aspects are susceptible to measurement, and what presented indicators actually show. . . . It may also be necessary to explain the interrelationships among measures . . . .
- An explanation of the reasons for changes in performance. . . . Users will likely want to know the reasons and what action management plans to take.

The importance of explanatory information is highlighted in the Governmental Accounting Standards Board (1992) report on service efforts and accomplishment reporting:

> Narrative explanatory information . . . can provide explanations of what the level of performance reported . . . means, the possible effects that explanatory factors might have on performance, and actions that have been (or are being) taken to change reported performance. Explanations are particularly important when comparisons with other jurisdictions or among similar components within the same jurisdiction are reported. They are also important in conjunction with reporting secondary, unintended effects of a service. (1992: 14–15)

In addition to this type of explanatory information, the method of data collection and analysis should be briefly outlined. This helps the reader judge the robustness of the evidence provided.

Relevant Costing Information

Performance reporting needs to be done in relation to the costs incurred in producing the results (the outputs, client benefits, or outcomes). Thus, reporting on performance achieved should directly include relevant costing information or be transparently related to the financial accounting system being used by the organization. In many jurisdictions, costing related performance is not readily available from existing financial systems. The lack of available and good costing information is a significant hindrance to credible performance reporting.

Parsimonious Reporting

Perhaps the most difficult aspect of good performance reporting is to identify and display those few pieces of performance information that tell the key elements of the story. The U.K. Efficiency Unit (1991: 3) suggests:

The aim should be for each Agency to have a handful of robust and meaningful top level output targets which measure financial performance, efficiency and quality of customer service, over and above whatever subsidiary performance indicators are required for the Agency's internal management purposes.

The challenge is often to be parsimonious while still ensuring that the information reported is representative of the performance of what is being reported on. A few key indicators are not effective if they do not reflect the operating environment and thereby present a distorted picture.

Purposeful Reporting

While being parsimonious is essential, it is also true that different users will have very different information needs and interests concerning the performance of the same program. These different users might be different levels within an organization (such as service deliverers, middle management, or senior management), or different organizations (for example, a Treasury office, Parliament, or an auditor general). For efficiency in reporting, one usually tries to make one report suit many different users. The result, however, may be that none are pleased. If the purpose of the performance reporting for each user is not clearly thought out, effective reporting will be elusive. In planning for performance reporting it is useful to explicitly identify the various audiences and their issues and concerns which the reporting should address.

Thus one should be parsimonious in reporting for a specific user, but if there are several key users or clients of the reporting, a number of different measures of performance or different presentations of performance may be needed. And with today's information technology, it may be only marginally more of an effort and cost to design careful, purposeful reporting for key users.

User-Friendly Reporting

The better efforts at reporting performance have clearly spent the extra time and money needed to prepare attractive, simple, and clear reporting directed at an intended audience. Raaum makes this point well:

An unrecognized challenge will . . . come in finding innovative ways of presenting the performance results. *Narratives and tables of numbers will probably not do the trick.* People not skilled or comfortable with numbers are not likely to be able or motivated to interpret the data. The challenge will be to find ways to present measured performance results in graphs, charts and other forms of visual aids. (Raaum 1992:24, italics added)

The performance of a policy or program can be quite complex, with several levels of objectives and sub-objectives required to properly describe what is being accomplished. Often this complexity is carried through to the reporting of performance, making interpretation difficult for all but the expert or the most persistent. An organized and logical display of the various components of performance addressed which is used consistently throughout can help in having user-friendly reporting.

Further, frequently those to whom performance information is provided have limited time to consider it. Providing the information in a concise format tailored to the specific audience will enhance the chance that the import of the information is communicated.

Communicating Performance Information

There is a tendency to assume that performance reporting will occur through reports. This is an appropriate vehicle for some audiences, but in most cases more thought and innovation is needed for effective communication. Oral reports (speeches, town hall meetings, briefings), video, electronic bulletin boards, on-line data bases, newspapers, pamphlets, brochures, and posters all could be more effective than the traditional performance report for some audiences. This is especially true when communicating with the public.

In her report analyzing the quality of performance reporting to the Australian Parliament, Funnell (1993: 1) suggests that an effective performance-reporting regime for Parliament is characterized by:

- A focus on outcomes achieved, including social justice outcomes.
- Clear links between strategies, reported outcomes and program objectives.
- Concise, readily understandable and balanced presentation.

Implementing Effective Performance Monitoring

Much has been written about implementing performance monitoring in an organization (OECD, 1994). Several other chapters in this book, including the final chapter 11, discuss implementation problems and solutions. Here we would like to make only a few points based on the foregoing analysis.

Performance Monitoring Takes Time and Costs Money

The commitment from senior management that is frequently called for, requires more than intellectual agreement. An effective performance-monitoring regime in an organization will require time and perhaps money, resources often thought of as being diverted from direct program delivery. But in saying this, the optics are all wrong. If effective delivery requires performance information and if managers were responsible for reporting to their clients on how well performance expectations were being met—and hence perhaps receive a form of political support for their programs—then effective performance monitoring would be seen not as overhead but as part of modern public management and be budgeted for.

We should be seeking cost-effective performance monitoring, but dollar costs are perhaps not the greatest problem, rather the time required of management and staff. If demonstration became part of a manager's responsibility, the attention and the time by the manager would be there. Further, if staff are involved and are empowered to design and use the performance-monitoring system, then attention will be there. If the results from performance monitoring were used to compare performance among units in an organization or among other organizations ("benchmarking," "encouraging a competitive spirit"), the attention would certainly be there.

Performance Monitoring Requires Enlightened Management and Oversight

Performance monitoring exposes problems and shortcomings with performance. As long as managers and governing bodies see problems and shortcomings as someone's fault, effective performance monitoring will not ensue, it cannot as the incentives are all wrong. We need to make learning from experience—learning organizations—a reality. One aspect of this is the need for rapid feedback to employees from the performance-monitoring system, so they can do something in response. Providing the information to employees only later on suggests the information is being gathered to punish someone by showing them how bad they were, long after they can do much about it.

Accountability based on demonstration of performance offers an important positive incentive. It requires managers to reward the identification of problems and their resolution. It requires managers to act more like coaches looking for opportunities to praise and encourage empowered employees who are able to demonstrate that they are in control, rather than looking for fault. It requires oversight focused more on results and less on prudence and probity.

Accountability for Program Performance

A recent Australian report states that "By definition, accountability requires assessment of performance. Quality performance information is thus required to properly meet accountability and reporting requirements" (Management Advisory Board and Management Improvement Advisory Committee 1993: 5).

Few would argue otherwise, yet quality performance information is often not forthcoming. A "blame apportionment" approach to accountability is unlikely to change this.

We have argued that accountability should be based on individuals seeking and being provided occasions to demonstrate the actual performance being achieved by their programs and services. In particular, it should be a public-sector manager's responsibility to demonstrate ("account," "report") to their publics on performance being achieved with tax dollars and with parliamentary and other authorities conferred.

Such a perspective would ensure that appropriate performance information were forthcoming.[5] And the experience gained with performance monitoring over the past twenty years can provide the practical guidance needed for responding to this demand for quality performance information.

This still would not completely solve the problem, since effective accountability for performance is not usually demanded by governing bodies, be they managers, central agencies, or parliaments. But even this might change if the "accountee" was providing credible, timely, and relevant performance information and demanding that it be paid attention to.

Finally, in light of the widespread public disenchantment with government, it is perhaps surprising that ruling governments have not made more effort at demonstrating through credible performance information their many ongoing accomplishments in terms of the programs and services they provide. Over and above their political and policy actions to convince their citizens of their good governance, routine demonstration to the public on the accomplishments of their programs and services might go some way to restore confidence in government.

Notes

1. Reasonableness allows for a sensible amount of regularity accounting. One is expected to follow laws and basic administrative rules of probity and prudence.
2. A good discussion of the issues surrounding a performance-based accountability regime can be found in a recent OECD (1994) report.
3. Others typically break up these two principles into finer detail. Thus, in providing general guidance to departments and agencies on reporting to Papliament, the government of Canada gives six "principles of disclosure": relevance, reliability, objectivity, completeness, materiality, and comparability (Treasury Board of Canada 1987). A report prepared for the British Columbia School Superintendent's Association (1992) suggests effective reporting must be understandable, credible, and useful. The Governmental Accounting Standards Board (1992) provides a detailed list of quality characteristics of performance information and is developing performance reporting criteria. The Auditor General of Canada (1992) suggested three criteria for reporting to Parliament: relevancy, reliability, and understandability.
4. Modern information technology provides for even greater flexibility in reporting by making performance databases available, so that just the right kind of performance information can be called up.
5. Some argue that performance information will not be forthcoming unless it is tied closely to the budgeting process. This has been the theory behind many previous attempts at institutionalizing performance monitoring in government. We suggest this is an unrealistic goal. Resourcing is the result of many factors (history, politics, social goals, the need to compromise, etc.) and performance information in most cases will not be the deciding factor for reaching resource levels decisions, certainly not at the center of government. In a democratic system, resources should be allocated to areas of government priority. Where expected results do not seem to be forthcoming in a priority area, we might get a better manager, redesign or reengineer the program, but we will usually still allocate resources. There is more hope for a more direct resource link at the operational level, where managers can use performance information to make incremental changes in their programs. Other chapters in this book confirm this view (see also OECD 1994: 46).

References

Auditor General of Canada. 1992. Report of *the Auditor General of Canada to the House of Commons*. Minister of Supply and Services.

Aucoin, P. 1990. "Administrative Reform in Public Management: Paradigms, Principles, Paradoxes and Pendulums." *Governance* 3, no. 2: 115–37.

Aucoin, P. 1990. "Comment: Assessing Managerial Reforms." *Governance* 3, no. 2: 197–204.

B. C. School Superintendents' Association. 1992. *Developing Indicators and Standards: Choosing Appropriate Measures and Targets of Education Performance.*

Barzelay, M. 1992. *Breaking Through Bureaucracy: A New Vision for Managing Government.* Berkeley: University of California Press.

Carter, N. and P. Greer. 1993. "Evaluating Agencies: The Next Steps and Performance Indicators." *Public Administration* 71, Autumn: 407–16.

The Economist. 1993. "The State of the State." 14 August: 57.

Efficiency Unit. 1991. *Making the Most of Next Steps: The Management of Ministers Departments and their Executive Agencies.* London: HMSO.

Eriksen, B. 1987. *Three Norwegian Initiatives in the Eighties.* Paper prepared for International Institute of Administrative Sciences.

Funnell, S. 1993. *Effective Reporting in Program Performance Statements.* Australian Department of Finance.

Government of Canada. 1990. *Public Service 2000—The Renewal of the Public Service of Canada.* Supply and Services Canada.

Governmental Accounting Standards Board. 1992. *Preliminary Views on Service Efforts and Accomplishments Reporting.* Governmental Accounting Standards Series.

Holmes, M. 1992. "Public Sector Management Reform: Convergence or Divergence?" *Governance* 5, no. 4: 472–83.

Management Advisory Board and Management Improvement Advisory Committee. 1993. *Performance Information and the Management Cycle.* Australian Government Publishing Service.

OECD. 1992. *Accountability: A Background Paper.*

OECD. 1994. *Performance Management in Government: Performance Measurement and Results-Oriented Management.* Occasional Paper No. 3.

Office of the Comptroller General. 1991. *Line Managers and Assessing Service to the Public.*

Raaum, R. B. 1992. "Measuring and Reporting Performance in Government." *Government Accountants Journal,* Fall: 19–25.

Task Force on Management Improvement. 1992. *The Australian Public Service Reformed—An Evaluation of a Decade of Public Sector Reform.* Australian Government Publishing Service.

Taylor, J. C. 1992. "Public Accountability Requirements." *Australian Journal of Public Administration* 51, no. 4: 455—60.

Treasury and Civil Service Committee. 1991. *The new system of departmental reports (5th Report, session 1990–91).* London: HMSO.

Treasury Board of Canada. 1987. *Guide to the Preparation of Part III of the Estimates.* Supply and Services Canada.

Treasury Board of Canada. 1994. *Treasury Board Manual: Review, Internal Audit and Evaluation.*

Treasury Board of Canada. 1995. *Service Standards: A Guide to the Initiative.*

Part III

Comparing Performance Monitoring in Policy Areas

7

The Performance-Monitoring System in the Korean Government, With Special Reference to Health Care

Myoung-soo Kim

Introduction

This study assesses the Korean government's performance monitoring system, specifically referred to as the Review and Analysis System (RAS), as it is operated at the central government level. It describes the system's components and the organizational and legal arrangements necessary for the RAS, both essential elements and important factors for accounting for its successful operation (Sabatier and Mazmanian 1980: 542).

Specifically, the study addresses the following questions:

- What are the major components of the RAS?
- How does the RAS work?
- Why does the RAS work?
- What problems does the RAS have?
- What improvements does the RAS need?
- What can we learn from the operation of the RAS?

Literature surveys and interviews were used to answer the above questions. RAS reports prepared by the Ministry of Health and Social Affairs (MOHSA), guidelines issued by the Economic Planning Board (EPB), and survey reports prepared by the Korea Institute for Health and Social Affairs (KIHASA) are some of the literature used in this study. For the interviews, a semistructured interview schedule was prepared containing items dealing with various aspects of performance-monitoring activities in the administrative agencies, and interviews were held with public officials in charge of monitoring activities in various ministries. The Family Health Program was selected to illustrate the RAS.

To begin with, the organizations involved in administering the health care system and the background of the monitoring activities will be described to give readers information on how the health care system is managed and how the RAS is operated in Korea. Then, a description of the components of RAS, a highlight of the problems of RAS, suggestions on the factors affecting the success of the performance monitoring system, and recommendations for improvements of RAS are made. Finally, conclusions on the lessons learned from the Korean experience and on the conditions under which Korea's performance-monitoring system can best function are described.

The Administration of Health Care and the Performance-Monitoring System in the Korean Government

MOHSA, one of the twenty-three ministries that comprise the Cabinet, administers the health care system in Korea. It also has jurisdiction over the affairs concerning national hygiene, prevention of epidemics, medical administration, pharmaceutical administration, and women and juvenile welfare. It administers five categories of major programs: (1) establishment of a medical security system for the whole nation; (2) improvement of the well-being of low-income families and the handicapped; (3) construction of a foundation for the well-being of the aged; (4) establishment of an effective disease-control system; and (5) strengthening of the food and drug management system (MOHSA 1992 4).

Each major program category embraces several programs. For example, the fourth category, "establishing an effective disease control system," in addition to being responsible for the Family Health Program (FHP) itself, embraces five other programs:

- Expanding public investment for controlling special diseases;
- Campaigning for health awareness and improving nutrition;
- Preventing the outbreak of epidemic diseases;

- Controlling chronic diseases; and
- Controlling drug abuse.

As mentioned earlier, the FHP is used in this study to illustrate the RAS. The FHP's objective is to enhance the quality of health of the whole population by protecting maternal health and lives, and by promoting healthy parturition and child rearing (MOHSA 1994, FHP 1994: 7). The FHP, which comprises two subprograms, the Family Planning Program and Maternity and the Child Health Program, is implemented by five organizations: MOHSA, the National Institute of Health (NIH), the Korean Institute of Health and Social Affairs (KIHASA), the Planned Parenthood Federation of Korea (PPFK), and the Korea Association for Voluntary Sterilization (KAVS).

MOHSA is in charge of overall planning, coordination, and maintenance of the national service network for FHP. It prepares program plans, issues guidelines for implementing program plans, and supervises program implementation. NIH is responsible for training program staff and health-related personnel throughout the nation. KIHASA has responsibility for survey, research, and evaluation in the field of family health. PPFK is responsible for the operation of family planning clinics and mobile vans in its provincial branch offices. KAVS is responsible for the training of family-planning designated physicians and the treatment of complications and side effects from sterilization (KIHASA 1991: 93).

The Bureau of Health and Social Affairs of each provincial or metropolitan government assigns targets in relation to FHP for city, county, and district governments, supervises health workers; and provides directives for program implementation while private family health centers established in the provincial and metropolitan areas provide medical manpower and care.

Health centers and maternity and child health centers located in municipal and county areas, respectively, and health subcenters in township areas provide both prenatal and postnatal care for pregnant women, assist in delivery, provide families with health-related education, administer protective inoculations, and keep records.

In addition, the Ministry of Home Affairs (MOHA) has overall control of provincial and special city governments, including the administration of local-level public health and medical care organizations, such as health centers and provincial hospitals. However, by the time all the provincial governors, city mayors, county administrators, and local legislators are elected in June 1995, as mandated by the local autonomy system law amended in March 1994, the authority of such central ministries as MOHA and MOHSA to control provincial and local governments will be weakened.

As for the Korean government's RAS, monitoring program performance has been coordinated by the Performance Evaluation Bureau of the Economic Planning Board since late 1981. The Bureau replaced the Office of Planning and Coordination (OPC) which used to be an arm of the Office of the Prime Minister and oversaw the coordination of the monitoring function from 1962 until late 1981.

The Bureau, composed of five divisions with about forty evaluators, is responsible for both the coordination of the monitoring and evaluation activities within the central government and public corporations, and the systematic evaluation of some important government programs. Monitoring activities are coordinated by the Guideline for Monitoring Program Performance, which is distributed each year to all the ministries and agencies and specifies the information required for various forms.

At the individual ministry level, the monitoring function is coordinated by the director of administrative management of the Office of Planning and Management. But each division of a ministry bureau is responsible for gathering performance data of the programs under its jurisdiction. However, since programs are developed by the central ministries and implemented by the provincial and local governments (county, municipal, and township), actual program performance data are collected by each implementing entity. Data collected at lower-level agencies are forwarded to a directly higher-level agency.

For example, township health subcenters, maternal and child health centers, county/city health centers, and provincial government units concerned, respectively, prepare monthly Family Health Program progress reports. The township health subcenter and Maternity and Child Health (MCH) center reports are forwarded by the first day of the following month to health centers which are located in counties and cities; these health centers have direct jurisdiction over township health subcenters and MCH centers. The health centers, in turn, aggregate the data contained in the lower-echelon reports, add a few pieces of information, and then forward their reports by the fifth day of the same month to the provincial/special city governments, which, in turn, prepare their reports and forward them by the tenth day of the same month to MOHSA. MOHSA then pools these data into the proper forms and forwards the report to the EPB. A summary report is prepared by EPB and is deliberated in a state council meeting which is presided over by the president.

History of Monitoring Activities in the Korean Government

Adoption of RAS as a performance-monitoring device in the Korean government dates back to 1962, when the then military government began to introduce techniques of military administration into its administration. At that time, the government introduced the Basic Operational Planning System (BOPS). It is said that these ideas were adopted from the American military administration as a way to rationalize the Korean military administration. Under BOPS each central administrative agency prepared its operational plans, which were then reviewed and coordinated by the Office of Planning and Coordination (OPC) of the prime minister's office with other plans that had been submitted by other administrative agencies. Plans were coordinated taking into account national goals and priorities. Once coordinated operational plans were determined, they became the guideline for agencies to prepare their budget requests. Finally, once the presidential budget had been deliberated and determined by the National Assembly, final basic operational plans were prepared.

RAS was adopted in order to monitor the performance of BOPS. Performance monitoring has been performed quarterly by each central administrative agency. The findings of the RAS activities throughout the government are aggregated by OPC, submitted to the state council for its consideration, and finally reported to the president.

The system is supported by the Constitution, the Government Organization Act, the Regulation of Governmental Planning and Review and Analysis, and the Guideline for Managing Presidential Election Commitments. For example, Article 89 of the Constitution provides that the state council, which is composed of the president, the prime minister, and the members of the Cabinet, consider "evaluation and analysis of administration of state affairs." Article 23 of the Government Organization Act provides that the Economic Planning Board take charge of "the matters of coordination of planning and review and analysis in the central administrative agencies." The Regulation of Governmental Planning and Review and Analysis sets forth such matters as: (1) preparation of major programs; (2) preparation of an implementation plan of major programs; (3) review and analysis in the central government and the Seoul city government; (4) actions taken by the heads of the central administrative agencies and by the mayor of Seoul on the findings of review and analysis, (5) reports by the minister of EPB of the actions on finding of review and analysis; and so on.

The Guideline for Managing Presidential Election Commitments (Prime Ministerial Order No. 225), issued to ensure successful fulfillment of the presidential commitments made during the last election by the incumbent president, has four main directives:

- That the authorities concerned with particular programs prepare plans for implementing them;
- That they not only report quarterly to the prime minister on the progress of their programs, but also notify the chairman of the board of Audit and Inspection;
- That the minister of EPB prepare countermeasures for those programs that have not moved as planned; and
- That the chairman of BAI monitor the progress of all the presidential programs and report to the president on the findings.

Major change took place in 1981 in operating RAS when the Economic Planning Board (EPB) took over the government-wide review and analysis function from OPC. This change resulted from the following criticisms: (1) that assignment of the planning function to OPC and budgeting to EPB was unreasonable; (2) that OPC lacked the ability to coordinate; and (3) that thus far, RAS had not brought about intended effects, such as improving the delivery of services based on the findings of review and analysis of programs (EPB Bureau of Performance Evaluation 1988: 38).

In the same year, EPB established the Bureau of Review and Analysis (BRA) to operate review and analysis activities throughout the government. The Bureau changed its name to the Bureau of Performance Evaluation (BPE) in 1984, and took on the additional responsibility of evaluating the performance of government-sponsored enterprises, more than 50 percent of whose capital is held by the central government. Currently there are twenty-three such enterprises.

The 1982 amendment of the 1972 Regulation of Government Planning and Review and Analysis contributed to the institutionalization and to the change of the concept of RAS as practiced within the government. The changes can be summarized as follows:

- The Bureau of Performance Evaluation (BPE) of EPB assumed a role of an evaluator of some programs of major national interest. When BPE finds problems in the course of evaluation, it recommends corrective actions to the head of the relevant agency.
- Beginning in 1983, each administrative agency began to undertake special analysis studies (SAS) of some new programs which were expected to face problems during implementation. When an agency finds problems as a result of SAS, it is expected to take corrective actions.
- Beginning in 1984, EPB acted as a metaevaluator, that is, an evaluator of evaluations done by each central agency. Since 1987, EPB has awarded prizes to the agencies which had been evaluated as performing good evaluations and taking appropriate corrective actions as the findings of evaluative work required.
- Findings of EPB studies, SAS, and of quarterly reviews analyses done by relevant ministries and agencies are aggregated biannually by EPB to be submitted to the state council for its consideration and the final presidential report. At the central government level, the RAS divides the programs subject to monitoring into two categories: the first category of programs is subjected to monthly monitoring, the second to quarterly monitoring. Most programs fall within the second category; programs subjected to monthly performance monitoring are ones that are regarded as very important and/or ones that appear likely to encounter problems in the implementation process.

Components of the Performance-Monitoring System in the Korean Government

As pointed out by Altman (1979 32), worthwhile performance-monitoring systems are composed of three major components: a data component, an analytical component, and an action component. The data component provides the framework for collecting data about the actual and expected performance of what is monitored, for example, government programs. The analytical component consists of information distilled through analysis of the raw data obtained from the data component, that is, measurements of program performance and comparisons of actual program performance with prior or expected or planned performance (Wholey 1979: 118; Poister 1982: 606–7). The action component refers to management's use of program-performance information produced by the analytical component.

Before describing the Korean government's performance-monitoring system, the RAS, according to the above framework, we need to first deal with the object of monitoring. Are all government programs indiscriminately subjected to monitoring? Or, is there any criteria applicable when selecting programs to be monitored? Certainly, not all programs administered by the administrative agencies are subjected to monitoring. Only those programs that meet certain criteria as established by the Korean government are selected for performance monitoring.

The programs whose performance is monitored fall into several, but not mutually exclusive, categories:

- those that have problems or are likely to encounter problems during implementation;
- those that require a large amount of money;
- those that are new;
- those that are related to the election commitments pledged by the incumbent president;
- those whose progress needs to be continuously measured and reported on;
- those which are set forth in the five-year Socioeconomic Development Plan and which are subject to implementation in the current year; and
- those programs found to need improvements through intensive analysis undertaken by the EPB, in policy evaluations undertaken by the Office of the Prime Minister, in policy audits undertaken by the Board of Audit and Inspection, and in audits of state affairs by the National Assembly (EPB 1992: 14).

The number of programs monitored have varied from year to year. For example, 1,120 programs were subjected to performance monitoring in 1982; however, in 1988, the number decreased to 651 (EPB 1988: 92) and, in 1993, to 461.

We now examine the three components of the Korean government's performance monitoring system.

Data Component

In the data component of a performance-monitoring system, raw data is collected at the program implementation level, for example, family health centers, maternity and child health centers, and health subcenters. In collecting raw data, measures of program performance have to be decided. Performance of the programs can be measured through a variety of measures. Different scholars propose different measures. An aggregation of the different measures proposed leads to six types of measures: (1) inputs; (2) activities; (3) outputs; (4) efficiency; (5) effectiveness; and (6) equity. The first three can be directly collected in the field, whereas the latter three can only be obtained from analyses of raw data. Therefore, the former are more relevant to the data component, whereas the latter to the analytical component.

Inputs are the resources used in carrying out the program activities and can be expressed in cost terms or in terms of person-hours (Weir 1984: 39). *Activities* are part of the elements of a program and can be measured in terms of workload. Workload describes the types of services to be performed and the amount of work required to deliver them (Altman 1984: 34). *Outputs* are the goods and services produced by the program activities.

Efficiency can be defined as the ratio of outputs to inputs. The ratio of the monetary value of outputs to the monetary value of the input resources used to produce the outputs, and the number of output units per person-hours are common measures of efficiency. *Effectiveness* measures describe the extent to which outputs meet defined performance objectives. Effectiveness generally is not concerned with inputs (Altman 1979: 34), but is concerned with a question of success in accomplishing a mission of a program (Usher and Cornia 1981: 232). *Equity* refers to fairness in the distribution of services among individuals, groups, or geographic areas, regardless of their ability to pay for them or to express a demand for them (Usher and Cornia 1981: 232).

Let us consider which types of measures are used in monitoring performance in the Korean government. An examination of reports published monthly by MOHSA reveals that data on program activities and outputs is collected at the field implementation level.

Some of the types of data contained in monthly reports are as follows (U.N. 1990: 60—61; Cho and Kim 1991: 161).

Data on the Family Planning Program:
- Total number of registrations
- Number of new registrations and drop-outs
- Number of monetary incentive acceptors
- Number of free medical service acceptors
- Number of termination operations by contraceptive methods
- Number of deliveries free of charge
- Number of hospitals for side-effect treatments
- Number of family-planning designated hospitals/clinics by method

Data on the Maternal and Child Health Program
- Number of new pregnant women and drop-outs
- Number of new infants and children and drop-outs
- Number of prenatal services
- Number of infant/child treatments
- Number of institutional deliveries
- Number of home deliveries
- Number of referral cases
- Number of educational sessions and participants
- Number of infants and children inoculated
- Number of high-risk women who received health examinations
- Number of infants and children who received health examinations
- Number of persons who received the second health examination and the results

Analytical Component

In the analysis component of a performance-monitoring system, measurements of program performance are aggregated and computed by using raw data, and actual performance is compared with planned or prior performance both at the field level and at the central government level. Since objectives are expressed in terms of inputs, activities (or tasks), outputs, and/or impacts (Wholey 1978: 56–57; Altman 1979: 33), the content of progress will vary from program to program, depending upon how program objectives are expressed.

As pointed out above, the Korean system collects data at the field implementation level on actual and planned performance. And from these data those measurements of activities, planned and actual, and outputs are aggregated both at the field and central government levels. And then, progress in achieving task (or activity-related) objectives (implementing activities, producing services, etc.) and input objectives (executing program costs) are measured. The data on inputs are easily obtained from the budgetary documents since they represent budgeted costs of the program in the monitoring process. Efficiency of the program is computed by using data on inputs and outputs.

As to the effectiveness of FHP, it might be thought one could use such social indicators as infant and maternal mortality rates which appear in the *Health Statistical Yearbook* and in the *Social Indicators of Korea* as proxy measures of effectiveness of all the health-related programs, including FHP. But the measurements of these indicators do not tell the effectiveness of a particular health care program. Since

TABLE 7.1
Content of a Review and Analysis Report

1. Title of the programs (with a statement of goals)
2. Program period
3. Activities of each program with planned performance and budgeted cost for each activity
4. Actual performance in terms of implementation of activities and execution of the budget
5. Comparison of planned and actual performance in terms of progress
6. Progress
7. Findings

FHP aspires to contribute to an increased health status of the target group, it should have an effect, positive or negative, on the measurements of those indicators.

The following output measures illustrate the measures used to monitor performance of FHP (MOHSA 1992).

- Broadcasting messages X number of times through TV and/or radio
- Distributing X number of copies of various brochures
- Holding educational sessions for X number of people
- Performing contraceptive operations for X number of people
- Distribution of X amount of money's worth of contraceptive devices
- Having X number of pregnant women and infants of low-income families registered
- Performing medical examination for X number of pregnant women and infants
- Having X number of infants and children inoculated
- Spending X amount of money for the above activities

Table 7.1 shows the kind of information contained in a typical review and analysis report. The format of these reports is the same throughout the Korean government because each ministry is required to prepare the quarterly report as specified by the Performance Evaluation Bureau of the Economic Planning Board.

Action Component

Action components of a performance-monitoring system may consist of decisions concerning program objectives, decisions concerning program elements or activities, decisions concerning performance measures, and decisions concerning monitoring (Wholey 1979: 118; Poister 1982: 606).

The Korean system is concerned mainly with progress towards achieving task objectives. Progress is measured by comparing planned with actual inputs, activities, and outputs. Action is based on the result of these comparisons. Therefore, as far as task objectives are met, the program in question is judged successful and the objectives are maintained. However, if objectives are not met, the administrative agency which has operated that particular program is required to identify causes for underachievement and to take proper measures to meet task objectives. Proper measures include changing program objectives, as in the case of increasing or reducing the performance level, and changing program activities, as in the case of deleting activities or adding new activities.

According to EPB, among the 461 programs whose performance had been monitored in 1993, 108 had met their objectives, 345 had been moving forward as planned, and 8 (or 1.7 percent) did not progress as planned (EPB 1994: 7). Of course, for these eight programs, corrective measures were to be taken by the ministries concerned.

Problems

As far as the performance-monitoring system in the Korean government is concerned, it can be said that it has been functioning relatively well. However, it has not been without problems. First, the effectiveness of the program is not directly addressed by the monitoring system. Infant mortality rate and maternal mortality rate are the most important performance indicators of the MCH Program, but they are obtained through a survey by EPB, not by MOHSA, in an effort to report on social conditions of the country. Certainly, it is more desirable to make MOHSA accountable for managing them, that is, collecting, aggregating, and analyzing data to obtain statistics on those indicators.

Second, since the current monitoring system is not computerized, it is difficult to obtain necessary information quickly and to manage programs in question more efficiently and effectively. A computerized monitoring system requires developing an indicator system for major programs which would be managed by the central ministries.

Third, the findings of program-monitoring activities are used to correct any delays in delivery of programs and to find reasons for the delays. But that is not enough. A more meaningful way for their utilization would be to link them also to the budgetary decision-making process. For example, if it appears that the program does not perform at a satisfactory level, that information should be taken into account when allocating the budget among programs.

Fourth, successful operation of a program performance-monitoring system depends upon the will of top management (Gore 1993: 89). However, their interest in the findings of program performance monitoring activities has not been consistent. For example, some presidents of the country, like presidents Park Chung-hee and Rho Rae-woo, personally made use of them, while others, like President Chun Doo-hwan, paid little attention to them.

Factors for Success

As mentioned earlier, the program performance-monitoring system in the Korean government, RAS, has been working relatively well, except for the problems alluded to above. Here it is thought worthwhile to find out what has made the system work as it does today. Although a variety of factors are responsible, the major ones are mentioned below.

First and foremost, the promulgation of rules and regulations governing the Review and Analysis System is attributable to its successful implementation. Within the Korean government, rules and regulations are generally well-abided by because they are the most important audit criterion against which operations of an audited entity are judged.

Second, assignment of the responsibility for facilitating and coordinating the monitoring activities within the central government to the prime minister's office, and later to the Economic Planning Board, seems to have acted as a contributing factor to its success. The EPB, which is at the vice-prime ministerial level, plays the role of coordinator between central ministries contending for power or for money, hence its directives are more readily complied with by central government ministries.

Third, especially during the early stage of institutionalization of the monitoring system, that is, the early 1960s, then president Park Chung-hee showed considerable interest in it, which helped it take root and move forward. His special interest in progress towards targets set for developmental programs made the system progress-analysis oriented, which put major emphasis on both program inputs and outputs.

Fourth, regarding the operation of the performance-monitoring system within MOHSA, a built-in rating system of program operation has contributed to its success. The rating system specifies evaluation items in six areas and weights assigned to each of them (MOHSA 1992: 86). These six areas are: (1) program objectives and actual performance; (2) performance by program elements; (3) preventive inoculation management; (4) results of on-the-spot inspections; (5) reporting of maternal and infants' deaths, and (6) performance of maternal and child health educational activities. Based on the results of the rating, those units or individuals who contributed substantially to achieving program goals are provided awards. The reward system is also operated by EPB. EPB provides awards to the ministry that did an excellent job of monitoring performance.

It was pointed out at one time that little checking had been done to ensure that the records were accurate (U.N. 1990: 55). However, that is not the case any longer. Program data collection and record-keeping activities are subjected to both internal and external audits, and a penalty is imposed on the cases which contain incorrect statistical figures (MOHSA 1991: 28; MOHSA 1992: 71). The rating system mentioned above differentiates the penalty. It is considered essential, of course, not to be penalized and consequently get a lower score, as this would endanger an administrative unit's chances of being rewarded an incentive bonus by the minister concerned, the prime minister, or the president.

Recommendations for Improvement

In spite of such a successful operation of the performance-monitoring system, improvements are warranted. Five recommendations follow.

First, the RAS needs to use performance indicators to monitor the effectiveness status of the programs in question (Hatry et al 1973: 12). In the meantime, it seems more appropriate for MOHSA to measure and manage such important indicators as infant and maternal mortality rates. Such an arrangement will make MOHSA respond much more quickly to unsatisfactory performance of programs under its jurisdiction. Since performance monitoring on its own does not address questions about cause and effect nor does it easily measure some of the more difficult aspects of performance, the RAS should expand its coverage to include evaluation of the effectiveness of programs.

Second, the performance-monitoring system needs to encourage disclosure of failures, that is, cases of underachievement of objectives, if it aspires to play a more meaningful role in the overall process of program management. It has long been said that failures indicate inability of the ministers concerned, and hence failures tend to be covered up, even intentionally. But as long as failures are not disclosed, it is impossible to design improvements for the system. It might be more recommendable to reward disclosure of failures and corrective actions taken rather than penalize those who disclose failures. It might take the form of a presidential citation of the ministers concerned at a state council meeting, or a ministerial citation of the directors general who did a good job of acting on the findings of the performance monitoring of their programs. The bottom line is to identify failures and to take corrective actions, rather than to cover them up, doing nothing about them.

Third, the performance-monitoring system needs to move well beyond mere description of program inputs and outputs and do more analytical work on the efficiency aspect of the programs, that is, the relationships between program inputs and outputs. A systematic analysis will probably reveal abuse and wasteful practices in the delivery of programs.

Fourth, the performance-monitoring system needs to be more closely linked to the budgetary process so that the information obtained in the monitoring process might be utilized in the resource-allocation process which follows. Occasionally utilization is claimed, but it should be more consistent.

Fifth and finally, the performance monitoring system needs to be computerized, so that it might retrieve necessary information at a time of need. Delayed information may be too late to be of any use.

Conclusion

The RAS as a tool of performance monitoring and evaluation in the Korean government has been operative for more than thirty years. The system has undergone some changes over time. However, as far as the monitoring component of RAS is concerned, its basic framework remains the same. One of its shortcomings is that it has not measured nor reported the status of the effectiveness of programs. Even if the monitoring function does not necessitate ascertaining causal links between programs and their outcomes, it seems desirable to monitor the effectiveness of the programs in question to determine the extent to which they are achieving their goals.

Other than that, we can say that RAS has succeeded in meeting the goal of analyzing and reporting the progress of programs, especially developmental programs, thereby contributing to their timely implementation in compliance with plans. From the Korean experience we can learn under what conditions a performance-monitoring system can work well. Those conditions are listed below.

First, as Sabatier and Mazmanian (1980: 544–45) suggest, appropriate statutes should structure the implementation process of the performance-monitoring system. Recognition of the importance of the monitoring and evaluation function in the legislation and promulgation of a regulation by presidential order necessary to implement RAS are examples of such statutory arrangements we can observe in the Korean case.

Second, there should be continuous support for the performance-monitoring activities from the government leaders and bodies, such as the chief executive, the legislature, courts, and hierarchically superior agencies. In the Korean case, the president's interest in RAS was a very important factor for its being institutionalized in the government.

Third, high levels of commitment and leadership of the central coordinating agency are also very important for the implementation of the performance-monitoring system government-wide. Such an agency provides the administrative agencies with guiding principles of the system and ensures that they comply with pertinent regulations and directives.

Fourth, a reward system seems to help the performance-monitoring system work better. The reward systems operated by EPB and MOHSA are good examples. The system rewards the good performance with commendations and/or bonuses, and penalizes the bad indirectly by depriving an agency or individuals guilty of poor performance of the opportunities to get rewards. It is important also not to penalize honest mistakes but to penalize failure to correct them in time.

References

Altman, S. 1979. "Performance monitoring systems for public managers." Public Administration Review 39, no. 1: 31–35.

Chelimsky, E., ed. 1985. Program Evaluation: Patterns and Directions. The American Society for Public Administration.

Cho, N. and H.O. Kim, eds. 1991. Korean experience with population control policy and family planning program management and operation. Seoul: KIHASA.

Dunn, W. N. 1981. Public Policy Analysis. Englewood Cliffs, N.J.: Prentice-Hall, Inc.

Economic Planning Board. 1992. The guideline for review and analysis for 1992.

Economic Planning Board. 1994. Review and analysis report of governmental programs for 1993.

Gore, A. 1993. From Red Tape To Results: Creating a Government that Works Better and Costs Less. New York: Random House.

Hatry, H. P., R. Winnie, and D. Fisk. 1973. Practical Program Evaluation for State and Local Government Officials. The Urban Institute.

Kruschke, E. R. and B.M. Jackson. 1987. The Public Policy Dictionary. ABC-Clio, Inc.

Ministry of Health and Social Affairs. 1994. Family Health Program for 1994. Seoul.

Ministry of Health and Social Affairs. 1992. Review and analysis of major programs administered during 1991. Seoul.

Ministry of Health and Social Affairs. 1991. Reference materials for the family health programs. Seoul.

Ministry of Health and Social Affairs. 1991. Family Health Programs for 1991. Seoul.

Performance Evaluation Bureau, EPB. 1988. Reference materials for review and analysis. Seoul.

Poister, T.H. 1982. "Performance Monitoring in the Evaluation Process." Evaluation Review 6, no. 5: 601–23.

Rist, R. C. 1990. Program Evaluation and the Management of Government. New Brunswick, N.J.: Transaction Publishers.

Rossi, P. H., and H. Freeman. 1982. Evaluation: A Systematic Approach (2nd ed.). Newbury Park, Cal.: Sage Publications Inc.

Sabatier, P., and D. Mazmanian. 1980. "The Implementation of Public Policy: A Framework of Analysis." Policy Studies Journal 8, no. 4: 531–653.

United Nations. 1990. Monitoring and Evaluating Family Planning Programmes in the 1990s.

Usher, Charles L., and G.C. Cornia. 1981. "Goal Setting and Performance Assessment in Municipal Budgeting." Public Administration Review 41, no. 2: 229–35.

Waller, J. D., et al. 1976. Monitoring for Government Agencies. The Urban Institute.

Weir, M. 1984. "Efficiency Measurement in Government." The Bureaucrat 13, no. 2: 38–42.

Wholey, J. S. 1991. "Using Evaluation to Improve Program Performance." The Bureaucrat 20, no. 2: 55–59.

Wholey, J. S. 1978. Zero-base Budgeting and Program Evaluation. Lexington, Mass.: Lexington Books.

Wholey, J. S. 1979. Evaluation: Promise and Performance. Washington, D.C.: The Urban Institute.

Wholey, J. S. et al. 1973. *Federal Evaluation Policy.* Washington, D.C.: The Urban Institute.

Wildavsky, A. 1979. *Speaking Truth to Power: The Art and Craft of Policy Analysis.* Boston: The Macmillan Press, Ltd.

8

A System for Monitoring and Control of Health Services: The Case of Mexico

Francisco Javier Casas Guzman

Introduction

This chapter describes the structure and operation of the Mexican monitoring and control system for its health programs, known as the National Health Sector Evaluation System. The approach used for the study parallels the one used in the previous chapter by Professor Kim who discussed the case of Korea. We have tried to maintain a homogeneous structure for the presentation to facilitate comparisons between the two systems.

We begin with a description of the special features of the political system in the United Mexican States (Mexico's official name) in order to provide the reader with a basic framework for understanding the National Health System, as well as the process carried out for its monitoring and control. Subsequently, the National Health System, the National Health Sector Evaluation System organization and its components are discussed, along with its legal basis. To provide a concrete case and to illustrate the system, the family planning program is chosen for discussion, due to the high priority assigned it for the health policy and social development of the country. The chapter concludes with a brief review of the main limitations to the successful operation of the health monitoring system and presents some conclusions about the results achieved.

To obtain data for the research, official documents issued by the Mexican government were reviewed (United Mexican States 1983, 1989a, 1989b, 1990, and 1991), complemented by data obtained through interviews with directors of the family planning division of the Health Department.

An Overview of the Mexican Political System

The foundations and the development of Mexico's modern social democracy are inevitably related to the Mexican Revolution and the 1917 Constitution. The social measures framed in the Constitution have their origin in society's demands which, politically articulated during the revolutionary process, took shape in the Mexican Constitution. The Constitution is the supreme law and brings together the essential rules to which a society must submit and provides the foundations of the legal principles of the political order. However, it is not rigid. Amendments to the Mexican Constitution reveal a concern on the part of the legislative branch to expand social guarantees.

Mexico is a federal state comprising a number of free and sovereign states, united in their internal rule. The states have their own jurisdictions and powers. Each state has its own constitution, laws, governmental structures, and resources.

The Mexican government is characterized by the division of powers: executive, legislative and judicial. Governmental plans and programs are prepared by the executive and approved by the legislative branch; in this way they acquire legal status. The implementation of these laws is the responsibility of both the central and decentralized administrative sectors. The central administrative sectors comprises government agencies (departments), while the decentralized administrative sectors are made up of quasi-public enterprises and other entities. The heads of the agencies and secretariats are appointed by the president of the Republic, and are obliged to implement his decisions.

The Mexican Health System

Mexico's Constitution includes health protection as a right for everyone. This right has motivated several initiatives that have created a variety of public institutions responsible for providing health services throughout the nation.

The secretariat of health, the Mexican Social Security and Service Institute, and the Social Security and Service Institute for Government Employees are the leading organizations of the federal government which provide health care. Since 1977, these agencies comprise the health sector and are coordinated by the secretariat of health.

In addition, there are several health-related institutions of the state or municipal governments, other social organizations (mainly depending on labor unions) as well as private institutions all of which provide health services.

Since 1983, all these institutions comprise the National Health System, regulated by the Mexican state. Today, the system has an estimated capacity to provide services to about 80 million persons, representing 95 percent of Mexico's population. Users pay for the services through different mechanisms, such as collective insurance fees, tax contributions, individual medical insurance, and others. In some cases, health care is free.

The Federal Government Planning Law establishes the obligation of government offices and agencies to conduct their activities in keeping with the objectives and priorities of the national planning process (United Mexican States 1989: 191). To this end, the National Democratic Planning System was established and standards were adopted for the processes of planning, scheduling, budgeting, control, and evaluation of government activities (United Mexican States 1989: 192).

As part of the National Democratic Planning System, the six-year National Development Plan, the medium-term sectoral programs, the annual operating programs, and special programs are drafted. These plans and programs are agreed on with the state and municipal governments. Further, through negotiation, agreements are reached for the participation of the social and private sectors in the execution of the plan and its programs. The plans identify which programs and actions should be monitored and controlled and also determine the frequency and the degree of detail with which monitoring should be exercised.

The development and performance of the health sector is governed by the National Health Program, which is coordinated by the secretariat of health. The purpose of the program is to upgrade health programs and services, and direct the distribution of human and financial resources. The National Health Program establishes six large health program categories (United Mexican States 1990: 25):

1. Promotion of the culture of health;
2. Universal access to health services, with equity and quality;
3. Prevention and control of disease and accidents;
4. Protection and basic cleaning up of the environment;
5. Contribution to the regulation of population growth;
6. Promotion of social welfare.

To implement activities under these categories, the National Health Program has thirty-one basic programs, six support programs, and nine strategic projects, monitored through the National Health Sector Evaluation System. This system comprises a set of structures, functions, guidelines, procedures, and resources, through which the information necessary for planning and evaluation is coordinated. It makes this information available for quantitative and qualitative analysis and appraisal of the results achieved in the operation of the programs and services of the institutions in the health sector.

The system provides a comprehensive set of performance targets and establishes methods and criteria for the uniform evaluation of the various health activities. It is dynamic in that it lends itself to updating targets required in strategic planning, and it is functional and feasible in that it bases its operation on the resource capabilities of the institutions (United Mexican States 1991: 8).

The Family Planning Program

The family planning program is part of program category (5) above, on the regulation of population growth. This program is a key element in the National Health Program since population size has been established as a central element of the 1989–94 National Development Plan.

Two central objectives are established in the National Development Plan with regard to population policy: the reduction of population growth, and the promotion of a distribution of the population consistent with the efficient utilization of territorial resources. These objectives are to be achieved within a framework of full respect for the dignity and free decisions of couples and the right of free movement in Mexico's territory, as set forth in the Constitution.

In this context, and in compliance with the provisions set forth in the General Laws on Population and Health and in the 1989–94 National Population Program, the National Population Council established the 1990–94 National Family Planning Program, which constitutes the frame of reference for the family planning activities of the agencies of the public, social, and private sectors. For the public sector agencies, the program is compulsory.

The National Family Planning Program establishes objectives and quantitative targets for monitoring progress and for analyzing results. It determines the processes for monitoring and systematic evaluation of the various family planning services. Over the past twenty years, the institutions and agencies comprising Mexico's health sector have engaged in activities designed to assess the performance of their programs and services, and specific methodologies and instruments have been established.

Beginning in 1980, as a consequence of the enactment of the Global Development Plan and the resulting sectoral programs, steps were taken to set up a sectoral evaluation system that would standardize institutional developments and lay the groundwork for a unified planning, scheduling, budgeting, and control process. This effort made it possible to structure the first National Health Sector Evaluation System, which began in 1985. The results were mixed since on one hand some agencies placed greater emphasis on the global evaluation, while others on assessing specific situations. Consequently, the system was revised and modified until it attained its present shape.

Special measures to promote and stimulate development of monitoring and evaluation on the part of the government are of two types: measures which aim to prevent noncompliance, and measures which accept certain cases of noncompliance—that recognize the need to learn from failures. Outstanding among these is the Law of Responsibility of Public Employees, which establishes sanctions of an administrative, civil, or penal nature for officials who fail to comply with the goals and objectives of programs for which they are responsible.

Organization of the National Health Sector Evaluation System

The organizational and functional system of the National Health Sector Evaluation System is based on the resources and infrastructure of the National Health System and is illustrated in figure 8.1.

At the national *level* the system involves the participation of the institutions responsible for establishing the overall evaluation policy, and for directing, applying, controlling, and supervising the evaluation

FIGURE 8.1
Information Flow for Evaluation:
Institutional Information System

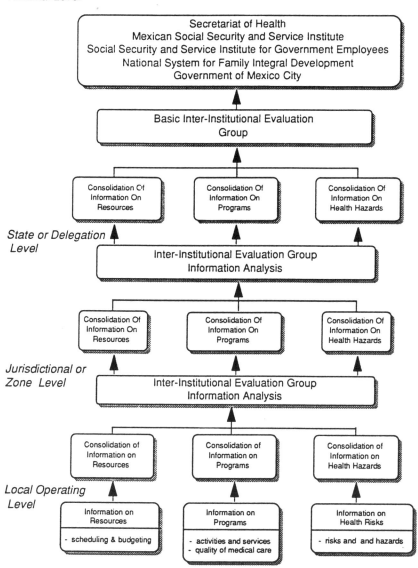

process and disseminating its results. The system also verifies compliance with the corrective measures proposed. At this level, the secretariat of health and the directors general of the Mexican Social Security and Service Institute, the Social Security and Service Institute for Government Employees, the National System for Family Integral Development, and the Health Services of the Mexico City government participate, along with the Basic Inter-Institutional Evaluation Group.

The *state* or *delegation level* (see figure 8.2) is responsible for evaluating the achievement of the state-level targets established at the central level and for making the adjustments so that the state component will appropriately respond to the state evaluation requirements. The secretariat of health participates at this level, together with senior health officials in the states, federal district, and Mexico City, and institutional delegates of the Mexican Social Security and Service Institute, the Social Security and Service Institute for Government Employees, and the National System for Family Integral Development. The Internal Administration and State Planning Committee and the Inter-Institutional Evaluation Group are also involved.

The *jurisdictional* or *zone level* is in charge of applying the laws decreed by the national level, taking into account the modifications established at the state level. The heads of jurisdictions of the secretariat of health, zone heads of the Mexican Social Security and Service Institute and the Social Security and Service Institute for Government Employees, and directors of the Mexico City regional hospitals participate, as well as those parties responsible for the evaluation activities, who also form part of the Inter-Institutional Evaluation Group.

The *local level* is in charge of evaluating local-level targets, based on adjustments made by the state and jurisdictional levels, and of incorporating local evaluation requirements. This level is made up of the directors of first- and second-level units and, with the provisions permitted by the state and jurisdictional levels or the availability of resources, of the parties responsible for programs and services. The parties in charge of the specific operation of programs and services from which the information used by the National Evaluation System is generated also participate.

The structure for monitoring and evaluating the National Family Planning Program reflects the program's general organization. Given the high priority accorded the program, the responsibility for its development lies primarily with the National Population Council, presided

FIGURE 8.2
Operation of the National Evaluation System:
State or Delegation Level

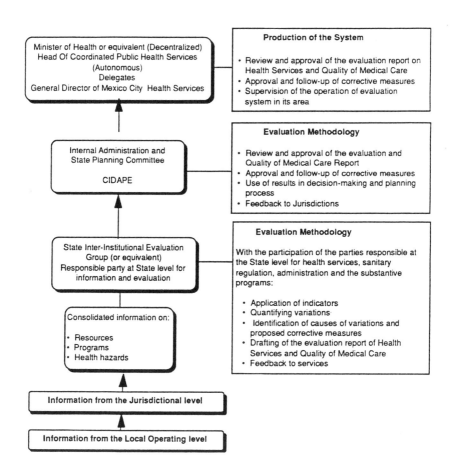

over by the minister of the interior, and composed of the senior representative of the related programs and services. The council is charged
with overseeing the proper coordination of the institutions of the National Health System in the specific area of family planning.

In order to assist the council, a family planning interinstitutional
group has been created by the cabinet responsible for the monitoring
and control of the council's tasks. This group is presided over by the
secretariat of health and consists of representatives of the Mexican
Social Security and Service Institute, the Social Security and Service
Institute for Government Employees, the National System for Family
Integral Development, the secretariat of the Navy, the Secretariat of
the National Defense, and PEMEX (the state petroleum company). It
also has the participation of the Mexican Federation of Private Family
Planning Associations, the Mexican Family Planning Foundation, the
Adolescent Counseling Center, and the Family Planning Council for
Youth.

The resolutions of the National Population Council in family planning are implemented by the institutions within the area of their responsibilities. A similar structure is seen at the level of each of the
states and the federal district, through the establishment of the state
population councils and the state interinstitutional family planning
groups.

Components of the National Health Sector Evaluation System

We will analyze the National Health Sector Evaluation System using the three components Altman (1979: 32) suggests for an effective
monitoring system: information, analysis, and action (see chapter 7):

The Information Component

A. Types of Measures of Performance.

The measures of performance used by the system can be grouped
together in ten categories: (1) inputs; (2) activities; (3) products; (4)
efficacy; (5) efficiency; (6) effectiveness; (7) quality; (8) congruency;
(9) adequacy; and (10) appropriateness (National Health System 1991:
10).

Inputs are the resources used in the execution of the planned activities. *Activities* are the main actions carried out by programs and are, in

another sense, the means that relate governmental action to the demands of the populace. *Products* are the goods and services provided through the program.

Efficacy refers to the potential of the program to achieve its objectives. *Efficiency* expresses the relationship between the objectives and resources utilized. This measure is applied in the analysis of the use of resources and infrastructure. *Effectiveness* consists of the degree to which the objectives have been accomplished. It includes the assessment of coverage, actual accessibility of priority groups to services, adequate implementation of the medical units, and the capability of the services to provide comprehensive service to the populace. *Quality* consists of the application of appropriate technology for medical care. It is measured by technical standards.

The foregoing measures are applied mainly to analyze and assess the quantitative results from the service provided. In contrast, to evaluate the performance of the organization, the criteria of *congruency, adequacy* and *appropriateness* are applied.

For the case of the programs under the National Health Sector Evaluation System control, the measurements applied with greater frequency are related to the inputs, activities, products, efficiency, and efficacy. The measurement of effectiveness and quality is conducted through specific studies that are not part of the general process.

For practically all the programs, data are collected on planned activities and actual progress achieved. In addition, information is recorded on the number of persons served, as well as on the current health risks and hazards. In particular, data is gathered on morbidity from certain illnesses which are subject to actions to improve sanitary conditions. Information on mortality is difficult to obtain in the short term and, accordingly, estimates are made based on samples.

The amount of information and the way in which it is broken down varies according to the management level.

In the case of the family planning program, the following measurements are mainly used:

- Results criteria are used, those measuring the impact of the program in terms of the general objectives, i.e. in terms of reduction of fertility and improvement of public health.
- Criteria of efficacy are used, both in terms of coverage of the program and with regard to the degree of accomplishment of the goals.
- Effectiveness criteria are applied in terms of the use of resources.

Depending on opportunity, coverage, and construction of the indicators used for control and evaluation, some data are obtained through surveys and special studies while others are generated on the basis of ongoing records.

Some examples of the types of measures used for monitoring and evaluation of the family planning program in Mexico are listed below:

- New users by area of application (urban and rural) and contraceptive method used;
- Users and equipment, by area of application and contraceptive method;
- First-time and subsequent visits by users;
- Family planning surgery by sex and area of application;
- Population enrolled in the institution and women in the fertile age by area of application;
- Number of service centers in which family planning service is provided, by area of application and service level;
- Budget and spending in the family planning program;

B. Monitoring Frequency

The frequency of monitoring varies according to the type of program. For example, in programs to control epidemic outbreaks, monitoring is very frequent, while in more or less standardized programs the frequency is less. In general terms, monitoring at the local (operating) and zone levels is conducted on a monthly or quarterly basis, while at the state and national level it is carried out quarterly, semiannually, or annually.

The Analytical Component

Among the elements necessary for monitoring, control, and evaluation are performance indicators. These provide an objective basis for analysis of the use of resources, the degree of use of the health infrastructure, the progress of programs in achieving their objectives, and the effect of these programs on the health condition of the population (National Health System 1991: 12).

Indicators in the national evaluation system are of two types: quantitative and qualitative. Quantitative evaluation is based on the indicators defined in the basic indicators table for evaluation of health services (United Mexican States 1991: 12), while the qualitative evaluation uses questionnaires to complement the quantitative information and which are designed specifically to identify the cause of any deviations detected.

Analysis of the quantitative results and the qualitative information supports the identification of any corrective measures required. These are formulated in a coordinated way among the areas that are responsible for conducting and implementing the programs, aiming at ensuring a clear assignment of responsibilities.

The national evaluation system is the practical application of the required indicators for evaluation at institutional and sectoral levels in national, state, jurisdictional, or local areas, and in medical units. The relationship between the national evaluation system and the various institutions translates in practice to each of these institutions selecting the indicators that are of greatest utility to evaluate their own programs, operations, and problems.

The institutional health administrative and service units responsible for planning and evaluating the health programs at the national level have established norms or criteria for comparison that make it possible to evaluate and compare the results of the programs. These norms consist of patterns of results or targets that provide an objective measurement of the various health goals. They are the quantification of the achievement of goals, coverage, resource productivity, and rates of health damage.

To establish these targets, the institutions take into account current technical norms. In the event that norms do not exist or that it is not possible to determine them, criteria are defined to permit effective measurement. Their use makes it possible to obtain a uniform evaluation at the technical-administrative level of whether the objectives have been achieved, whether the strategies developed and the goals reached are within the norms established for program execution, and the degree of progress in compliance with the agency's goals and objectives.

Primary data are converted into indicators for analysis as follows: the units that provide health service record their activities and prepare quantitative reports that are consolidated for specific periods of time (for a vaccination campaign, every day; for control of recipients of family planning methods, every month; etc.) At the same time, the resources applied are recorded by health unit, measure, and item for the purpose of determining the efficiency of their use. Later, in meetings held in zonal or jurisdictional units, comparison is made on the services provided against planned targets to determine whether there are any appreciable deviations. Similarly, a comparison is made of cost figures against authorized budget.

If significant deviations are found, the possible causes are investigated: lack of demand on the part of the population, lack of personnel, lack of medication, lack of promotion of the service, and so forth. The investigation is carried out either directly through interviews with personnel and users of the service, or indirectly by linking the indicators about program use with resources used.

Consider a specific example. The health service in Xochitepec, a town in which there are 1,000 women of fertile age, is targeted to provide a certain method of family planning service to 450 of them. Of these, 30 percent should be new users and the rest active users (this proportion is also determined through norms). Similarly, a determination is made of how many users will use hormonal methods, how many will use contraceptives, and how many will undergo surgery (60 percent, 30 percent, and 10 percent, respectively). To provide the service, a budget of 9,000 new pesos is authorized, of which 4,500 will be used to pay personnel and 4,500 for supplies such as contraceptives, interuterine devices, surgical material, etc.

According to the health registry reports, 500 women made use of the service, of whom 200 were new users and 300 active users. Sixty women chose surgical methods, and 440 other methods. These figures show:

TABLE 8.1

Measure	Goal Targets	Progress Achieved
Total users	450	500
By Type:		
New users	30%	200 (40%)
Active Users	70%	300 (60%)
By Method:		
Hormonal	60%	265 (53%)
Contraceptive	30%	175 (35%)
Surgical	10%	60 (12%)

The targets of 450 users, 30 percent new users and 10 percent using surgical methods were all exceeded. There were 50 (11 percent) more users than targeted, the new user target was exceed by ten percentage points (or 33 percent) and the target for surgical users exceeded by two percentage points (or 20 percent). While this is good, we need to know at what cost.

The data are that 9,500 new pesos were spent, 4,500 for personnel and 5,000 for supplies:

Cost Item	Progress Budget	Actual
Personnel	4,500	4,500
Materials and Supplies	4,500	5,000
Total	9,000	9,500
Unit Cost per User	20	19

With this data, we can see that while the planned budget target was exceeded by 500 pesos, the overall efficiency of treatment improved by 5.2 percent: the target was twenty pesos per user and it actually cost nineteen pesos per user. Using more detailed cost data one could assess the efficiency of the surgical treatment.

More generally, performance targets are prepared for each level of the health system previously described. Data is collected and aggregated at each level in the system to determine the extent to which the targets have indeed been met. The whole system is linked from top to bottom:

The Local Operating Level. Based on the primary data gathered on activities and services, health risks and hazards, actual levels of achievement are compared with the targets established by the higher levels in the hierarchy and the basic table of indicators for evaluation of health services (CBIESS, in Spanish). The evaluation methodology shown in figure 8.2 begins at this local level with the application of indicators, quantifying variations, and so forth. For information required by the state level and jurisdictional or zone level, an evaluation report on health services and the quality of medical care is prepared.

The Jurisdictional or Zone Level. The zone level consolidates this information and constructs the measures of performance for the targets set for this level, according to the CBIESS. Again the same methodology outlined in figure 8.2 is followed, but at this jurisdictional level. A report on the health services and the quality of medical care is drafted and submitted to the head of the state delegation institution, following its review by the state interinstitutional evaluation group.

The State Level. The relevant zone reports are consolidated, as shown in figure 8.2, and the state level performance measures established in the CBIESS are constructed. Using these reports, and subsequent to a review and analysis by the state interinstitutional evaluation committee, the state-level health services evaluation report is drafted and submitted to the heads of the institutions in the state development planning committee.

The National Level. Each national institution receives the performance reports from the various state delegations and head offices. In addition, using information from the epidemiological surveillance system, the impact measures contained in the CBIESS are assessed and compared with the targets established, and the variations of greatest significance are identified.

Using the state evaluations, a health-services evaluation report is drafted and submitted to the head of each institution. The institutional evaluations serve as the basis to put together the comprehensive health sector evaluation which is sent to the interinstitutional evaluation group. The secretariat of health is responsible for putting together the health sector evaluation report and disseminating it (figure 8.3).

The Corrective Actions Component

Figures 8.1 to 8.3 illustrated the flow of information in the National Health Sector Evaluation System and how corrective actions are taken at each level. As we saw, at each level in the system performance is compared with targets to determine progress made and areas where corrective measures may need to be taken. Analysis of these results provides information on the causes of the shortcomings and a basis for taking appropriate corrective measures. Obviously, in some cases, corrective measures can be taken immediately while in others they need to be reviewed first by higher levels.

For the case of the family planning program, the decisions taken and corrective measures adopted are shown in figure 8.4.

Within each of the institutions in the program, the evaluation results obtained serve as a base for several stages of control: identifying of the possible deviations, determining if they are important, and deciding on what should be done to correct problems. In the State Population Council, progress is analyzed, and decisions made regarding the redirection of the strategies and actions for each institution. The family planning interinstitutional group is placed in charge of the follow-

FIGURE 8.3
Operation of National Evaluation System: National Level

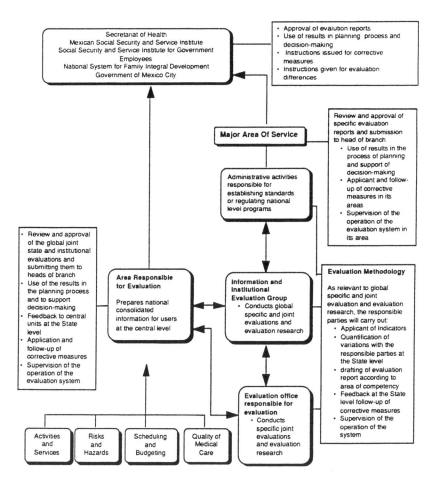

State Services and Head Offices of Services

FIGURE 8.4
National Family Planning Program Control and Evaluation Process

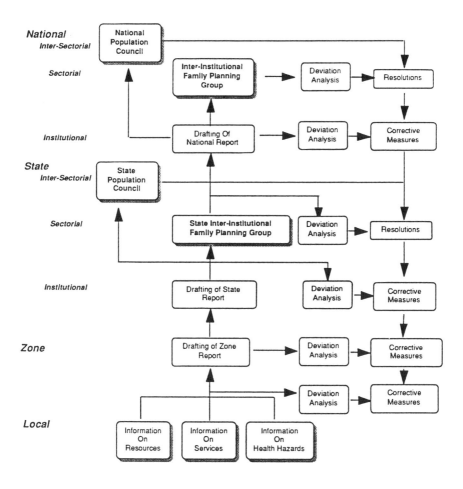

up of these decisions. A similar process is carried out in the National Population Council, but in this case the reports on the progress and results of the family planning program are augmented by the data obtained from surveys and special studies in order to reach agreement on the actions necessary to achieve the program objectives. The follow-up of these measures is the job of the family planning interinstitutional group.

Legal Foundation of the System

We have seen that Mexico has a fairly elaborate and well-developed monitoring and control system in place in the health sector. We have also seen that evaluation, as an ongoing and systematic administrative instrument, is part of the control, oversight, and evaluation system for the federal and public administration and state-owned enterprises. A key reason for the existence of the health sector is its legal basis in Article 26 of the Constitution. Three main legal measures are provided:

1. The Planning Law (published in the Official Gazette of the Federation on 5 January 1993) which establishes the principal elements of the nation's planned development, the obligatory nature of these elements for organizations in the federal public sector, the approaches and methods for the coordination of governmental action, and—most important for our subject—the obligatory requirements for controlling and evaluating progress of programs and services against results achieved.

2. The Health Law (published in the Official Gazette of the Federation on 7 February 1984) which sets forth the procedures and forms to be used by the Mexican government to comply with the constitutional precept of health protection for citizens, the organization and regulation of health services, the supervisory function of the secretariat of health, and its specific role in the control and evaluation of health services.

3. The Law of Responsibility of Public Employees (published in the Official Gazette of the Federation on 31 December 1982) which determines the preventive measures and sanctions in place for obtaining compliance by federal government officials for the responsibilities entrusted to them.

These legal precepts provide the specific framework of the control and evaluation system for health services.

Auditing the System

The audit or inspection function is very important in the National Evaluation System. By constitutional decree, both the executive and the legislative have the authority to inspect and examine the actions executed by public organizations. Effective audit further ensures that the evaluation system is operating in a reasonably honest way.

Under the executive, the inspection function is carried out by different institutions. The federal government can inspect all activities where federal resources are involved, thereby extending its scope throughout the national territory. It executes the audit function through the secretariat of the general controllership of the federation (SECOGEF, in Spanish) which subsequently carries out audits through the internal control bodies of all departments and state enterprises.

In addition, the state governments audit the use of their resources, in their specific domains. The audits are carried out in a fashion similar to the federal level: control bodies carry out the audits, coordinated with the federal controllership, when required.

The legislative is empowered to examine the way in which laws are applied and fulfilled, allowing them to audit all legislative processes. The inspection body of the legislative is the technical body of the chamber of deputies, which carries out the reviews and evaluations.

Thus we see that the internal control bodies of all the health institutions carry out planned audits on the service delivery processes and on the control systems, including those concerning information. Thus, a complete review is made in order to ensure that the process of service delivery complies with requirements, and that the performance information is recorded and processed fully and accurately. The results, including observations on noncompliance, are submitted to those directly responsible for the execution of the programs. Follow-up is done and if the irregularity persists, sanctions are applied to those responsible.

SECOGEF oversees these audit practices and carries out its own audits directly or through external auditors. In addition, SECOGEF holds periodic follow-up meetings with head officers of departments and state-owned enterprises. Something similar occurs at state and municipal levels, where the internal control function is performed by each institution or by the control body of the state government. For those service programs that are financed by international agencies,

SECOGEF has been empowered to perform specific audits on the management and control of the contributed resources.

The "Contaduria Mayor de Hacienda" performs the audit functions along with the analysis and approval of the national accounts. For this, the processes from which information is generated are reviewed, and revisions made to the National Health System.

Main Limitations

But of course, even with its legal mandate and follow-up audit work, the National Health Sector Evaluation System is not working as well as it should be. Without question, the main limitations to its operation are related to the complexities introduced with the decree consolidating the National Health System. On the one hand, since 1977, when it was decided to divide the secretaries and state agencies into sectors, important progress has been made in interinstitutional coordination within the health sector. Nevertheless, the autonomous relationship with which the social security institutions operate, constitutes an obstacle to carrying out the sectoral monitoring and evaluation guidelines. They are subject to their own basic laws. This is particularly true for institutions with diverse priorities. What is needed is for the institutions to make the necessary adjustments in their programs so that the production of data for the control of sector-wide programs can be improved. Concurrently, adjustments in the procedures used for monitoring and evaluation are needed in order for the national system to be more effective.

A similar situation occurs with regard to the institutions of the state governments. Since state governments are constitutionally free and sovereign, they tend to implement the guidelines of the federal government according to their own needs, which are not always consistent with the needs of the national system.

In addition to these difficulties in coordinating the various levels of government and their institutions, there remain conceptual and methodological issues. As was mentioned earlier, the evaluation system mainly focuses on measuring inputs, activities, products, and efficiency. The use of quantitative effectiveness and quality criteria for control and evaluation of health services remains limited due to the difficulty of determining which specific variables to measure and what targets to set. These issues are usually addressed through *ad hoc* evaluation studies and research. In terms of assessing organizational performance using measures of congruency, appropriateness, and adequacy, the diversity in the development and structure of the institutions has made it to date practically impossible to apply homogeneous approaches and variables.

The problems faced by the system for control and evaluation of the family planning program parallel those found in the National Health Services Evaluation System. They are in essence due to the fact that the National Health System is not yet fully matured. A particular challenge consists of increasing the participation of the state and municipal governments and getting the institutions of the public, social, and private sectors to act in a more coordinated fashion.

Conclusions

We have seen that the National Health System has shown unequal growth, making difficult the job of monitoring and evaluation. This arises from complexities inherent in the size of the country (almost 2 million square kilometers), the number of Mexicans (a little more than 86 million inhabitants), the federal Constitution (the states are free and sovereign), and the diversity of health service institutions, public as well as private, all with different and occasionally contradictory objectives.

To this are added, especially in the last ten years, the effects of the economic crisis on health services, outstanding among which are: deterioration in the purchasing power of the population, reduction of resources available, limited growth in the installed physical capacity, lack of investment in technology and equipment, and a rise in demand for services on the part of users.

All these factors make monitoring and evaluation more complex, and in particular make it difficult to determine the causes of noncompliance with plans and programs and to then improve the programs where the state of health of the population is concerned.

It is not surprising then that the major developments of the monitoring system occur with programs directed at quite specific problems, for example, increasing population growth, numerous cases of measles, cases of bouts of diarrhea, and so forth. The government decision to give these programs priority has resulted in reasonably homogeneous methodology and focus for their coordination, information, planning, and control. Furthermore, it has been possible to determine the impact of these programs; for example, decrease in fertility and birth rates, decrease of mortality rates from measles and gastrointestinal diseases, and so forth.

The value of the National Health Evaluation System is evident in its effect on timely decision making, making it possible to adjust, for example, the cohort of fertile women which need to be made more familiar with family planning programs, tactics to assure a greater coverage of vaccine programs, and so forth. There are, however, short-comings.

We have seen that the system deals mainly with quantitative aspects rather than qualitative ones; for example, the number and cost of the services provided instead of their quality. The result is that if the quality of the service is reduced, it may be difficult to know accurately if the programs are really being effective in dealing with the problems they were originally intended to address.

Secondly, it has not been possible to overcome inappropriate use of information. For example, comparisons among the costs of services given by different institutions frequently do not take into account the technological differences in service delivery in institution. This can lead to incorrect interpretations that sometimes are translated into er-roneous decisions. In situations where the organizations compete for major resources, this situation may prevent the development of an effective monitoring system common to all institutions because part of their information is withheld. Indeed, this is one of the main factors that have hindered the consolidation of interinstitutional agreements in the health sector.

A final problem that requires a solution for improving the monitor-ing and evaluation system is the lack of common information technol-ogy. The major public health institutions of Mexico have a great deal of data processing equipment. However, they operate independently and do not have the capacity to network. This affects what can be done as well as the overall quality of the information. In addition to technological differences, there is an inadequate information policy within the National Health System. This diversity is manifested even within each institution. Integrating information in the sector is an enor-mous problem. It results in an inefficient monitoring and evaluation system, and damage to the health programs themselves.

References

Altman, S. 1979. "Performance Monitoring Systems for Public Managers." *Public Administration Review* 39, no. 1: 31–35.

United Mexican States. Federal Executive Branch. 1983. *National System of Democratic Planning, Secretariat of Programming and Budget.*

United Mexican States. Federal Executive Branch. 1989a. *Planning Law, Laws and Codes of Mexico*, Editorial Porrua, S.A.

United Mexican States. Federal Executive Branch. 1989b. *National Development Plan*, Secretariat of Programming and Budget.

United Mexican States. Federal Executive Branch. 1990. *National Health Program, 1990–1994.* Secretariat of Health.

United Mexican States. National Health System. 1991. *National Evaluation System.*

9

Measuring Police Performance

Richard C. Sonnichsen

Effective law enforcement is the goal, not only of police agencies themselves, but also of the public they serve. Assessing the success of law enforcement activities, however, has been notoriously difficult and little consensus has formed around models of police productivity or effectiveness. Measurement criteria tend to focus on process variables while output and outcome indicators, arguably more difficult to identify and agree on, have been largely ignored.

Particularly ignored by law enforcement researchers has been the measurement and evaluation of the performance of police investigative activities. Attempts to measure and quantify the activities of police investigators have been largely confined to the traditional statistical accomplishments, for example, arrests, convictions, and property recovered. Determining the actual impact of police investigative activities has been an illusive endeavor.

This chapter will examine the development of performance measurement in police agencies and identify the particular factors that contribute to the difficulty in measuring police effectiveness. International examples of different approaches to police performance measurement will be examined by reviewing the most recent attempts to measure police performance in Canada, Germany, the United Kingdom, Sweden, The Netherlands, and the United States. Notable among the changes is the recognition of the public as a consumer of performance information and an acknowledgment of the public's role in helping define police priorities and the methodology for judging the success of police activities. Additionally, the implementation of community-based policing in many police departments makes law enforcement more accountable to the public it serves and moves police agencies away from the traditional "enforcement" model of policing toward a "community" based model. This redefinition of police priorities and the inclusion of the public as an actor in police activities will require new indicators of performance.

A review of the police literature reflects growing recognition of the limitation of measuring law enforcement effectiveness based on traditional crime statistical indicators (Silbermann 1981; Whitaker, et al. 1982; Schneider 1991; Wiebrens 1993). It is also clear that there is no single criterion of police effectiveness, and attempts to summarize police agency performance with any single measurement have the potential to be misleading. In chapter 3, Zapico-Goñi questions the reliance on the 3Es as performance criteria and suggests the necessity to develop new performance measures in light of the public-sector reform movement.

The measuring of police performance is not an exact science. Indicators may give some insight into police activities, but the indicators are rarely definitive and must be interpreted with a degree of subjectivity. A prime example of this dilemma is in Western society where there are conflicting ideas about the purpose of police activities. Conflicts arise among police officials, politicians, judicial officials, public administrators, and citizens about the priorities and purpose of police activities. Citizens may be interested in police responsiveness to their needs while public officials may focus on police efficiency. Certainly there are differences in the views of civil rights leaders and police officials over the purpose of police activities. Any system of performance measurement needs to be responsive, not only to the needs of the police but also the needs and diversity of public opinion and the requirements of interested government officials.

In Chapter 3 Zapico-Goñi introduces the emerging role of public managers working in today's complex environment and learning to deal with uncertainty. The successful public manager will be required to be creative and innovative. This is particularly true in the area of police performance measurement. It is unlikely that any police performance-measurement system will provide a complete picture of the effectiveness of police activities and their impact on the community.

However, because it is difficult it should not be viewed as an insurmountable barrier to determine the effectiveness of police agency performance. Whitaker, et. al., (1982) suggests that there are three issues that need to be considered when discussing the issue of police agency performance: (1) the lack of consensus about what police should do; (2) the lack of knowledge about the social consequences of police activities and about how other social conditions also influence the safety and well-being of the community; and (3) the obstacles to collecting valid data about what police do. Whitaker suggests that measuring police performance is a learning process that undergoes constant change as the nature of police work itself changes over time.

Wiebrens (1993) argues that some of the problems associated with the measurement of police performance are neither the fault of researchers nor of management but rather organizational systems flaws that occur from misunderstandings among organizational actors about the measurement of performance. According to Wiebrens, attempts to effectively measure police performance will be futile unless there is shared agreement about what is to be measured and the criteria for making judgments about performance. He believes that unless there is a "shared logic" between police executives and researchers, police officials will always be able to offer arguments and alibis regarding the validity of any particular performance measurement.

The focus of traditional police performance has been on process indicators. Some of the inherent problems in the use of these traditional statistics are:

- Law enforcement statistics can be easily affected by police managers with adjustments to resource allocation in specific areas and shifts in emphasis to statistically fertile areas. Statistics produced under these conditions may not accurately reflect crime problems.
- Crime rates are only partially influenced by police enforcement.
- Arrest rates do not convey the relevance of the individuals apprehended.
- Conviction rates tend to reflect the workings of the judicial system and not the effectiveness of the police.
- There are difficulties in translating law enforcement policy level concepts, for instance safe streets, into specifically defined and precisely measurable performance indicators.

These problems pose a challenge to those involved in accurate performance measurement in law enforcement. The problems enumerated above occur in law enforcement but they also contain a generic quality endemic in measuring public-sector performance. Mayne and Zapico-Goñi notes in chapter 1 that reform in performance measurement is occurring in all public sectors and argues that effective performance measurement is essential if meaningful public-sector reform is to occur.

Impetus for Performance Review

Interestingly, the field of performance measurement has gained momentum in the last twenty years, more specifically in the past decade. This impetus for increased interest in performance measurement has its origins in a number of sources, both internally in police departments and externally among government agencies and the general public. The following are some of the driving forces which helped shape the current state of performance measurement in the six countries surveyed in this chapter.

External Factors

- Increased interest by central government agencies for improved financial management;
- Greater demand for accountability by central government agencies and budget oversight bodies;
- Demand for improved police services by the public;
- Decreased availability of human and financial resources;
- Increased interest by funding bodies and senior administrators for data demonstrating which programs and which activities within programs work;
- Shift in emphasis from traditional police performance measures of activity to interest in outcome and impact measures;
- Mandated performance and effectiveness data in budget requests; and
- Fear of crime and disillusionment by the public over the effectiveness of police agencies.

Internal Factors

- Need of better performance data by senior police administrators for input into resource distribution decisions;
- Increased recognition by police administrators of the value of effective and efficient delivery of police services;
- Recognition of the public as a customer for police services and a major stakeholder in police performance; and
- Increased complexity of crime and sophistication of criminals requiring new measures to accurately portray police performance.

Police officials have recognized these factors and begun to rethink the traditional approach to performance measurement. The following discussion will examine police and government efforts in six countries to implement improved approaches to measuring police performance.

Canada

In Canada, both Canada Customs and the Royal Canadian Mounted Police (RCMP) have recognized the law enforcement challenges of the 1990s and are attempting to confront this challenge by developing effective performance indicators in their respective services. Canada Customs has begun to review performance measures used to measure the results of Customs enforcement activity. This review has been prompted by the increased sophistication of criminals, an increase in the number of shipments and travelers across Canadian borders, and pressures to streamline transaction processing and provide protection to Canadian society.

Traditional performance measures for Canada Customs have consisted of informal and ad hoc feedback from users and clients, formal surveys of participants, established management information systems, as well as occasional studies, program evaluations, and internal audits (Revenue Canada 1991). Recognizing that these sources may not be adequate for the future, law enforcement officials in Canada Customs are seeking improved performance information, focusing on the outputs produced by their enforcement activities coupled with the deterrent effect.

A report published in July 1991 (commissioned by the Customs Enforcement Directorate) recommended ten possible performance measures for investigations (Revenue Canada 1991). These performance measures are based on the stated enforcement objectives of Canada Customs and are designed to illustrate the "relationship between the immediate or visible outputs of enforcement activity and some of the broader compliance aims espoused by the organization."

These ten indicators are:

- Number of cases completed and value of assessments per person-year;
- Ratio of assessments and penalties to program expenditures;
- Prosecutions initiated;
- Percent of prosecutions successfully resolved;
- Average case turnaround times;

- Sources used as the basis of new cases;
- Percent of investigations assessments confirmed through adjudications;
- Ratio of investigations assessments and penalties to total departmental commercial enforcement actions;
- Ratio of actual collections to annual investigations assessments and penalties; and
- Deterrent effect.

The use of deterrent effect as a performance indicator mirrors the trend in law enforcement toward using public opinion as input into assessing the performance of law enforcement.

In 1990, the RCMP, in response to a Treasury Board mandate to improve performance measurements, developed the following five performance indicators intended to refine and be used in assessing agency performance (RCMP).

- *Efficiency*: the ratio of outputs (goods or services) produced to the inputs (dollars) expended over time;
- *Productivity*: the ratio of outputs (goods or services) produced to the inputs (person years or time) expended over time;
- *Level of service*: the ratio of the standards established to define the manner and/or timeliness in which the outputs (goods or services) are produced for the client to the actual manner/timeliness of produced goods/services;
- *Quality of service*: the extent to which the outputs (goods or services) produced have conformed to the specifications of the client. Client "reaction/response" to those outputs provided may be either formal or informal; and
- *Effectiveness*: the extent to which the objective(s) of the program(s) has/have been achieved.

The RCMP recognizes that the overall assessment of performance must also take into consideration managers' assessments, program evaluations, internal and external documents, and other available material relevant to the program being assessed.

This multiindicator approach to evaluating the effectiveness of police organizations utilized by both Canada Customs and the RCMP has been supported by research conducted among senior police managers in Canada (Schneider 1991). Although the two most commonly mentioned productivity indicators among the senior officials surveyed were crime levels and enforcement (i.e., arrests, clearances, and solvencies), Schneider also found that the groups studied were not tied to traditional police performance indicators but recognized that a more comprehensive multiindicator approach was needed. Eighteen of the twenty-four managers involved in the study described an effective police force as one that is responsive to the needs of the community.

Sweden

In Sweden the budget process covers a three-year period and mandates the use of performance and effectiveness criteria. Police activities in Sweden are under the direction and oversight of the Swedish National Police Board (SNPB), a central government agency. The SNPB uses performance indicators internally to assess performance and productivity of the 118 Swedish police districts; externally, this information is used by SNPB when presenting their budget to Parliament. Performance indicators are also used in Sweden by the National Audit Bureau (NAB), an oversight agency similar to the Government Accounting Office (GAO) in the United States. The NAB uses performance indicators during their review and evaluation of police activities.

Since 1975, Sweden has had a computerized crime statistics system (Knutsson 1991). The Central Bureau of Statistics processes, compiles, and publishes statistical data from all of the 118 police districts. This system stores data on both reported crimes and man-years of investigative effort. Performance indicators can then be generated by dividing crime data by resource data. These data are monitored by the SNPB on a quarterly basis in the police districts and annually for all 118 police districts.

The following performance indicators are currently used in Sweden to measure the performance of criminal investigative activities (SNPB 1991):

- *Workload*: measured as the number of reported crimes divided by number of man-hours registered for the investigative programs;
- *Productivity*: measured as number of crimes turned over to the prosecutor's office divided by the number of man-hours registered for each investigative program;
- *Case Flow*: measured as (for each reporting period) the number of reported crimes not investigated, divided by the number of reported crimes during the reporting period
  — the number of reported crimes where police investigation resulted in a "cleared case" in the sense that it was determined that no crime was committed, the perpetrator was under age, etc., divided by the number of reported crimes during the reporting period

— the number of crimes investigated and turned over to the prosecutors office divided by the number of reported crimes during the reporting period;

• *Handling Time*: the average calendar time in days from the date a crime is reported until the case reaches a termination point as defined by the case flow measure; and

• *Quality*: proportion of the number of crimes turned over to the prosecutor that he decides to prosecute.

One of the factors impacting the Swedish police is a marked decline in resources allocated to criminal investigations during the past decade, to about 14 percent of total police resources. During this same period, however, work load and productivity have increased and the "clearance rate" has remained constant.

The role of the SNPB is changing, moving away from operations toward a more strategic evaluative role of the Swedish police system. Recognizing the importance of monitoring and evaluating police performance, the SNPB is experimenting with a measuring instrument (E-Factor) designed to allow crime clearance comparisons among the 118 police districts, controlling for certain demographic factors that are beyond the control of police authorities (Knutsson 1991). Demographic factors hinder police activities in some areas, but have minimal effect in others. By controlling for these factors, it becomes possible to calculate an expected clearance factor which then can be compared with the actual clearance rate. The difference between the actual and expected clearance rate is the E-Factor, which should normally fluctuate around zero.

The E-Factor can be used as an analytical tool to probe the causes of both positive and negative performance deviations. The E-Factor highlights differences in resource allocation to specific criminal activities, procedural approaches, and investigative techniques among the police districts. The E-Factor is not, per se, a performance indicator, but an analytical tool to be used in conjunction with performance indicators to analyze and compare performance variations (Kuntsson 1991). This is a new approach by Sweden in evaluating police performance and insufficient data have been collected to determine the validity of this approach.

Germany

Germany has had limited evaluations, particularly at the national level, of the effectiveness of its police force (Zimmerman 1993). Police resource allocation is primarily based on traditional police statistics plus local demographic data. Much of the evaluation of police performance is done by the staffs of the larger police departments.

Despite several research attempts to develop a scientific basis and sophisticated performance indicators to measure and evaluate police activities at the national level, none has been satisfactory and Germany continues to use the traditional police statistics to measure the performance of their police forces. Data are generally collected about the number of investigations, the number of arrests, the number of overtime hours worked by investigators, and other process data indicating the work activity of police investigators. These data are used by local police commanders for planning and resource allocation, but is insufficient for effective use at the federal level.

The German police community recognizes these limitations of traditional police statistics for use in developing strategies against crime. In 1982, an effort was made by the Bundeskriminalant (BKA) to predict the future trends of crime and develop strategies for both prevention and attacks on prevalent crime problem areas. A committee of experts, "Prognose-Gremium," was established in the BKA to facilitate decision making about the future development of crime. Its purpose was to evaluate crime data and to develop tactics and strategies to combat crime. Although the committee no longer exists, the BKA continues to conduct research in this area.

In 1990, the Permanent Conference of the Interior Ministers and Senators of the Federal States established a work group to develop criteria for deciding personnel needs for the next ten years. In September 1992, they reported that "data concerning the time spent on individual activities [does not] yield sufficiently precise information about the needed police strength for one particular Federal state or for the entire Federal Republic, and such data, [is insufficient] to make a prognosis for the future" (Zimmerman 1993). The work group concluded that it was not possible to calculate a formula to accurately predict police personnel needs by using work load data.

United States

In the mid–1970s the Federal Bureau of Investigation (FBI) in the United States recognized the inadequacy of traditional investigative performance measures to accurately account for the distribution of scarce personnel resources and effectively portray the accomplishments to external oversight and funding entities (Sonnichsen 1987). Prior to the mid–1970s, the FBI focused on quantitative output and caseload statistics as indicators of workload and performance.

Caseload was eventually recognized as a purely quantitative measurement without a qualitative essence, thereby rendering complexity distinctions among cases impossible. The quantitative approach to measuring outputs, such as arrests, convictions, fines, savings, and recoveries was also devoid of qualitative interpretation. In a classic example of "what gets measured, gets done" the special agents in charge of FBI field offices were pursuing those investigations that generated performance statistics which were used to judge agent performance. With the FBI measurement system unable to distinguish case quality or complexity, the conviction of two petty car thieves appeared to represent superior performance to the conviction of one major criminal figure or one corrupt politician.

In an effort to redirect resources to the major criminal problems identified in FBI field office territories, the emphasis on caseload and traditional accomplishment statistics was reduced and field offices were encouraged to identify priority investigative targets and devote sufficient resources to cause a major impact in these areas. This major philosophical reorientation toward resource distribution and performance measurement, redirected the FBI investigative effort away from the quantity of work to the quality of work. This concept of "quality over quantity," was successfully piloted in four field offices and on 28 August 1975 Director Clarence Kelley directed all FBI field offices to:

> . . . initiate a careful review of investigative matters with a view toward bringing those of marginal importance to a logical conclusion at the earliest possible time. In the future, field offices should strive for early resolutions of such cases, should attempt to give improved time service to leads from other field offices, and concentrate investigative effort on the major criminal and security problems within their respective territories . . . I am aware of the fact that this approach to our investigative responsibilities represents a change in our traditional utilization of agent manpower. However, I feel this is an important step in placing this organiza-

tion in a position to more aggressively meet the criminal and security problems facing us. I am convinced that a quality approach will best enable the FBI to fulfill its mission.

With a change of this magnitude in the investigative activities of the FBI, sweeping changes in the reporting of accomplishments had to be effected if the FBI was to maintain credibility and continue to secure adequate funding during congressional budget hearings. Objective evaluation of the FBI as a prominent public agency would have to include qualitative descriptions of case activities and not be based solely on traditional quantitative performance measures.

In order to monitor and evaluate the utilization and performance of FBI resources, FBI activities were grouped into eleven investigative programs and given priority rankings. To accomplish this the FBI designed a resource management information system (RMIS) that captured agent time expenditures, differentiated by significant cases of a quality nature designated as priority case indicator (PCI) cases. Resource expenditures were matched with accomplishment results, the quantitative outputs now supplemented with the qualitative explanations. Continuous review of the comprehensive RMIS information underscores the shifting of FBI priorities to priority areas with reported accomplishments in high priority programs. This new approach to investigations has been successful and allowed the FBI to develop major cases in organized crime, financial crimes, and public corruption, without any funding reductions.

The Netherlands

In November 1989, the Dutch government integrated the state and municipal police forces as part of an effort to accomplish a more efficient and effective public sector (Wiebrens 1993). In April 1994, 148 municipal police forces and seventeen state police districts were merged into twenty-five regional forces and one national force (Wiebrans 1994). This effort by the Dutch reflects an interest in streamlining the public sector by reorganizing police forces into larger and more effective units, and applying new approaches to public management. These reforms will require new relationships to be developed among the police authorities and oversight institutions. Underlying this new approach to managing and judging police performance is the concept of "steering at a distance," allowing greater autonomy to the police districts in accomplishing results once agreement has been reached on what the intended results should be (Wiebrans 1994).

Accompanying the reform is the introduction of a police performance model developed by the ministry of justice research and documentation center (RDC). The RDC model uses a series of performance matrices depicting not only police products (cleared up crimes, fines, warrants, etc.) but also police achievement in the areas of service to the public (public confidence, levels of feeling safe/unsafe, levels of unreported crimes, etc.) (Wiebrens 1993).

Merging police performance in both products and services into one matrix for all police entities allows comparisons to be made among police districts. This final matrix provides insights into the performance of each police entity and whether their performance was average, below average, or above average compared to other departments. At the end of 1992 the RDC model was implemented and tested in Rotterdam-Rijinmond, a new police region and other regions are expected to implement the model.

Currently the Dutch are developing four types of instruments to be used as a comprehensive monitoring system of police performance:

1. The police monitor will be a nationwide survey held every two years providing planning and resource allocation data as well as performance data.
2. Output measurement will create an inventory of all possible police outputs and assign an average production time to each output, thereby developing a productivity indicator. Also being developed is another indicator measuring those police activities that are necessary but do not lead to tangible and measurable outputs, such as crowd control at public functions.
3. Quality controls will be established defining minimum standards for all police activities. The police forces will be audited every four years.
4. Regional police budgets will be audited and compared.

These four instruments combined will provide a comprehensive review of police activities and performance on a three- to four-year cycle.

United Kingdom

The English Audit Commission, in a report published in December 1990, cites strengthening of the performance review system as the key to more effective policing. The audit commission proposed a diagnostic model for reviewing performance in crime detection that relies on analyzing the underlying statistics on crime "clear-ups" and examining the reasons for the differences in clear-up rates among the forces. By analyzing the underlying reasons for variations among forces, successful approaches to combating crime can be identified. (This is similar to the E-factor approach used in Sweden.)

New Scotland Yard introduced in 1992 its "Plus Nine Approach" to measuring police performance. Five core operational functions have been developed: (1) twenty-four hour response service; (2) crime management; (3) traffic management; (4) maintenance of the Queen's peace; and (5) public reassurance. For each of these core functions, suggested performance indicators have been developed. By collecting and displaying quantitative data in a graphic format the metropolitan police will be in a position to judge the performance of police activities in these selected areas.

Developments in Measuring Police Performance

In chapter 1, Mayne and Zapico-Goñi refer to the citizen as a consumer of services and a partner in governance. The long-term effect of this trend in public partnership is that in the future, it may be insufficient to just provide police services if the quality and effectiveness of these services cannot be demonstrated to the public. A major advancement in the field of measuring police performance has been the recognition that the traditional focus on inputs and processes should be reordered toward collecting and analyzing data on output and outcomes. Canada, Sweden, the United Kingdom, The Netherlands, and the United States have all reoriented this approach to data collection to reflect the increasing demand for improved information on the effectiveness of police activities.

By refocusing performance measurements on the outputs and their consequences, that is, outcomes, police agencies are required to continuously monitor and analyze the effects of their activities and resource distribution. Deemphasizing input and process measurements obligates that police identify important crime issues and effectively distribute resources for impact. The outcome approach to police performance relegates input and activity measurement to an intermediate performance measure and not an end result.

Another critical improvement in measuring performance has been the attempt to incorporate explanatory, qualitative information along with data on police statistical accomplishments to assist in differentiating the complexity and the quality of cases. The movement in this direction allows judgments to be offered regarding resource distribution and decisions made about police effectiveness.

New approaches to measuring law enforcement performance require coordination and cooperation among police agencies and government entities. Identified major crime problems require the application of significant resources for protracted periods of time with the potential for limited available performance data during periodic routine performance measurement reporting timeframes. Allowances for these situations must be negotiated between police, funding, and oversight bodies with the expectation by all participants that complex criminal activities do not usually succumb to traditional police efforts. Extraordinary, creative, and complex investigative activities are not appropriately described by traditional police statistics and timeframes.

Future of Police Performance

Reviewing the difficulties in advancing police performance measurement should not obscure the positive accomplishments that have been made. There is a hazard that dwelling on the difficult aspects of measuring police performance may detract from the positive advances made by police agencies. To approach police performance measurement it is first necessary to understand that it is highly unlikely that a system of measurement will ever be developed that comprehensively measures all relevant variables of police operations yet is sufficiently sensitive to differentiate among departments in different geographical regions. Some of the multiple pressures on police to measure performance are contradictory. There are inherent conflicts in the goals and objectives of the public and police officials, as well as budget constraints. Police performance measurement will likely always result in an incomplete picture of police activities due to the complexities of internal police variables, external community expectations, and the very nature of crime as an enterprise that defies precise definition, varies by region, and fluctuates due to events beyond the control of either police or government.

However, one potential positive effect of renewed interest in police performance is the requirement for all those concerned with the outcomes of police activities to conceptually address and rigorously examine the basic mission of policing in light of public interests. Discovering multiple and sometimes conflicting demands for services has had the beneficial effect of causing police agencies to review their activities and establish priorities. Limited resources, coupled with increased demand for police services requires that police rank the demands for their services and justify their resource distribution.

However difficult the prospects for accurate measurement of police performance appear, there are positive approaches that are useful in determining the effectiveness and efficiency of police activities. Any data collected on police performance give some indication of performance. Police performance measurement has been described as a "learning strategy" where cooperation among those involved in designing, measuring, collecting data, and interpreting results leads to more useful information about police performance (Whitaker 1982).

In chapter 3, Zapico-Goñi questions the reliance of the traditional 3Es as performance criteria and suggests the necessity to develop new performance measures in light of the public-sector reform movement. In the future, quantitative statistical data will need to be supplemented with qualitative descriptive data to explain variances and allow more accurate interpretation of different levels of performance and diverse approaches to the solutions of criminal activity. Without qualitative data, the use of traditional statistical accomplishments limits valid comparisons among police entities.

As performance measurement techniques and strategies continue to be developed, evaluation may become increasingly useful as a tool to supplement performance data. A periodic, comprehensive evaluation of a police program or entity, including not only statistical data, but a detailed examination of the crime problem, the social context, and all relevant variables, may be helpful to those charged with the responsibility for judging police performance. Periodic evaluation of police activities provides valuable insights into both the process and outcomes of police efforts and supplements the traditional collection of performance data. An independent evaluation staff can perform an invaluable service to executive decision makers by furnishing in-depth, unbiased information on how programs work.

Drawbacks to evaluation of police agencies are the expense involved in comprehensive evaluations and the difficulty in generalizing the results to other settings. Nevertheless, a police agency that develops continuous evaluation procedures for its programs and units can, over time, gain valuable insights into performance variation among its subgroups. Coupling regularly collected performance data with periodic evaluations produces a combination of qualitative and quantitative data that allows comparative judgments of performance.

Conclusion

The six countries referred to in this chapter have all recognized the inadequacy of traditional police performance statistics in light of the increased complexity and sophistication of criminal problems. New approaches to measuring police activities are being developed to supplement traditional methods and reflect the growing awareness of the public as a major stakeholder in the behavior and performance of police agencies. The use of qualitative descriptions of police investigations has been recognized as a necessary supplement to quantitative data, which can be misleading and subject to manipulation. No single criterion will accurately portray police performance, however the multiindicator approach being developed will enhance the public's ability to properly judge police performance as well as furnish police executives with the necessary data to make operational and resource decisions.

Improved performance measures will contribute to improving police performance. By examining performance data, police agencies will be better able to respond to the demands for their services. However, performance data is but one ingredient in determining the quality of police performance. It should be used as part of the input, along with other available information to determine if police agencies are responsive to the criminal problems that affect their communities.

References

Government of Canada. 1991. *A Proposal for Measuring Enforcement in Canada Customs.* Ottawa: Revenue Canada.

Government of Canada. Undated. *Operational Plan Framework: A Guide to Performance measurement.* Ottawa: Royal Canadian Mounted Police.

Government of England. 1991. *Core Performance Indicators.* Metropolitan Police, Plus 9. London.

Government of England. 1990. *Effective Policing—Performance Review in Police Forces.* The Audit Commission for Local Authorities and the National Health

Service in England and Wales. Number 8, London.

Government of Sweden. 1991. *National Swedish Police Board Performance Indicators and Criteria for the Criminal Investigative Activities.* Stockholm: National Swedish Police Board, Financial Division.

Knutsson, J. 1991. *Performance Indicators and Criteria.* Response to Personal Inquiry. Stockholm: Research Unit, The Police College.

Schneider, F. 1991. "Police Organization Effectiveness: The Manager's Perspective." *Canadian Police College Journal* 15, no. 3.

Silberman, G. 1981. "New Methods in Criminal Justice Evaluation." In *New Directions for Program Evaluation: Federal Efforts to Develop New Evaluation Methods* no. 12, ed. N. Smith. San Francisco, Cal.: Jossey-Bass.

Sonnichsen, R. 1987. "Communicating Excellence in the FBI." In *Organizational Excellence*, ed. Joseph S. Wholey. Lexington, Mass.: Lexington Books.

Whitaker, G. et al. 1982. *Basic Issues in Police Performance.* Washington, D. C.: U. S. Department of Justice,

Whitaker, G. 1984. *Understanding Police Agency Performance.* Washington, D. C.: U. S. Department of Justice.

Wiebrens, C. 1993. "Of Alibis, Arguments, and Measurement: The RDC-model for Police Performance Measurement," paper presented at the A.S.C. Conference, Phoenix, Ariz.

Wiebrens,C. (1994). Personal correspondence. Research and Documentation Center (RDC), Ministry of Justice, The Hague, The Netherlands.

Zimmerman, H. (1993). Personal correspondence. German senior staff police academy. Munster, Germany.

10

Monitoring the Efficiency, Quality, and Effectiveness of Policy Advice to Government[1]

John Nicholson

Introduction

The practice of regularly monitoring the performance of public programs is widespread in developed countries and generally recognized as being essential to good government.[2]

Notwithstanding this increased emphasis in recent years on program evaluation and performance monitoring in the public sector, examples of such activity specifically in relation to policy advice are rare, despite the undoubted importance that policy advice plays in the role of many, if not most, government agencies. Typically, most agencies will be responsible for the provision of policy advice to government at some time. Some agencies will see policy advice as their principal responsibility. Regular monitoring of that advice would, therefore, seem necessary, and yet the available evidence suggests that very little is being done. Why?

One reason may be the relatively immature development of program evaluation and performance monitoring that exists at the moment in many countries and the consequent concentration on the less difficult issues for the time being. Another may reflect a considered view that the costs of undertaking such activity exceed the benefits.

Yet another may be a belief that, while potentially useful, it is too difficult. For some, it may simply not be seen as serving any useful purpose at all.

This chapter considers the case, not only for monitoring the performance of the *program*, but also for systematic monitoring of the *advice* provided to government by the civil service and on which a policy decision about a particular program will be influenced. It also points to some examples where policy advice has been evaluated and argues that, although possibly more difficult, the activity of policy advice is as open to measurement as is program performance and the benefits of so doing may be significant.

A word on definitions. The term *monitoring* is used throughout this chapter to include both measurement and reporting. *Policy advice* is defined as the giving of formal advice to government ministers by civil servants suggesting a particular state of events or proposed course of action in relation to existing or proposed government programs. The term *agency* is used to include all the various references to public-sector bodies, for example, departments, agencies, ministries, and so forth.

Why Monitor Policy Advice?

The reasons for choosing to monitor the performance of policy advice are fundamentally no different than the reasons for choosing to monitor the performance of the program itself.

First and foremost, performance monitoring is a management tool that, if used properly, will assist decision making, thus leading (hopefully) to better outcomes for the community. There is abundant evidence available to suggest that decision makers are using the results of their program monitoring to bring about needed changes in their programs. At the simplest level, this may be little more than an adjustment to the program administration leading to greater efficiency in program delivery. At the other end of the scale, it might involve a fundamental change to the program policy itself, to improve the effectiveness of the program, in terms of its outcomes.

Secondly, it acts as an accountability mechanism. The provision of policy advice costs the taxpayer money, both directly, in terms of the resources consumed in preparing the advice, and indirectly, in the economic effects such advice might have on future government decisions. The community has a right to know that that money is being well spent.

If then, there are good reasons for monitoring the performance of the policy advice function, why is it the case that there is such little evidence of its occurrence throughout the world? A significant factor must be that the right incentives do not currently exist. There is little pressure for change in an area which many would consider as too difficult and of marginal value, particularly when there are so many other areas of public-sector reform with which governments can concern themselves and where the benefits are more immediately apparent. There is, however, increasing evidence that this is likely to change.

For many countries, one of the most significant areas of public-sector reform has to do with the changing nature of accountability. Typically, electors are expecting greater accountability from their elected representatives, with one consequence being that the traditional roles of the bureaucracy, vis-à-vis the parliament, are having to be rethought and often reformulated. It is unrealistic to expect that this increased demand for public-sector accountability will not spill over into calls for greater accountability by the bureaucracy for government decisions in which they have played a large part. The difficulty, of course, is in determining to what extent the bureaucracy has actually played a part in the final decision and hence might be called to account. Some of these issues are considered below.

Some Inherent Complications

Policy advice is not provided in a perfectly objective, value-free environment. As Wilenski (1986) observed:

> The myth is sustained that although public servants are actively involved in the policy-making process, and sometimes vigorously support the adoption of certain policy lines, this support is based on a profession and detached assessment of the options. It is quite clear, however, that many of the most important issues on which senior policy makers are required to advise—such as the level of pension benefits, the level of protection that should be afforded a particular industry, the siting of an airport, the division of expenditure between government and non-government schools, the overall size of the budget—are all issues in which values play a large part in guiding a public servant to advocate a particular position.

Taking it one step further, there is ample international evidence to suggest that, on occasions, policy advisers simply "get it wrong" and provide poorly developed advice on which subsequent decisions are (at least partly) made.

While it will not be possible, or perhaps even desirable, to totally eradicate the value-laden nature of policy advice, it should be possible to improve the quality of such advice by firstly, recognizing those attributes which go to making up "good" advice and secondly, instituting an appropriate monitoring system to ascertain whether or not those attributes are attained. Obviously, this will not guarantee better decisions, but it is a step in the right direction.

Inevitably, there are significant difficulties to be faced in any attempt to monitor the policy-advising function. Such difficulties, however, should not be used as an excuse for doing nothing, even though in some cases the extent of those difficulties may lead to the adoption of a pragmatic, second-best solution. Nevertheless, if it can be shown that such monitoring is leading to better decision making and/or increased accountability, then there is, prima facie, a strong argument in its favor. The major difficulties are summarized below and examined in more detail throughout the chapter:

• It may not be easy, or even sensible in some cases, to try to establish a direct causal link between the policy advice and the eventual policy adopted by the government. Neither may it be possible to accord an unequivocal relationship between the government decision and the final outcome. Other factors may substantially affect the result. That is not to suggest that the policy advice has no value, only that it has to be recognized that the eventual policy will probably be the result of many and varied factors, some of them quite extrinsic to the development of policy advice by civil servants. Nonacceptance of advice does not necessarily lower the inherent quality or "value" of that advice. While such a link is necessary in trying to measure the effectiveness of the policy advice, it will be less so if the major concern is to do with the *efficiency* or *quality* of the process.

• The difficulty in establishing a causal link is made even more so by the fact that the timeframes over which policy advice is developed can be very long. Equally, there can be a significant period of time between the giving of the advice and the eventual policy implementation. Finally, there may be a long lead time between the advice and the eventual policy outcome.

• As suggested above, governments increasingly look to many different sources for their advice, and the weight to be placed on the importance of the civil service advice, in terms of the final policy decision, vis-à-vis the rest of the advice received may be difficult to sensibly assess.

• It is not always possible to separate the policy-advising function from the policy-administration function,[3] or at least, where such separation does take place, it is important to recognize the interdependence of each. For example, while the U.K. "Next Steps" initiative has been largely concerned with achieving exactly such a separation, it has long been recognized that the development of policy advice cannot be successfully achieved without input from the policy administrators. The U.K. Prison Services Agency is an example of a "Next Steps" agency which has been given a specific policy advice role as part of its framework document.

• The costs of monitoring the policy advice might outweigh the perceived benefits.

• It may not be possible to institute an acceptably objective method of assessing performance.

• An assessment system must be sophisticated enough to recognize, and take account of, the changed circumstances that may have occurred since the original advice was prepared.

Choosing what to Monitor?

At one extreme, monitoring could concentrate just on the efficiency of the *process* of policy advising, while at the other, it could seek to establish a causal link between the advice and the eventual *outcome*, and thereby create an accountability relationship that generally does not exist at the moment, at least not in the traditional Westminster system of government. This chapter argues that while the former is necessary, it is not sufficient, but the latter may prove to be more than is possible or even necessary.

Performance measures can be grouped under a variety of classifications. For simplicity, they are hereunder considered under the general categories of efficiency, quality, and effectiveness. We will examine the implications of measuring policy advice for each of these categories.

Efficiency

It is axiomatic that performance monitoring is easiest when the concentration is on efficiency issues—the relationship between outputs and the inputs used to produce them. The reasons for this are several, but primarily reflect the fact that *quantitative*, and hence relatively objective, rather than *qualitative*, and therefore often more subjective, measures are the norm. Another important reason is that we are usually able to develop performance *measures* of efficiency rather than having to rely on performance *indicators*, as is more often the case when measuring quality and particularly, effectiveness. The distinction between measures and indicators is not always clear and some countries, such as Australia, prefer to use the term performance information to cover both concepts. Others find the distinction useful, arguing that a strictly quantifiable *measure* is to be preferred to an *indicator* which implies less certainty about the degree of certainty to be afforded the information.

Given the experience we now have with developing information about program efficiency, it should not be too difficult to develop a reasonably comprehensive understanding of what is meant by efficient policy advice. For example, one would expect, as a minimum, to measure such attributes as quantity, timeliness of preparation, and cost per unit of delivery.

Quality

Whereas assessment of efficiency may be regarded as relatively trivial, an assessment of the quality of the advice is more problematic. Quality here refers to the extent to which the nature of the output and the delivery of the output service meets the government's objectives and, where appropriate, the users' needs. It is immediately apparent that there is a much greater degree of subjectivity involved with measures of quality than there is for efficiency measures, thereby making comparative analysis more difficult. Nevertheless, if we are to provide information more useful to decision making and accountability than that which is inherent in efficiency measures alone, such measurement, albeit largely subjective, is necessary. Subjectivity need not mean inequity, provided the nature of the subjectivity is well understood and account is taken of its existence and effect.

How then, do we assess the *quality* of policy advice? A prerequisite to any attempt to answer this question is to define what we mean by 'quality' advice. Like the much vaunted term "excellence," quality can have many shades, dependant on who is making the judgement. While it is probably true that the final arbiter must be the recipient who, for the purpose of this chapter, we are assuming to be the responsible government minister, Blakely's (1991) view that "the acceptance of policy advice by the Minister or Cabinet is not the sole measure of quality" is undoubtedly correct. There can be a multitude of reasons unrelated to the quality of the advice that will lead to the advice not being accepted, particularly in those public sectors where the provision of advice is meant to be at arms length from the political process.

The attributes necessary to measure quality might include the following:

- *accuracy*—the facts in the papers are accurate and reliable;
- *comprehensiveness*—all material facts have been included;
- *timeliness*[4]—the information provided is up to date;
- *responsiveness*—the information is sensitive to realities and anticipates developments;
- *clarity*—the information is logically and concisely set out and uses plain English;
- *practicality*—the recommendations are practical;
- *appropriateness*—the recommendations are relevant and useful;
- *fairness*—the recommendations provide a balanced, objective and equitable view;
- *cost-effectiveness*—the solutions are cost-effective and comparative costs are provided; and
- *consultation*—there is evidence of adequate consultation with interested parties.

It is immediately apparent that there is the potential for conflicting views on the appropriate balance to be struck between some of these attributes, for example comprehensiveness and timeliness. The answer lies in a common-sense approach that recognizes that the priority of one attribute over another will be dependent on the circumstances of the situation.

We now return to the question of *how* we might formally[5] assess the quality of policy advice. Assessments can be undertaken either internally by the organization itself, where typically there is a high degree of self-interest, or externally, where there may or may not be any direct self-interest. A combination of internal and external assessment may also be appropriate in some cases. As a generalization, the determining factor in whether a review will be undertaken internally or externally could be expected to depend on the purpose of that review. To the extent that the review is for decision-making purposes, the most likely course would be for the review to be undertaken internally. On the other hand, if the purpose is primarily about ensuring accountability, then one might expect there to be a greater reliance on external review.

An obvious starting point to determining the quality of the advice is to ask the recipient, that is the responsible government minister. An example of this approach exists in New Zealand (1992) where "the Minister's views of the relevance and quality of the advice are sought in the context of quarterly and year-end performance reviews." Ministers are asked to assess the quality of advice, using a five-point scale, on the attributes of purpose, logic, accuracy, options, consultation, practicality, and presentation. As noted by Scott (1992), "Ministers need to tell their Chief Executives plainly when the advice they are receiving is not up to standard. . . . If Ministers do not get satisfaction they need to inject their disquiet forcefully into the Chief Executive's performance assessment, and thus their pay and/or ultimately, the non-renewal of their contract." In the New Zealand example, a minister's proclivity for so doing is undoubtedly helped by the requirement for "explicit contracting between Ministers and departments for the purchase of policy advice outputs" (Scott, 1992).

This type of approach would appear to be the exception rather than the rule however. One reason may be that, at least in a Westminster system, where the government of the day is served by a civil service which is theoretically supposed to remain politically neutral and not become involved in partisan controversies, it could be expected that on occasions ministers will receive advice that they will not like. This may reflect the fact that the quality of the advice is poor, or it might be the case that the advice simply does not accord with the minister's own views. Of course, the continued provision of policy advice that is known to be contrary to the minister's views is not quality advice, regardless of its analytical rigor. In such circumstances, advisers have a responsibility to provide advice based on the known ministerial view, having previously made it clearly understood that they do not necessarily agree with that approach.

For a system of ministerial assessment to work, therefore, it seems that an essential prerequisite is that there be a clear understanding and agreement between the minister and his or her advisers on exactly what constitutes good quality advice. This has been recognized in New Zealand where a recent initiative requires increased specificity in the quantity, quality, and cost of policy advice outputs (New Zealand, State Services Commission, 1992).

Another approach might be to set up specific review units, tasked with the independent review of the policy advice using the criteria described above. For their results to be credible, these units would need to be independent of the organization being reviewed and staffed with suitably qualified, professionally respected people. Even then, given the often complex nature of policy advice involving several different sources, their task will be difficult. It will not be made any easier knowing that their assessment may be hampered by the need to respect a degree of confidentiality between ministers and their advisers. Nor will they be helped by the fact that they are reviewing the process with the perfect vision that comes with hindsight.

From within existing sources, other potential methods of external assessment include the parliament through its various review committees, international bodies such as the Organization for Economic Co-operation and Development (OECD) and the International Monetary Fund (IMF), other government departments and, of course, the auditors, although generally none of these bodies will be as well-placed to provide such specific assessment as will ministers or specialized review bodies.

Most of the above methods are concerned with external review. Equally, there are various internal methods that can be adopted to monitor the quality of the advice. Most government agencies have a system, albeit not always formalized, whereby they internally review their working practices from time to time, and for those agencies where policy advice is an integral part of their function, these reviews can throw some interesting light on the quality of the advice they are giving. An example from Australia, which involves internal assessment coupled with external assessment, is the Department of Finance which annually reviews its just completed federal budget process. In large part, this review is concerned with examining the quality of the advice the department has prepared for its minister and other ministers involved in budget deliberations. As part of these postbudget reviews, both ministers and officials from other departments are invited to attend and offer their views on the successes and failures of the process. It is the Department of Finance's view that such reviews have helped them to provide high quality advice to government.

Yet another approach could be to institute a process of peer review, whereby other policy advisers, either internal or external to the agency, periodically examine and report on the quality of the policy advice and the management of the process. The danger in internalizing the peer review process is that self-interest might possibly lead to less than perfectly honest and frank reporting by the reviewing team. On the other hand, externalizing the process may lead to it becoming administratively cumbersome and difficult to manage.

Notwithstanding the difficulties identified above, the use of peer review has much to recommend it, as independent, well-informed senior policy advisers, who are themselves well-regarded, are arguably the best judges of quality in policy advice. For the review to be creditable, it would probably best be undertaken by an external body acting independently and without any other agenda. It would not be appropriate, for example, for external bodies such as audit offices, who clearly and correctly have their own agenda, to be involved in the process.

The peer review process could concentrate on the process of the policy advice function, as has been done in New Zealand, or could go further and consider the quality of the outputs.

Finally, it is important to note that a good deal of policy advice assessment is undertaken either directly or indirectly through periodic program evaluation. Using another Australian example, in recent years the Department of Foreign Affairs and Trade undertook an evaluation of its "Relations with Asia" program, a program whose major function is the provision of policy advice. "As well as establishing the client focus approach to evaluating this type of program, it also formulated some specific performance indicators for the provision of policy advice. In brief these were the timeliness, accuracy, comprehensiveness and responsiveness of the advice provided" (Australia, Department of Foreign Affairs and Trade, 1993).

Also, as individual or team performance appraisal becomes more widely practiced in public-service agencies, it is often the case that part of that appraisal process is to do with the policy advice skills of the individual or team.

Problems with Measuring the Quality of Policy Advice

None of the approaches discussed above are without their problems, some of which have already been mentioned. The following discussion expands on those and also considers some others.

Probably the most important consideration that has to be taken into account is that any process, while bringing benefits, will also bring costs. As in other areas of public policy development it is useful, perhaps essential, to attempt a specification of both the expected benefits and costs from a particular action and for decision makers to be aware of those costs and benefits before a final decision is made. The difficulties inherent in such analyses are well-known and an area such as policy advice might be expected to be even more troublesome. Nevertheless, it is a necessary prerequisite to a successful outcome.

Another difficulty relates to the particularly subjective nature of any assessment of this type, particularly in the case where the assessment is being undertaken by one person. Given that inevitable subjectivity, it will not be a simple exercise to develop a system of assessment which is, and is seen to be, fair. Certainly, subjective, qualititative advice can be very solid and robust, but often is not. To a large extent this subjectivity can be lessened by ensuring a common set of assessment criteria. Also, it might be useful in some circumstances to introduce a moderating process to make the result as objective as possible. While nothing will entirely eradicate this subjectivity, it should be possible for it to, at least, be controlled to the point where it does not prevent useful information being collected.

Another problem, akin to the issue of subjectivity, is the difficulty in extricating that part of the final advice that relates to a particular individual or group. An assessment of quality must incorporate the concept of added value, but determining the component parts of that added value may be very difficult. Typically, for example, the final advice would have gone through a process of considerable consultation both individually and collectively, the effects of which would be to "muddy the waters" somewhat.

Finally, there is the problem referred to throughout the paper of the importance of recognizing that any assessment will be carried out after the event with the obvious advantage of being done when all the facts are known. It would be rare that any particular piece of advice would not have been improved had additional information been available at the time. In practice, this should not prevent a reasonable assessment of quality being undertaken, provided there is a common understanding by both the adviser and the assessor of what is meant by quality and the assessment criteria is clearly set down. It becomes much more problematic if an attempt is made to link the advice with the eventual outcome.

Effectiveness

Effectiveness refers to the extent to which the objectives of a policy have been achieved and the relationship between the intended and actual effect of outputs in the achievement of objectives. Attempting to link the policy advice process to the eventual outcome of a particular policy is far and away the most controversial issue and would be dismissed by many as totally inappropriate. The basis of such an argument is that officials are responsible for *advising* ministers but it is governments who make policy and responsibility for those policy decisions must always rest with the government of the day. This view is illustrated in the approach adopted by New Zealand where there is a clear distinction made between outputs, for which officials are held accountable, and outcomes, for which the government is responsible. While, on the face of it, this clean divarication is quite appealing, it is increasingly being seen as too simplistic, even among Westminster-style governments where the principal of separation of responsibilities is the strongest.

Mather (1993) wants to go further, arguing that "in reality, power is shared between ministers and their senior civil servants" and what are needed are "departmental structures which will make this explicit and hence introduce meaningful accountability." His solution, supporting Rose (1991), is to introduce departmental policy directorates whose membership would include ministers, senior civil servants, and outside experts on contract, thereby "help(ing) to end an absence of civil service responsibility by linking officials to policy successes or failures."

While a committee approach of this type may work to help share the blame (in practice, successes are of much less interest), the important question is whether or not it will lead to either better decision making or improved accountability. Unless the quality of the advice can be improved by this method, which seems unlikely as the players in the process will not have changed, but only been rearranged into different playing positions, it is difficult to see how decision making might be improved. Its justification must rest on its ability to improve accountability.

The difficulties associated with this are akin to the issues raised previously. In particular, ministers (and Cabinet) will, increasingly, have received advice from several other sources as well and it is usually not possible to establish a direct causal link between the advice of the policy-adviser, even in the broadened format proposed by Mather, and the final government decision. Such a link seems essential to establishing accountability.

Also, there are the problems identified above having to do with hindsight. Trying to establish accountability after the event, when information may be available that was not at the time of the advice, is fraught with difficulties. The nature of that information is also important. To what extent should a civil servant be held accountable for a government decision that, after the event, has been shown to be totally unacceptable to the electorate but was, nevertheless, based on sensible, rational, and economically sound advice at the time?

Going further, the failure of government policy might be a result of poor program administration rather than poor policy advice per se. Particularly in those areas of the public sector where policy development and program administration are closely linked and interrelated, the division into separately accountable units may not be possible.

In practice, the difficulties involved in developing a system which could fairly and accurately monitor the link between the policy advice and the eventual outcome would probably make the exercise unproductive. It is not obvious that it would improve decision making, and while it might ameliorate accountability to some extent, the costs of so doing are likely to outweigh the benefits.

Nevertheless, while stopping short of recommending an approach which attempts to measure the eventual outcome of a government decision and to specifically link that outcome back to the original policy advice, it is quite possible to imagine an approach which recognizes that a sensible consideration of the policy advice in terms of the eventual outcome, may be useful. For example, there must be many instances of policy work which do allow for assessment of whether the advice "worked" in the way it was intended. Such assessment would include questions such as:

- Was the analysis of the problem correct when the advice was accepted?
- Where policy decisions have followed closely the advice given, did the analysis of the solution accurately predict the outcome?
- If the advice was not accepted, what were the reasons?

While answers to such questions will not automatically lead to the provision of "better" advice, they will point to areas of potential concern and might be expected to lead to alternative approaches in the future.

There are some existing examples of interest. In 1993 the Australian Department of Prime Minister and Cabinet formally reviewed its policy-advising function in relation to the carer's package and in the same year the Treasury reviewed its policy-advising role in relation to an inquiry into the Australian banking industry. While it has to be said that none of these early evaluations have proved to be particularly insightful into the effectiveness of the policy-advising function in so far as its impact on outcomes, they have shown that it is possible and, most importantly, potentially useful, to address an issue which had previously been considered "too difficult" by most.

Conclusion

This paper argues that monitoring the performance of policy advice is equally as important as monitoring the performance of any other government program, albeit potentially more difficult in some cases. At the very least it should be possible to develop a system that measures, not only the efficiency of the advice process, but also the quality of the advice itself. Whether or not, or to what extent, it is sensible to attempt to measure the effectiveness of the policy advice by directly relating it to the policy outcome is considerably more problematic.

The successful use of a performance-monitoring system depends on its simplicity, practicality, and acceptance in terms of its perceived objectivity.

A pragmatic approach would suggest that what is immediately needed is a broader understanding and acceptance of the value of monitoring policy advice, and the best way to achieve this is through "small steps" or to quote another metaphor "learning to walk before you run."

One way of achieving this acceptance is for international examples of successful implementation to be widely studied. What seems increasingly certain is that, if the civil servants are not prepared to take the lead in this area, others will. Increasingly, demands for greater public accountability are evident, including from academics, journalists, and not the least, politicians. In Australia, for example, there have been regular calls from parliamentary committees for improved performance information, including for policy advice. As the calls for "value for money" in public expenditure, coupled with greater accountability by government, ring around the world it is foolhardy to assume that a component of public policy so obviously integral to achieving these objectives, will be left untouched.

Notes

1. An earlier version of this chapter was published in Uhr and MacKay (1996).
2. Recognizing that the form policy advice takes is very dependant on the style of government that exists in a country, this paper is primarily, although not exclusively, concerned with the Westminster style of government.
3. This paper does not attempt to make any such distinction, preferring to restrict itself to those areas of government that have as their primary function the provision of policy advice to government, such as the policy advice unit of a coordinating agency in central government.
4. This concept is not to be confused with the timeliness of the preparation of the advice which has been used earlier as an example of an efficiency measure.
5. There are various informal assessment mechanisms already in place, such as irregular dialogue between advisers and ministers, acceptance of advice by senior officers, and ultimately career progression.

References

Blakely, R. 1991. "Achieving Performance: Preparing Policy." In *Managing for Results* New Zealand Institute of Public Administration Research Papers VII, no. 20.

Department of Foreign Affairs and Trade (1992). *Program Performance Statements 1992–93.* Australia:

Mather, G. 1993. "Responsibility, Accountability & Standards in Government. *Memorandum to the Treasury & Civil Service Select Committee.*

State Services Commission (1992). *The Policy Advice Initiative: Opportunities for Management.* New Zealand.

Treasury 1992. *Annual Report For the Year Ended 30 June 1992.* New Zealand.

Rose, R. 1991. "The Political Economy of Cabinet Change." In *Britain's Constitutional Future*, ed. S. Haselar. London: Institute of Economic Affairs.

Scott, C. 1992. "Review of the Purchase of Policy Advice from Government Departments." *Public Sector* 15, no. 2: 19–24.

Scott, G. 1992. "Ensuring the Quality of Policy Advice." Address to Australian Investment Conferences Conference, 1 July 1992.

Uhr, J. and K. MacKay (eds.). 1996. *Evaluating Policy Advice*. Federal Research Centre, Australian National University and Commonwealth Department of Finance. Canberra.

Wilenski, P. 1986. *Public Power and Public Administration*. Sydney, NSW: Hale and Ironmonger.

11

Performance Monitoring: Implications for the Future

Eduardo Zapico-Goñi and John Mayne

The introductory chapter anticipated the need for effective performance monitoring in order to realize the benefits expected from the new trends in administrative reform, such as "affordable excellence," "managerialism," and "public partnership." This need is corroborated in other chapters which provide illustrations of the use of performance monitoring to assess how well public managers have responded to citizens' demands, and how public resources have been used to achieve results. Richard Sonnichsen in chapter 9 on measuring police performance presents a broad and very representative list of reasons for the need for better performance monitoring: decreasing resources and pressures to improve financial management, greater demand for accountability, demand for better police services, recognition of the public as a customer and a major stakeholder in police performance, and increased complexity of crime and sophistication of criminals. Sylvie Trosa in chapter 4 identifies value for money and accountability in the United Kingdom, and resource allocation and decentralized decision making in France, as major reasons for the need for effective target setting and performance monitoring.

Obstacles to Performance Monitoring

While the need and demand for performance monitoring are widely recognized, bringing about effective monitoring depends on both overcoming serious implementation obstacles and dealing effectively with organizational conditions faced in the public sector today. Chapter 1 discussed the complexity of current public management and identified four factors which mitigate against effective performance monitoring: uncertainty, diversity, interdependence, and instability. As we saw, specific obstacles to performance monitoring in the public sector have been identified in previous research, including: multiple and conflicting interests, ambiguity of goals and objectives, difficulties in measurement, interdependence among multiple organizations involved in related programs, resistance to measurement, and unintended behavioral effects. Evidence of these obstacles and some of the ways around them are well illustrated in the chapters. The findings in the chapters support the analysis presented in the introduction on lessons learned from the past, such as the importance of involving managers and their clients in defining and developing indicators, being parsimonious and ensuring the interests of various stakeholders are monitored, focusing on results which can be influenced, and continuously reviewing and updating performance indicators.

In chapter 2, Terje Nilsen reminds us about the ambiguity of political objectives, unclear expectations for performance, complex interaction among government activities and/or their consequences, and difficulties in measuring some activities. Trosa (ch. 4) discusses several agencies in the United Kingdom which have found difficulties with performance measurement, including the drivers' license delivery agency with "several clients with conflicting interests, the drivers, the car manufacturers, the insurance companies, the police . . . ." She also mentions changes over time in the goals of agencies as another difficulty in setting targets and indicators. In chapter 10, John Nicholson highlights the diversity of values as a complicating factor in choosing the standards for measuring policy advice and the unknown causal link between policy advice and its effect.

Rolf Sandahl in chapter 5 refers, among other difficulties, to the reduced usefulness of performance information "the more changeable is the society" and to the increased difficulty in assessing the results of government activities due to the increasing interdependence or integration of policy sectors and different constituents. He also signals the ambiguity of goals and the lack of interest and weakness at the central ministerial level, to explain the limited use of performance information in much decision making in government.

Sonnichsen (ch. 9) identifies four sources of difficulties arising in measuring police performance that may be extended to other areas of public services: lack of consensus on police goals, uncertainty about the social consequences of police activities, uncertainty about what defines safety—the intended result, and obstacles in data collection.

In the health-care monitoring systems in Korea and Mexico, Myoung-soo Kim in chapter 7 and Javier Casas Guzman in chapter 8 identify a common difficulty for performance monitoring in a complex policy sector: the multiplicity of interrelated institutions and administrations dealing with, and responsible, for the performance of the health-care system. Both conclude that diversity and lack of organizational coordination are two of the main obstacles for effective performance monitoring.

These difficulties with performance monitoring have frequently limited the scope of performance measures in use to those dealing mainly with efficiency matters, as Eduardo Zapico-Goñi points out in chapter 3. In general, there is a lack of effectiveness and impact measures. Several authors illustrate this. Sandahl (ch. 5) refers to the annual budget report in Sweden using mainly output measures "with high degree of detail." Trosa (ch. 4) found an emphasis on "simple and measurable targets and indicators" in the United Kingdom. Not surprisingly, measuring the performance of research and development type of activities, as Nicholson shows (ch. 9) regarding policy advice, uses even more limited measures. In most cases, the usual explanation for the limited scope of measures is the inability to control the external factors affecting program impacts. John Mayne in chapter 6 argues that a better explanation is that frequently the incentives in an organization do not support the use of performance information, in particular where accountability regimes are seeking to find fault rather than rewarding good performance.

However, the difficulties and limitations found are not seen as reasons to stop efforts to introduce and develop performance monitoring in all fields of government intervention. The general belief in the necessity for performance-monitoring tools for public managers remains high, as does the belief that the difficulties faced can be overcome. Indeed, the comparative experiences discussed in the various chapters will help in designing and introducing appropriate performance-monitoring systems.

In addition, the chapters illustrated suggested approaches to developing effective performance-monitoring systems in complex environments which have received less attention in the literature. Figure 11.1 outlines the approaches discussed in the book and summarized in this chapter.

The next section considers the main specific approaches suggested here for confronting the difficulties of designing and implementing performance monitoring in a complex public-sector environment: leadership and support from the center, building the right incentives, and using complementary program evaluation. Other points raised in the chapters call into question the assumptions behind performance monitoring as well as the models of current administrative reform. The subsequent section focuses on the inherent design limitations in the current administrative reform assumptions about sound public management performance. The more the public management context is characterized by the factors outlined in the figure, the more the instruments discussed should be considered and new criteria for success developed.

Approaches for Effective Performance Monitoring Under Complexity

A Leadership Role from Central Departments

A core issue of several chapters related to the need for active and competent leadership from a central unit to ensure the implementation of effective performance monitoring. This need, of course, depends on the reason why performance monitoring is being pursued. The interest of public managers in using performance monitoring themselves may be quite independent from the interest in central units. Any agency or manager could develop their own performance-monitoring system without the center playing a role. However, if performance monitoring is to be part of an overall initiative, in particular, a shift from a traditional direct type of control to a more flexible, strategic, and distant type of control, then the need for firm central leadership seems clear.

But the specific role of a central unit and the way it exercises its

FIGURE 11.1
Performance-Monitoring Problems and Solutions

Complexity and its Confounding Factors	Related and Derived Problems for Decision Making	Solutions and Approaches Proposed for Effective Performance Monitoring	
		Instruments Discussed	Reinventing Criteria of Success
Uncertainty: unknown cause-effect relationships, difficult measurement or data collection (chapters 2, 3, 4, 10, 9)	limited scope of traditional performance indicators in use

unintended effects | Central leadership | Maximizing *utility* in straightforward management contexts • Economy • Efficiency • Effectiveness |
| **Interdependence**: interaction among units, organizations, policies, and constituents (chapters 2, 5, 7, 8)

Diversity: multiple and conflicting values and interests (chapters 4, 5, 6, 7, 8, 9, 10)

Instability: changing goals, policies, and environment (chapters 3, 4, 5) | ambiguity of goal definition

inability to control external factors

lack of coordination among interdependent actors

resistance to performance monitoring

irrelevance of goals and policies | The right incentives • positive accountability • rewarding learning • focus on clients

Evaluation as a complementary too | Maximizing *adaptability* in complex, strategic management contexts • Diagnosis • Design • Development |

leadership need to be discussed. The relevant question is: What is the role of central units during and after decentralization? This question raises issues of contract management, performance partnerships (Office of Management and Budget 1995: 153), and the appropriate accountability system in a decentralized management regime.

With decentralization the changes in the responsibilities of the central unit are not just quantitative but also and more importantly qualitative. Public-sector reform initiatives such as contract management, budgeting for results, and decentralization in general demand improvement in the management capabilities in both decentralized agencies and in central units. The former need to undertake better performance monitoring and reporting. The latter need to not only understand performance monitoring but also be able to provide leadership for the introduction, development, and coordination of a government-wide decentralized management system among interdependent organizations, including performance monitoring. If during the process of decentralization, agencies resist improving their performance monitoring or cannot cope with the conditions of autonomy, the center must actively play a leadership role in promoting performance monitoring in agencies so that the government as a whole can learn from its experiences and each organization does not have to begin from scratch.

Nilsen, using the experience of the United Kingdom and Canada, argues (ch. 2) that the introduction of performance monitoring as part of a broad scale reform in government requires strong central unit leadership. In the United Kingdom, as also pointed out by Trosa (ch. 4), the central unit was supported by strong political will, pushing performance monitoring to the forefront of the reform agenda. In Canada, without equivalent political support, performance monitoring played much more of a supporting rather than leading role.

Some might argue that after decentralization the new role of the center is more limited, circumscribed to coordination and postevaluation (Shick 1990: 33). In this book we have argued in favor of the need for the center to play a qualitatively "stronger," albeit different, role than before decentralization. Trosa (ch. 4) compares the roles of central units in the United Kingdom and France, showing how quite different approaches can be used, depending on the underlying purpose assigned to performance monitoring. France saw performance monitoring as a useful and essential tool for moving towards decentralization and hence stressed the use of experiments and learning, guided by the center. In the United Kingdom, she argues, performance monitoring was seen more as a tool for a decentralized form of accountability, and hence as a form of control, with the center playing more of a traditional oversight role.

We suggest that after decentralization the performance of the government-wide management system heavily depends on adequate, strategic leadership from the center. The central unit has to pay special attention to increasing pressures towards fragmentation in a system struggling to work under a new type of accountability based on strategic direction and demonstrating performance (Mayne ch. 6). Independent behavior might follow decentralization and competition for resources if there is no special effort from central units to improve coordination (Zapico-Goñi ch. 3). This central role is essential not only to maintain a unified central government, but also for the effective performance and management of the whole system. Guzman (ch. 8) illustrates this when referring to the performance of health services in Mexico as monitored better where the government had identified a clear priority. After decentralization, it is necessary to increase the capability of the center for strategic leadership, overall priority-setting, negotiating, and designing the rules of the new decentralization game, building proper channels of communication, and developing institutional capacity for coordination and conflict resolution (Zapico-Goñi ch. 3), and for evaluation and accountability in order to ensure the coordinated functioning and integrated learning of the decentralized parts of the government.

The new types of performance measurement (the 3Ds) suggested in chapter 3 by Zapico-Goñi and discussed later in this chapter help to define further the role of the center in government reform under conditions of uncertainty. Sandahl discusses the case where interest and support from senior officials and central departments does occur if the performance measures chosen are considered relevant and credible. This also suggests the need for redesigning the performance criteria. Nilsen's analysis (ch. 2) on the roles played by central units seeking better performance monitoring in government administrative reforms in the United Kingdom,, Norway, and Canada illustrates the need for central guidance and evaluation to increase the capacity for *diagnosis*, *design*, and *development* of the system under reform. The reformers in the first two countries have not undertaken any systematic evaluation of the reforms, and hence limit their capacity for "differentiation and adaptation" (mainly diagnosis and design). In Canada, central units responsible for performance monitoring have moved towards "learning and adaptation" (mainly capacity for design and development). But before further elaboration on these concepts, let us first consider the other strategies suggested to deal with the implementation obstacles mentioned earlier.

Overcoming Measurement Difficulties with Incentives

One of the key ways to overcome resistance to performance monitoring is to introduce incentives which create a working environment that requires and supports good performance monitoring. Proper rewards and penalties will generate a real demand and an effective supply of performance measures for managers.

Mayne in chapter 6, argues that one of the critical factors influencing the use of performance monitoring is the appropriateness of reporting and accountability systems. But effective accountability is a weakness of most public-sector reforms. Although most reforms propose increasing accountability, often these are merely broad proposals and, in any event, focus on the negative face of accountability (preventing or punishing misbehavior) rather than the positive side (promoting or guiding desired performance). The organizational learning potential of accountability regimes has been largely neglected in government managerial reform. In a similar line, given that failures and underachievements are not adequately recognized in the Korean health-care monitoring system, Kim (ch. 7) points to the need for encouraging disclosure of problems by focusing the system on rewards rather than on imposing penalties. A focus by organizations seeking greater accountability through rewarding performance for results rather than for proper procedures will enhance the development and use of performance information.

As Mayne (ch. 6) discusses, an important emerging incentive for effective performance monitoring in many countries is the demand by citizens for better evidence that they are getting value for the taxes they pay. Sonnichsen (ch. 9) discusses the increased realization that the citizen is a real and active customer of police services. Most public-sector reform initiatives now include a service quality component and, in particular, a service standards component. These typically include both explicitly telling government service users what service they can expect to get and reporting back to those users on performance achieved against the standards (OECD 1994). This public accountability requires service units to have effective performance-monitoring systems, as does the increasing importance of taking into account the interests of the various stakeholders involved in any service delivery.

Zapico-Goñi (ch. 3) shows how the traditional budgeting incentives reward misspending and the "spending fever at the end of the fiscal year." Most modern budget management initiatives focus on adequate flexibility in spending controls, shifting towards performance monitoring to encourage cost consciousness in managers, and greater productivity. However, this approach with its business-style incentives, can only go so far in an era of shrinking budgets, reduced scope for rewards, and a focus on immediate operational productivity. Zapico-Goñi argues for different criteria of success in budget management and financial accountability, to reflect more relevant performance measures. In times of instability, the budget office should reward and motivate spending behavior adaptation (the 3Ds) rather than just maximizing traditional values of sound management (the 3Es).

Performance Monitoring and Evaluation as Complementary Tools

The usefulness of viewing performance measurement and program evaluation as complementary management tools was stressed in several of the chapters. This complementary role has three different aspects. In the first case, elements of performance which are difficult (or expensive) to measure through ongoing performance measures, can often be more appropriately handled through periodic evaluation studies. For example, in most cases performance measurement per se will not be able to say much about cause-and-effect relations: whether the program operations have indeed caused or contributed to a particular outcome result. An evaluation is required to try to sort out the various contributing factors. We have stressed in chapter 1 the importance of explanatory material in interpreting performance measures; often evaluation can provide the needed interpretation. We also suggest that measuring the 3Ds type of performance will frequently require evaluations. In these ways, weaknesses in a performance-monitoring system can be buttressed through strategically conducted evaluations.

Secondly, (and conversely) where conducting timely in-depth evaluations would be too expensive or intrusive, a well-designed performance-measurement system can often track proxy indicators of performance and provide reasonably reliable signals when things go astray.

Nilsen (ch. 2) discusses the need to combine both performance assessment approaches, and also discusses the choice made by Norway to apply performance monitoring for operational management and program evaluation for strategic management. Sweden has an annual report mainly focused on performance measures and an in-depth budget request based on more thorough program evaluation. Canada and the United Kingdom have in the past adopted less balanced approaches stressing evaluation and performance measures respectively. Both now appear to be trying to correct the imbalance.

A third complementary approach is using program evaluation to develop good performance measurement. Kim reports (ch. 7) on a built-in evaluation system in the Ministry of Health and Social Affairs in Korea aimed directly at the improvement of the performance-monitoring system. The system included internal and external evaluations as well as audits of data collection and record-keeping of performance-monitoring activities. A good evaluation ought to generate a number of relevant and useful performance measures.

The complementary nature of performance measurement and program evaluation should be obvious but it appears not to be with each treated in its separate literature and practice. Critiques of performance-measurement systems tend to discuss the difficulty of developing credible indicators with no reference to the possibility of evaluation, and critiques of evaluation talk about the expense and lack of timeliness of evaluations without mentioning how performance measurement could complement such studies. An all inclusive performance monitoring framework and measurement strategy is needed to best take advantage of the complementary nature of performance measurement and evaluation.

Redesigning Performance Monitoring in Complex Settings

In Search of New Criteria of Success: From 3Es to 3Ds

Enlightened leadership from the center, building the right incentives for the use of performance information in an organization, and combining both performance measurement and evaluation to comprise performance monitoring will go some way to overcoming many of the obstacles raised in implementing effective performance monitoring.

However, major obstacles, such as instability, interdependence, diversity, and, in general, uncertainty can often best be addressed, we suggest, by rethinking the nature of performance monitoring (see figure 11.1). We need to reinvent performance monitoring and the criteria of successful performance to match today's organizational realities.

According to the studies presented in this book, success with both performance monitoring and more generally with current management reforms requires responding to several sources of uncertainty.

The definition of sound performance proposed in the introductory chapter reflects the need to take uncertainty and other change-factors into account in its focus on the need for continued relevance: A well performing public program or service is one that is providing, in the most cost-effective manner, intended results and benefits that continue to be relevant, without causing undue unintended effects.

This definition and the need for *continued relevance* has important implications for the measurement of organizational performance and the models chosen by current reforms to improve public administration. In this respect, it is important first to clarify how uncertainty affects and influences public managers' performance.

In a context of uncertainty about outcomes of programs and/or policy instability, the ability to properly *redefine* goals and intervention modes is a precondition of success for public managers. The capacity and skills of managers to be economic, efficient, and effective—the 3Es —in achieving goals may be not enough if the goals are changing or outcomes cannot be readily anticipated. In fact, the greater the organizational uncertainty, the more distorted will be the performance-monitoring system in use (Carter 1991: 98) and the less relevant the use of the 3Es model for performance monitoring and assessment. This is because the model assumes the availability of precisely defined and stable objectives and a well-known (or at least widely accepted) cause-and-effect relationship between organizational activities and outcomes.

However, it is widely recognized that today public managers work under considerable uncertainty. This is due to the increasing complexity of public programs, the diversity of interests at stake (as illustrated by the health-care systems in Korea and Mexico—ch. 7 and 8), and the constant change which characterizes the public sector today. Managers must have a capacity for readjustment and adaptation. This situation does not allow us to realistically assess organizational performance just on the basis of traditional types of performance monitoring. There is, rather, a need for (a) other sources of information to complement an ongoing measurement system based on the 3Es; and/or (b) new measures designed that capture the capacity of managers to identify, respond to, and cope with unanticipated problems and outcomes.

The first approach would use the traditional 3Es at least as "tin-openers"—signals for further study—(Carter 1989) to monitor performance and complement these measures with program evaluation. In the second approach, new measures or criteria of successful performance are proposed for assessing the management capacity of *diagnosis* of new problems, *designing* new solutions, and *developing* or getting support for their implementation—the 3Ds of Metcalfe (1991) discussed by Zapico-Goñi (ch. 3):

> *diagnosis*—the identification of new problems or the redefinition of current problems, taking into account changes in the environment and the interests of stakeholders, building a common perception of the problem;
> *design*—the formulation of new solutions, including the incentives to solve new problems identified, and the adaptation of organizational and interorganizational structures and strategies;
> *development*—the actual implementation of new solutions as a learning process, coping with resistance to change, redefining problems and solutions during implementation, and learning from experience.

The 3Es and 3Ds approaches are not incompatible alternatives. Designing and using performance measures as "tin-openers" means interpreting the level of success achieved by public managers in the framework of the 3Es and looking for the reasons why managers could have achieved better results. The 3Ds model, on the other hand, looks at adaptive performance and demands in part questioning the definition of objectives, the cause-and-effect relationship and the values underlining the public-sector intervention. There is a parallel here between the 3Es vs. 3Ds distinction and the single vs. double loop organizational learning discussed in an earlier book in this series by Leeuw, Rist, and Sonnichsen (1994), and the interorganizational learning discussed by Metcalfe (1993).

The 3Ds approach is more relevant for monitoring and assessing performance under uncertainty. Rather than examining how well performance criteria based on the 3Es have been met in cases where these criteria become obsolete or irrelevant, assessing performance from a 3Ds perspective looks at how well organizations and their managers

- respond to multiple pressures and unexpected challenges;
- exhibit flexibility in the face of changing circumstances;
- work cooperatively within networks of organizations when delivering new programs; and
- adapt to a changing and uncertain environment.

In a context of uncertainty, we suggest that public managers' performance should be assessed with regard to their capacity for adapting to new problems beyond the traditional concerns of cost reduction, productivity, and quality improvement of current services. In such a context, maximizing flexibility rather than maximizing short-term utility is a different and more relevant criteria of success.

Public Managers' Roles and Performance Monitoring Under Complexity

Let us discuss the measurement of adaptive performance by considering performance monitoring and the main roles played by public managers in different organizational contexts. Metcalfe and Richards (1990: 35, ff) have reviewed and summarized the literature in this regard. In figure 11.2, the four role possibilities depend on the combination of two key variables: (a) concern with procedures vs. concern with results; and (b) stability (certainty) vs. change (uncertainty).

FIGURE 11.2
Public Managers' Roles (*)

Change

Integrator (negotiator) Development	**Innovator** (strategist) Diagnosis & Design
Administrator (bureaucrat) Equity	**Producer** (executive) Economy, Efficiency Effectiveness

Procedures .... *Results*

Stability

* (adapted from Metcalfe and Richards 1990: 39)

Consideration of these variables results in four roles:

- the *Administrator*: a bureaucrat concerned mainly with putting appropriate procedures in place in an equitable manner;
- the *Producer*: an executive, mainly concerned with achieving fixed objectives and being effective in an efficient and economical manner;

- the *Innovator*: a strategist, concerned with adaptation to changes in the environment; and
- the *Integrator*: a negotiator, with skills to persuade those affected by changes in order to implement and develop new ideas.

This classification does not mean to suggest that each public servant can or should play one single role. They represent a collective profile. Most public servants could and should be playing more than one role at different times. What is important here is the extent to which those working under instability or uncertainty are or are not encouraged by a performance-monitoring system to perform as "innovators" and "integrators" rather than mere "administrators" and "producers." Sound performance-information systems should capture and provide incentives for the appropriate management role depending on each context.

Public servants have traditionally emphasized concern with legal compliance and the formal aspects of government action. As mentioned in chapter 1, their roles have been identified with the equitable administration of procedures (the "Administrator" box in figure 11.2). Current reforms in public administration perceive public servants more like executive managers, responsible for policy implementation, delivering services to the public, concerned with obtaining more with less (OECD 1993), getting things done by effectively using public resources, and achieving value-for-money (i.e., the "Producer" box in figure 11.2). From this perspective, good managers are not supposed to put into question public policies and objectives, but just to get higher quality results more efficiently.

This common view, however, is based on three assumptions which do not reflect the realities of public administration today: (a) an artificial separation between policy formulation and policy implementation—public managers just implement their political masters' programs; (b) the view that public managers' performance should be neutral and not affected or influenced by the variety of interests of stakeholders; and (c) the belief that managers do this under conditions of certainty about the expected results and a stable environment.

A separation of policy and operations. The first assumption implies that objectives are clearly defined within firm policy frameworks, and are based on neutral, nonconflicting values which provide unquestionable and fixed standards for managers to work towards. Their work is to execute the decisions of others. According to many current administrative reforms, managers are supposed to focus on achieving specific results and their performance is to be assessed in relation to anticipated values of economy, efficiency, and effectiveness under a fixed framework of reference. The assumption is that policies and objectives are given parameters transmitted to public managers from political levels.

This assumption has been questioned for some time. We suggest that a more realistic and useful formulation is that public managers do in fact influence policymakers during policy formulation and target setting (Selznick 1957: 56). In this view, effective performance from public managers requires effort in both achieving and defining goals: the *relevance and feasibility of anticipated achievements* is also the responsibility of public managers. Nicholson illustrates (ch. 10) this argument when he questions New Zealand's approach of making officials responsible for outputs and ministers for outcomes. Although accepting that this separation is appealing, he considers it very simplistic, arguing that meaningful accountability should be based on the recognition of power sharing between ministers and senior public servants. Officials formally influence outcomes through policy advice. This influence along with other sorts of informal influence on political levels help to define goals. The case of Sweden is very clear in this respect since their small central ministries depend on the specialist knowledge to be found in the larger autonomous agencies (Sandahl ch. 5). Trosa (ch. 4) also provides a good illustration of this point in the United Kingdom when explaining how, despite official rhetoric presenting the traditional view of ministers setting policy and public managers implementing it, in actual practice it was the agencies, not ministers, who proposed targets to be negotiated with the center of the department. She found that agency managers have much better information on implementation problems and on hence feasible policy options.

Public managers' active participation in policy formulation is as important as the work they do on execution. Their role in reality is not just to execute programs but also to help redesign them. Objectives are not given and externally fixed. Good performance might require redefining rather than achieving objectives.

None of this reduces the central role of politicians in setting policy direction and defining policy objectives. It is merely to say that they are, and should be, assisted in this process by public-sector managers.

Neutral public managers. Current administrative reforms have not paid enough attention to one of the most important factors of uncertainty in public management: value diversity (Smith 1978: 22). Designing performance monitoring and accountability systems in the public sector cannot neglect the existence of multiple, and often conflicting, sources of performance legitimacy. Whose expectations should public managers respond to? Trends in administrative reform highlight the importance of "client" type of accountability from public managers to citizens, as consumers or users of public services. However, Trosa finds agency clientele being divided by contradictory interests. Furthermore, other sources of legitimacy such as the legislative body, departmental hierarchies, professional peers, unions, and other stakeholders have expectations that influence decision making. All these forms of interdependence should be taken into account in developing effective performance-monitoring and management systems, and would be exceedingly difficult for a neutral, anonymous public servant to do well.

Guzman (ch. 8) shows similar findings when referring to the diversity and autonomy of institutions at different levels of government, making integration of the health-care system difficult. The need for a broader social construction of performance measures and standards is increasingly recognized as a condition for the proper design of performance-monitoring systems Nicholson points this out (ch. 10) as an "inherent complication" for monitoring policy advice. Even recognizing some difficulties of the approach, Nicholson argues in favor of using peer review as a monitoring system of policy advice and presents New Zealand as a case where the process of policy advice has been subject to peer group review.

Policy advice and public administration on many important issues are not value-free. Neutral detachment and professional objectivity of public managers' involvement in policy making is increasingly seen as a myth. Metcalfe and Richards (1990: 45) point out that, "The notion that civil servants are politically neutral, anonymous and powerless agents of ministerial will is far removed from the facts of contemporary administrative life."

There are a number of factors today which require the active involvement of public servants in policy development: the requirement for more client consultation on program design and delivery, the need to appear in front of legislative committees, and the increased attention paid by the media to senior public servants. Access to information legislation further opens up the bureaucracy to questions and criticisms, and frequently requires a response and explanation by public servants.

Some countries involved in current initiatives of decentralization (the United Kingdom, New Zealand, Canada) seem to be clinging to the concept of a neutral and anonymous public servant. Others with administrations traditionally decentralized (Sweden) (Murray, 1992), or in an advanced process of decentralization (Australia) (Task Force on Management Improvement 1992: 505–6) already recognize the need for an involved, but still professional, public servant.

A stable environment. As for the third assumption, it should be clear that policy is built today within a very dynamic and uncertain framework. Public managers therefore should be concerned with designing and applying responses to new challenges. They should be responsible for improving the organizational capacity for adaptation: to do new things and work in different ways. Whether they realize it or not, they are finally responsible both for redefining problems they confront and for identifying the most relevant issues to be addressed (i.e., choosing priorities).

Trosa (ch. 4) presents several examples showing that "target setting is a continuous process of rectifying, correcting errors and interpreting situations." The problem is that the central units and ministers are "not always aware of these uncertainties." Qualitative analysis is the solution proposed by the Next Steps, however this analysis has to go beyond mere explanation of whether expected results were achieved, by questioning the rationale of the given targets as "intended results and benefits that continue to be relevant." The instability of many public-sector situations affects the performance criteria and the type of measures to be used.

In summary, the context of public management today is characterized by uncertainty, interdependence, diversity, and instability, leading to repeated rapid, radical, and unanticipated change (Wildavsky 1993: 5). Working under this complex situation requires public managers to focus their attention on the other two roles in the upper side of figure 11.2: identifying new problems and designing readjustments (the Innovator), and getting the support needed to proceed with actual readjustment (the Integrator). Savoie (1994: 7) in a study on governance and globalization concludes "[National governments] will need na-

tional civil services with the capacity to be creative, to seek out compromises, to educate, and to initiate change."

Although most managers need to play all four roles (administrator,
producer, innovator, and integrator), which one they should be concerned with at a point in time should reflect the specific circumstances
faced rather than be dictated by history or training. Performance monitoring should also be consistent and compatible with public managers'
roles and circumstances.

Measuring Performance Adaptability

In circumstances of instability and uncertainty, successful public
managers must create the organizational capacity for adaptation
(Metcalfe and Richards 1990). This means having the capacity for:

• *Strategic innovation.* Having the ability to innovate (the Innovator): gathering information on future unexpected variables and not
simply searching data on known ones; reformulating problems taking
into account different interests (*diagnosis*); defining new objectives
and tasks; redesigning organizational strategy and structure to reflect
changes in the environment; and adapting accountability systems to
reflect different sources of legitimacy (*design*); and

• *Adaptive implementation.* Having negotiating skills to gain support for implementing new ideas for change (the Integrator): guaranteeing good information on new initiatives; coordinating relevant actors; mobilizing support; encouraging a culture striving to improve
and receptive to learning and change; building coalitions; persuading
those affected to accept change; and providing the system with new
meaning (*development*).

Our consideration of the roles of public managers today provides a
new expanded framework for measuring and assessing performance.
The 3Ds model provides the relevant criteria for measuring adaptive
management performance by encouraging efforts for effective *diagnosis* of new problems, *design* of appropriate solutions, structures, and
strategies and *development* of adaptive implementation approaches.

Operationalizing these performance concepts in each policy area is
a challenge. It requires qualitatively different information from what is
traditionally available and new know-how and creativity to transform
the 3Ds model into concrete criteria to assess adaptive performance.
Despite these difficulties, effective performance monitoring should be

able to capture the most relevant components of performance to motivate managers in the right direction. Performance assessment which is biased towards any one of the four manager roles discussed will not support a balanced functioning of government. Effective performance monitoring requires a proper match among the management environment, the various public management roles and the criteria of success implicitly suggested by measurement.

Experiences analyzed in the book provide useful illustrations of the need for a 3Ds perspective on performance. Nicholson offers a good example of the need to incorporate new criteria to measure and assess policy advice in cases of uncertain outcomes. He suggests that in these cases, performance assessment should include questions such as "Was the analysis of the problem correct when the advice was accepted?" (a criterion assessing *diagnosis* capacity); or "Where policy decisions have followed closely the advice given, did the analysis of the solution accurately predict the outcome?" (related to *design* capacity); and "If the advice was not accepted, what were the reasons?" (connected with learning and *development* capacities).

Kim and Guzman (ch. 7 and 8) show the need for public managers to focus on integrating the diversity of interdependent institutions and their priorities in order to improve the coherence of the systems for effective performance monitoring (related to the capacity for *development* and *design* respectively).

When analyzing policing in the United States, Sonnichsen (ch. 9) provides another example of the necessary shift from the 3Es to the 3Ds. He starts with a critique of the traditional FBI approach to performance monitoring with the classic quote: "What gets measured, gets done." The FBI measurement system could not distinguish different levels of case quality or complexity, encouraging police action bias towards a producer-manager role of generating performance statistics. Efforts in the FBI to concentrate resources on major criminal and security problems demanded balance in the performance-monitoring system between quantitative and qualitative information. As Sonnichsen concludes:

> . . . complex criminal activities do not usually succumb to traditional police efforts. Extraordinary, creative and complex investigative activities are not appropriately described by traditional police statistics.

In this case, the 3Ds would provide more appropriate criteria to measure police success defined in general as the capacity of the police to respond to more sophisticated crime. Sonnichsen's discussion presents a good illustration of the type of role to be played by police managers under uncertainty with the 3Ds as criteria of success: *diagnosis* or capacity for reviewing current police activities, identifying and selecting priority crimes according to public interests; *design* or capacity for restructuring resources, investigating, innovating in police strategy; and *development* or capacity for implementing the responses to new crimes. The relevant strategic management role of police managers as "innovators" is to "conceptually address and rigorously examine the basic mission of policing in the light of external public interest" and as "integrators" to get support for implementing new programs consistent with their basic mission.

The need to measure more than the 3Es has been addressed in some literature. The 3Ds as criteria of success for public management under uncertainty was first presented by Metcalfe (1991 and 1993) and was specifically linked to interorganizational learning. A book edited by Leeuw, Rist, and Sonnichsen (1994) looks at cases where performance monitoring (mainly program evaluation) have lead to what Argyris (1982) has called "double loop learning," the ability to look beyond the traditional 3Es perspective on success and fundamentally reexamine objectives and current ways of delivering government programs. Mayne (1994) discusses the formal evaluation regime in the government of Canada which, in addition to examining the traditional issues of whether programs have met their objectives (a 3Es issue), also is meant to review the continued relevance of objectives (a diagnosis issue) and asks whether there are quite different ways of delivering programs (design issues). In this case, one could measure adaptive performance by assessing the extent to which institutional evaluation in fact addressed these 3Ds issues.

The Canadian Comprehensive Auditing Foundation (1987) published a major study on auditing effectiveness which provided an expanded definition of effectiveness, one which goes beyond the scope of the traditional 3Es. Several of the twelve attributes of effectiveness presented implicitly refer to aspects of 3Ds performance, in particular, the continued relevance of objectives being pursued (diagnosis), and responsiveness, "an organization's ability to adapt to changes" (p. 21) (design and development). Numerous jurisdictions in Canada have been working with the broader effectiveness scope outlined by the Foundation.

Of the 3Ds, the *development* element seems to have received the least attention in terms of measurement and public sector reform. It involves examining the extent to which management has been successful in implementing changes and has coped with resistance to change. Here, as for all the 3Ds, measurement would seem to require study based examinations and involve more qualitative and exploratory analysis. This, plus the fact that by their very nature the 3Ds challenge the status quo in public administration, suggest that adopting the 3Ds as the basis for performance monitoring will be difficult in all but the true learning organizations or, even more difficult, learning networks of organizations.

Although the 3Ds present challenges, their relevance when considering public-sector performance under uncertainty is evident. A pragmatic approach to performance monitoring may be to build a balanced mix of both performance monitoring based on the 3Es and a set of evaluations based on the more relevant 3Ds. As we anticipated in the introduction to the book, "there is no universal way to design performance monitoring systems." The balance required depends on the opportunities and challenges of each organizational situation. The choice of appropriate mix would depend on the degree of uncertainty under which managers work. To the extent that agencies have straightforward and undisputed objectives and deal with well-defined, homogeneous tasks and predictable outcomes, the 3Es-based performance monitoring and traditional evaluation will probably cover most of the management information needs. For organizations working in complex situations with objectives subject to different views and interpretations such as policy advice, and highly professionalized public services, for networks of organizations such as the health services in Mexico and Korea, and for central units dealing for instance with administrative reform, the need for evaluating the 3Ds is highest.

Implications for Future Performance Monitoring

Despite important obstacles, there is a persistent interest in, and recognition of the need for, effective performance monitoring as a key component of government administrative reform. Performance monitoring is not a new idea, but success has often proven illusive. As Trosa and others in the book have shown, success has often been limited to the use of simple and quantifiable performance measures (economy, current cost reductions, productivity), targeted on what can be easily measured.

We suggest that in addition to valuable learning from past experience with performance monitoring, a complementary new perspective is needed, one which would focus less on the technical aspects of designing measurement indicators and more on the cultural aspects of organizations and their relation with their environment and other organizations. It would consider the capacity of managers, organizations, and networks of organizations for adaptive learning.

Further improvements will depend on overcoming resistance to implementation within and outside the organization, and adapting performance monitoring to accommodate organizational conditions, culture, and interorganizational relations. The comparative experiences presented in this book suggest future directions for performance monitoring. Some of the lessons are more pragmatic or instrumental such as the need for a leadership role from central units, the readjustment of accountability regimes to develop the right incentives, and complementing performance measurement with program evaluation. In addition, other more fundamental suggestions have been made for redefining the criteria of success and redesigning performance monitoring to better match the variety of the public manager's roles. Performance monitoring needs to capture criteria of success more relevant for public managers working today under increasing uncertainty, diversity, interdependence, and instability.

References

Argyris, C. 1982. *Reasoning, Learning, and Action.* San Francisco, Cal.: Jossey-Bass .

Canadian Comprehensive Auditing Foundation. 1987. *Effectiveness Reporting and Auditing in the Public Sector.* Ottawa.

Carter, N. 1989. "Performance Indicators: Backseat Driving or Hands off Control?" *Policy and Politics* XVII, no. 2: 13–38.

Office of Management and Budget. 1995. *Making Government Work: Budget of the United States Government, Fiscal Year 1996.* Washington, DC:

Leeuw, F. L., R. C. Rist, et al. 1994. *Can Governments Learn? Comparative Perspectives on Evaluation & Organizational Learning.* New Brunswick, NJ: Transaction Publishers.

Mayne, J. 1994. "Utilizing Evaluation in Organizations: The Balancing Act." In *Can Governments Learn? Comparative Perspectives on Evaluation & Organizational Learning.* ed. F. L. Leeuw, R. C. Rist and R. C. Sonnichsen. New Brunswick, NJ: Transaction Publishers.

Metcalfe, L. and S. Richards. 1990. *Improving Public Management.* London: Sage.

Metcalfe, L. 1991. "Public Management: From Imitation to Innovation," paper presented at the Annual Conference of the International Association of Schools and Institutes of Administration (IASIA), Kota Kinabalu, Sabah, Malaysia, 28 July–2 August.

Metcalfe, L. 1993. Public Management: From Imitation to Innovation. In *Modern Government*, ed. J. Kooiman. London: Sage.

Murray, R. 1992. "Modernization of Public Sector in Sweden," paper presented in the conference *Public Management Modernization in the 90s*, INAP, Madrid.

OECD. 1993. *Performance Measurement*. PUMA (3) 93. Paris.

OECD. 1994. *Service Quality Initiatives in OCED Member Countries*, background paper for a Symposium held 7–8 November, 1994. PUMA (94) 13.

Savoie, D. J. 1994. *Globalization and Governance (Summary)*, research paper no. 12. Canadian Centre for Management Development. Ottawa.

Selznick, P. 1957. *Leadership in Administration*. Chicago, Ill.: Row, Peterson and Company.

Smith, D. 1978. *Value Biases in Performance Assessment*, paper delivered at the 1978 Annual Meeting of the American Political Science Association New York Hilton Hotel. August 31-September 3.

Task Force on Management Improvement. 1992. *The Australian Public Service Reformed—An Evaluation of a Decade of Public sector Reform*. Canberra: Australian Government Publishing service.

Wildavsky, A. 1993. "¿Qué necesita saber el manger público?' Una formación para la gestión pública." *Ekonomiaz*, 26 no. 2 cuatrimestre. Departamento de Economía y Hacienda. Gobierno Vasco, España.

Contributors

Francisco Javier Casas Guzman is currently undersecretary for energy operations, Ministry of Energy in Mexico City. He has occupied diverse governmental positions such as coordinator of Industrial Promotion in the "IMCE," general director of analysis and operation of energy and mines in "SEPAFIN," manager of supplies in the Federal Commission for Electricity, chief administrative officer, chief of unit vigilance officers and undersecretary "B" in the General Controllership of the Federation. He has authored two books and several articles.

Myoung-soo Kim is professor of public administration and policy at the Hankuk University of Foreign Studies in Seoul, Republic of Korea. He served as president of the Korean Association for Policy Analysis and Evaluation during 1993 and 1994. He has published widely on program evaluation, public auditing, and central and local legislature, and is author of *Public Policy Evaluation* and coauthor of *Public Auditing*. Dr. Kim is president-elect of the Korean Association for Policy Studies, policy advisor to the chairman of the Korean Board of Audit and Inspection, and is leading a fifteen-member group evaluating performance of Seoul City Corporation.

John Mayne currently is an audit principal in the Office of the Auditor General of Canada. From 1992 to 1994 he was the manager of the Services Standards Initiative for the Treasury Board Secretariat and formerly was director of evaluation policy at the Office of the Controller General. He served as president of the Canadian Evaluation Society from 1985 to 1987. Dr. Mayne has published numerous articles on program evaluation, policy analysis, and performance measurement, and is coeditor of several books on evaluation.

John Nicholson served as a military officer with the Australian Army serving in Vietnam, Papua New Guinea, and Thailand before joining the Australian Public Service in 1984. He worked with the Department of Housing and Construction for twelve months prior to his move to the Department of finance in early 1985. Mr. Nicholson spent three years in London as regional manager, was a member of the Resource Management Improvement Branch for two and a half years, including eight months as a/g assistant secretary, has been director of the Evaluation and Consultancy Group for the past two years and is currently a/g assistant secretary with the Transport and Government Division. Mr. Nicholson lectures regularly at universities in Australia, as well as at innumerable conferences both in Australia and overseas.

Terje Haugli Nilsen is now a private consultant whose main interests are in the areas of corporate planning and the use of evaluation in organizational development. He has held several senior positions in the public and private sectors, managing program evaluation studies. His academic training is in economics, Oslo University.

Rolf Sandahl is currently audit director in the financial management department at the Swedish National Audit Office. Dr. Sandahl's main fields of research are on evaluation methodology and policy instruments on which he has published several books and articles.

Richard C. Sonnichsen is retired from the Federal Bureau of Investigation after thirty years of service, the last fourteen as deputy assistant director in charge of the Office of Planning, Evaluation, and Audits. He is currently an evaluation and management consultant and member of the adjunct faculties of the University of Southern California and Central Michigan University. He is active in the American Evaluation Association and publishes on the topic of internal evaluation. He received his B.S. in forestry from the University of Idaho and his M.P.A. and D.P.A. from the University of Southern California. He resides in Sandpoint, Idaho.

Sylvie Trosa has a doctorate in Public Law from University Paris-

Sorbonne. She is currently the assistant secretary for the resource management improvement branch in the Australian Department of Finance. Previously, she has worked as deputy for the Scientific Council for Evaluation in France, where she was involved in several evaluations and published several articles on evaluation methodology. Prior to this, she was in charge of the evaluation division of the department of equipment in charge of Roads, Social Housing and Transport. She has also been responsible for the doctorate seminar on evaluation at l'Institut d'Etudes Politiques de Paris for three years. She has been the French delegate for the Performance Measurement Program of the OECD for the past five years and has published several reports for the OECD.

Joseph Wholey is a professor of public administration at the University of Southern California and a fellow of the National Academy of Public Administration. His work focuses on the use of strategic planning and performance monitoring to improve budget decision making, program effectiveness, and public confidence in government. Wholey is author, co-author or editor of eight books and many reports, book chapters, and journal articles.

Eduardo Zapico-Goñi is currently an advisor in the Budgetary Office of the Presidency of the Central Government in Spain and recently advisor to the director general of the Instituto de Estudios Fiscales in Madrid. He worked for ten years (1985–1995) at the European Institute of Public Administration in Maastricht, the Netherlands where he became associate professor and was head of the Unit of Public Management for a two-year period. He regularly teaches public administration in several universities and professional schools. Dr. Zapico-Goñi has written and coedited several books and professional articles on budgeting and public management.

Index

The International Institute of Administrative Sciences
and Its Working Group on Policy and Program Evaluation

The International Institute of Administrative Sciences (IIAS) is a scientific institution, whose vocation is international, specializing in public administration and the administrative sciences. Its field covers all questions which concern contemporary public administration at the national and international levels. Imagined already as early as 1910 by administrators and politicians and established in 1930 by the International Congress of Administrative Sciences held in Madrid, the IIAS is the first of the specialized institutions to affirms, worldwide, its scientific willingness to resolve the problems and challenges of national and international administration.

The purpose of the IIAS is to promote the development of administrative sciences, the better operation of public administrative agencies, the improvement of administrative methods and technics and the progress of international administration. Its history demonstrates its capacity to respond to the needs of the industrialized and developing countries, as well as to those in transition. Owing to its attributes and great experience, the IIAS is a unique organization which is comprised of 48 Member States, 9 Governmental International Organizations, 49 National Sections and 54 Corporate Members.

A large part of IIAS activities is devoted to information (IIAS publications, its quarterly International Review of Administrative Sciences, published in French and English, and its information and documentation service attached to its Library) and to expertise and consultancy. The Institute responds to specific requests of governments, international organizations or any other agency. But most IIAS research activities are carried out in the framework of its annual major meetings (Congress, Conference or Round Table) and its Working Groups (12 currently).

One of these Working Groups, and one of the most productive, was launched in 1986 and, since this date, has been working on Policy and Program Evaluation. Since its beginning, the Dr. Ray C. Rist has presided, the group meets once a year and, in the framework of sub-groups, prepares books which present the findings of their intensive research. The latest book, *Monitoring Performance in the Public Sector,* presents the efforts of one of these sub-groups.

IIAS, rue Defacqz 1 box 11, B-1050 BRUXELLES, BELGIQUE